lídia jorge

in other words

por outras palavras

Portuguese Literary & Cultural Studies
2 Spring 1999

LÍDIA JORGE

lídia jorge

in other words
por outras palavras

Portuguese Literary & Cultural Studies is a multilingual interdisciplinary peer-reviewed journal published semi-annually by the Center for Portuguese Studies and Culture at the University of Massachusetts Dartmouth. The journal addresses the literatures and cultures of the diverse communities of the Portuguese-speaking world in terms of critical and theoretical approaches.

Manuscript Policy

Portuguese Literary & Cultural Studies welcomes submission of original and unpublished manuscripts in English, Portuguese, or Spanish appropriate to the goals of the journal. The first page of the submission must include the following: (*i*), name, mailing address, e-mail address, and appropriate phone and fax numbers; (*ii*), a brief biography, not exceeding a quarter of a page, with reference to institutional affiliation, no more than three publications, and current research; (*iii*), a half-page abstract of the content of the article or review. The article itself may not exceed 20 pages and should be submitted along with the above information in a single digital file. All of the information must be in the same language. *PLCS* encourages electronic submission in the form of an attached document addressed to greis@umassd.edu. Submission in hard copy and 3.5" diskette (in a protected envelope) may also be sent by regular mail to *Portuguese Literary & Cultural Studies*, Center for Portuguese Studies and Culture, University of Massachusetts Dartmouth, Dartmouth, MA 02747, USA.

Manuscripts should be in accordance with the *MLA Style Manual and Guide to Scholarly Publishing* (latest version) with parenthetical documentation and list of works cited. The author is responsible for the accuracy of all quotations, titles, names, and dates. Notes must be manually typed out at the end of the article (before the list of works cited), regardless of whether they were entered as footnotes or endnotes into the word processor.

The preferred digital format for submissions is, in order, (*i*), the latest version of MS Word (Windows), (*ii*), the latest version of MS Word (Macintosh), or (*iii*), any previous version of MS Word (Windows or Macintosh). The first page mentioned above should have a reference to the format and version in which the article was saved. Font and sizes as close as possible to the style of the previous issue of *PLCS* should be used throughout the text.

Subscription Information

The annual subscription (2 issues) for institutions is $40.00 and $20.00 for individuals. Single issues may also be purchased for $15.00. From outside the United States add $12.00 for shipping and handling.

Inquiries should be sent to *Portuguese Literary & Cultural Studies* Subscription, Center for Portuguese Studies and Culture, University of Massachusetts Dartmouth, Dartmouth, MA 02747 USA, or by e-mail to: greis@umassd.edu.

Advertising

Portuguese Literary & Cultural Studies accepts advertising that is of interest to scholars in the field of Portuguese, Brazilian, and Luso-African Studies and Critical Theory. Further information is available by contacting the Center for Portuguese Studies and Culture, University of Massachusetts Dartmouth.

Cover

Photography: Luís Ramos, *Lídia Jorge with a Photograph of Herself as a Child of 18 Months*, 1991. In *A Imagem das Palavras*. Comissariado Português Para a Europália 91. Lisbon: Contexto, 1991.

ISSN 1521-804X

Printed by American Printing, Inc., New Bedford, Massachusetts

Table of Contents

Reviews

Introduction

Portuguese Literature is currently enjoying an unrivalled and long overdue revival outside the Portuguese-speaking world. For instance, in the United States, Harold Bloom paid tribute to the outstanding originality of Fernando Pessoa by citing him among the ten greatest twentieth-century poets in the world in his *The Western Canon* (London: Macmillan, 1995). In Europe, meanwhile, the Frankfurt Book Fair, where Portugal was featured as a special theme country in 1997, placed Portuguese writers in the limelight. But surely the most fitting and coveted recognition came when the 1998 Nobel Prize for Literature was awarded to José Saramago, an honor bestowed for the first time to a writer whose native tongue is Portuguese.

Despite this recent "boom," people in English-speaking countries are still visibly less familiar with foreign literature in general, and the literary output of a perceived small country such as Portugal in particular, than their continental European counterparts. In countries like France or Germany, for instance, a significant number of major contemporary Portuguese authors seems to have warranted translation and dissemination alongside the obvious giants (Eça de Queirós, Pessoa, and lately Saramago). It comes as no surprise, therefore, to note that several of Lídia Jorge's novels are currently available in translation in those countries. By contrast, to cater for an English-speaking audience, only her best-known work, *A Costa dos Murmúrios*, has been translated so far (*The Murmuring Coast.* Trans. Natália Costa and Ronald W. Sousa. Minneapolis & London: University of Minnesota Press, 1995).

This special thematic issue of *Portuguese Literary & Cultural Studies* hopes to redress the balance, for Lídia Jorge is undoubtedly one of the foremost Portuguese novelists to have emerged since the April 1974 Revolution. Like other prolific post-revolutionary writers, she has ten titles to her credit in the space of two decades. "Amazing" is probably the right word for an author whose fertile imagination has tackled such varied topics as the impact of the April 1974 Revolution and that of the African colonial wars at one end of the spectrum, and the all-encompassing nature of an elusive father/ daughter relationship in a small village at the other. The relevance of her work is unquestionable, for her fiction explores the contradictions present in contemporary Portugal, taking in the differences between rural and city-based experiences, between various generations, and between men and women. Her thematic spread, moreover, is matched by a remarkable stylistic virtuosity. Her unconventional prose can be precise or it can swell in a lyrical mode. Her narrative strategies are just as versatile: her prose oscillates between collective and more individual narrating voices, including the occasional use of male narrators.

In 1980, her first work, *O Dia dos Prodígios*, was immediately hailed as a revelation for its incomparable stylistic and thematic originality and was awarded the prestigious Ricardo Malheiros prize. The writer Vergílio Ferreira may be cited here to represent the views of the critical establishment, as he confidently proclaimed the "afirmação poderosa e súbita de um grande escritor." What was sincerely meant as the ultimate accolade, "the appearance of a great writer," nevertheless encodes a stark and intrinsic contradiction. Can a woman writer be a great author irrespective of her gender? Or is it rather not the case that she was considered great *at the expense* of her gender? I would argue, and so do the majority of the contributors to this issue, that it is impossible to read Lídia Jorge without reference to her gender. Indeed, part of her originality lies precisely in being a voice from the margins, in providing a fresh and female perspective on major (or so deemed) historical events, and in engaging in the process of recovering events, voices, and positions often considered minor by the dominant order.

The present volume features an array of essays on some of her best-known fiction. Special attention is devoted here to *A Costa dos Murmúrios*, undoubtedly her most celebrated novel at home and abroad. The importance of its central theme—a personal recollection of colonial wartime in Mozambique that engages in dialogue with the highly fictionalized account featured at the outset of the book—would amply suffice to justify the interest it has elicited. But the original treatment which Lídia Jorge affords to her chosen theme enables her to problematize a wide range of issues close to the heart of modern readers (be they Portuguese or not), including personal and collective identity, memory, history, language, and representation itself. Here in the present volume, this novel is the focus of three pieces that develop incisive and insightful parameters of analysis focusing on the role of memory and the portrayal of women to cast a new light on this seminal text.

Three further essays consider some of her other more accomplished novels: *O Dia dos Prodígios* (1980), *Notícia da Cidade Silvestre* (1984, awarded the Cidade Lisboa prize), and finally *O Jardim sem Limites* (1995). The latter received mixed reviews when it first appeared, but it is nevertheless crucial to our understanding of Lídia Jorge's perception of contemporary Portugal. *O Dia dos Prodígios* brings to life the collective voice of rural Portugal. By contrast, her third novel, *Notícia da Cidade Silvestre*, takes place in the urban environment of Lisbon and signals Lídia Jorge's departure from the collective to a more individual, and even intimate, perspective. A decade later, *O Jardim sem Limites* revisits the capital city in the 1990s, using again a collective gaze to inscribe the tremendous changes which have occurred in people's way of life and outlook, insofar as modernization, membership of the European Union, and a new cult of the image have all contributed to a sense of *fin-de-siècle* emptiness in the new generation. In so doing, the novel looks back to that other novel that in the Portuguese imagination stands as the emblematic *fin-de-siècle* masterpiece *par excellence*, *Os Maias*. This is her most "realist" work to date, a fact which may account for the mixed reviews it initially attracted.

Only three of Lídia Jorge's novels are not analyzed in detail here. *O Cais das Merendas* (1982), her second novel, provided a complementary perspective on *O Dia dos Prodígios*. In fact, Lídia Jorge has been the first to acknowledge that they were conceived in parallel. Much has been written on *O Cais das Merendas* already (see bibliography), unlike *A Última Dona* (1992), which critics have somewhat neglected. Perhaps not coincidentally, the latter is her only work to date to make predominant use of a male perspective. Nevertheless, Ana Paula Ferreira makes sufficient references to it in the course of her essay on *A Instrumentalina* to emphasize that it occupies a significant place in Lídia Jorge's literary production. One novel which would have most certainly warranted a full-length article here, were it not for reasons of space, is Lídia Jorge's most recent and prodigious *tour de force*, *O Vale da Paixão* (1998). We have included, however, a perceptive and in-depth critical review by Elfriede Engelmayer, who gives us a flavor of this outstanding work, showing it to be one of Jorge's most powerful and symbolic novels built on intimate and haunting memories.

Although Lídia Jorge's reputation rests primarily on her novels, one should not forget that she has also published successfully in other genres. She has briefly ventured into the theatre, with a play, *A Maçon* (1996), that centers on Adelaide Cabete, one of the leading figures of Portuguese feminism during the first two decades of this century. Despite this foray into drama, Lídia Jorge remains above all a prose fiction writer. In this context, due credit should be given to her not only as a novelist, but also as the author of a number of short stories published in book-form under the titles *A Instrumentalina* (1992) and *Marido e Outros Contos* (1997) respectively. The two essays on her short stories which are included here reveal without a doubt that while these tales may productively be read to cast light on her novelistic works, they also deserve to stand as masterpieces in their own right. Ellen Sapega, in particular, lucidly argues that far from being a minor genre, the short story, by virtue of its very "shortness," is able to do things differently from longer narratives. Indeed, this genre seems lately to be attracting renewed interest from writers and critics alike, a tendency to be applauded given that Portuguese-speaking countries have long since boasted outstanding practitioners of the genre, including the Brazilian Clarice Lispector or more recently the Mozambican Mia Couto.

Since this issue of *Portuguese Literary & Cultural Studies* focuses on the multifaceted literary achievements of Lídia Jorge, most readers will surely agree that the article section closes with a *chave de ouro* by foregoing academic criticism in favor of Jorge's own words, firstly in a piece entitled "O Romance Contemporâneo," followed by Stephanie d'Orey's interview with the writer. The essay, originally read aloud in London in June 1996, analyzes the resurgence and vitality of the novel as a genre in the context of post-revolutionary Portugal. In so doing, the author situates herself within a generation intent on using the novel (as opposed to poetry) as a privileged medium to reflect (on) contemporary reality and makes an impassioned case for the genre's potential. Jorge's own ability to realize, challenge, and stretch the potential of the novel in her own work makes her one of the most distinguished and versatile writers of fiction in contemporary Portugal.

In conclusion, I wish to thank the contributors and editors who have been so willing to devote themselves to this common project. In particular, I should like to acknowledge Paulo de Medeiros, who initially inspired me to produce this volume, and Victor Mendes, who took over thereafter. And my gratitude goes to Lídia Jorge, too, for her receptiveness to my numerous requests and, above all, for being the writer she is.

Cláudia Pazos Alonso

Articles / Artigos

(Re)Telling History: Lídia Jorge's *O Dia dos Prodígios*

Lígia Silva

To the memory of my friend Maria Luís

All historical evidence is but the partial *visibilia* of *an entire invisible* world.[1]

O Dia dos Prodígios, written in 1980, was Lídia Jorge's first novel and is a celebration of as well as an ironical perspective on the 25 April 1974 Revolution. Lídia Jorge, who belongs to what Eduardo Lourenço called "a geração literária da revolução,"[2] did indeed write about the revolution and its consequences, but not from the point of view of "official discourses," that is, of those who write History, but rather from the point of view of those who in one way or another make up the unwritten reality of History. Through fiction, Lídia Jorge recovers that "entire invisible world" mentioned above, the world of the oppressed and the silenced. *O Dia dos Prodígios*, according to Lourenço, is "exigência de 'fala,'"[3] (a demand to speak) in opposition to the silence imposed on Portuguese people for almost fifty years of Salazar's dictatorship. In this sense the novel can be read as a "metaphor for April 25," as Jorge herself remarked in a lecture at the Universidade de Lisboa in March 1986.[4] In *O Dia dos Prodígios* and in Lídia Jorge's subsequent novels such as *O Cais das Merendas* (1982), *A Notícia da Cidade Silvestre* (1987), or *A Costa dos Murmúrios* (1988), the privileging of the word and the world of the dominated men and women suggests the possibility of multiple discourses that reflect the diversity of experiences where issues of class, gender, and race intermingle. It also opens up a space for a reading of the different experiences of women in a variety of social relations, contradicting the essentialized notion of women as a homogeneous entity.

In this paper I will attempt to show how Lídia Jorge brings to her text a diversity of languages or "world views" in a way which recalls Bakhtin's conceptualization of each language as "a kind of ideology brought-into-speech."[5] In this way, Lídia Jorge opens up possibilities to read *O Dia dos Prodígios* as a site of conflicting and possibly liberating "languages-in-use,"[6] which unsettles the patriarchal myth of one monologic language of truth.

Prodigious writing against silence

Bakhtin, in his theory of the novel, contends that heteroglossia are an amalgam of socio-ideological languages, where

> (...) all languages are specific points of view on the world, forms for conceptualising the world in words, specific world views, each characterised by its own objects, meanings and values. As such they all may be juxtaposed to one another, mutually supplement one another, contradict one another and be interrelated dialogically.[7]

This dialogical and dynamic conception of language implies a constant tension between two opposing sets of forces, which Bakhtin terms the centripetal and centrifugal forces of language. The centripetal forces work towards unification and stability of meaning, while the centrifugal forces introduce multiplicity and decentralization. This constant struggle defies "ideological unification and centralization,"[8] and as Herndl has suggested "is political and raises questions of power."[9] Insofar as it acknowledges the existence of different experiences mirrored through different languages and transforms each and every speaking subject into an "ideologue,"[10] Bakhtin's concept of the novel as a "social heteroglossia" offers the possibility for a better understanding of the different relations between the different social subjects in a particular society.

Lídia Jorge, in choosing to depict the rural, almost illiterate people of a small village in the Algarve, is deliberately constructing for us what I would call a "partial heteroglossia" as an act of resistance to centralizing tendencies and as a political accusation pointing to the marginalization of the rural poor. Lídia Jorge brings to her text the real atmosphere of the village with its smells, its habits, and especially the transcription of the oral speech of the villagers with their regional dialect, their jargon, and their swear words. Lídia Jorge also transcribes into the text the typical way they speak in the Algarve, where the vowels at the end of the words are closed: that in the text is transcribed by the past tense of the verbs ending in "i," such as "salti, pegui, di, atiri" (22). *O Dia dos Prodígios* conveys the idea that communication is impossible, not only between the urban and the rural world, but also between men and women, by drawing on specific techniques that remind us of oral discourse, with the continual shifting of narrative perspectives and points of view. I would suggest, then, that this struggle or dialogical relation between different discourses works as a reply to the homogenizing idea of the authoritarian discourse of Salazar's dictatorship, where people had no voice at all. These voices can be considered as "centrifugal forces," and what could be perceived as monologues are in fact dialogues in a Bakhtinian sense in that they resist and are acts of opposition to a monological discourse that wants to silence them. *O Dia dos Prodígios* starts with a brief introduction where we read, "E falamos todos ao mesmo tempo. (...) Seria bom para que ficasse bem claro o desentendimento." Characters will all talk at the same time; that is, no one will have a dominant voice. Each of their discourses, as well as the discourse of the heterodiegetic narrator, will interpenetrate each other in a dialogic relationship. The third-person narrator, controlling the development of the story, gives insight into the lives and interior of the characters, assuming the position of different narrative voices, and so participates in the polyphony of the text.

According to Bakhtin,

> (...) the word... exists in other people's mouths, in other people's contexts, serving other people's intentions: it is from there that one must take the word, and make it one's own.[11]

If, as Bakhtin claimed, one's own discourse emerges from other discourses and eventually will be able to free itself, Lídia Jorge, by bringing to her text "o desentendimento" of all characters' different ideas and intentions, is granting them the possibility of liberation through discourse. I will analyze *O Dia dos Prodígios*, arguing that in her construction of the novel as a "patchwork" of different discourses, or a "polyphony of voices," Lídia Jorge adopts an aesthetic form that uses representations of language to explore and denounce different forms of oppression in terms of class and gender, and thus also constitutes a form of liberation.

O Dia dos Prodígios is set in Vilamaninhos, a small remote village in the Algarve, where nothing ever happens. As a result, "A povoação vai ficando um ovo emurchecido. Que fede, gorado, e não gera" (21). Vilamaninhos does not produce anything anymore, and "nada avança" (139) because the young have been forced to leave, "Todos tinham abalado para as suas pátrias" (75), since there was no future for them in the village. Those who have stayed were tired of being voiceless, ignored by the politicians in the capital; the only way to survive was to seek refuge in their own dreams and hopes. These dreams and hopes, which are different for each of them, are reified in the sudden and mysterious appearance of a flying snake, which they see as "O pressentimento que antecede os grandes acontecimentos" (43). We are transported into an atmosphere of magic and fantasy to account for their daydreaming, their belief in the possibility that one day something would happen to change their lives, because although they feel powerless to change their own destiny, they see the snake as an omen, as a sign of "(…) crença (…). Não de surpresa (…) Antes de *inconformação*" (69). This resistance towards a fascist authoritarian politics that advised them to adopt "resignação" (81) and thus, silence, "(…) tão pequena é esta terra. E tão grande o seu silêncio" (170), is registered by bringing their voices to the text as a way of asserting themselves as autonomous subjects.

The leitmotiv of *O Dia dos Prodígios* is a need for change, but they have to wait, "Vão tão lentos os dias nesta espera" (150), a slow and painful expectation that is soon going to descend into disillusion and frustration. The news of a revolution that has taken place in the capital is brought by the only radio in the village, belonging to Pássaro Volante, and Maria Rebôla breaks the news saying, "(…) em Lisboa os soldados fizeram uma revolução para melhorarem a vida daquela gente? Uma re vo lu ção" (133).

Later on, Jesuína Palha also talks about the revolution as if it were happening far away and was going to have no consequences for them at all. Jesuína's double-voiced discourse, because it expresses simultaneously two different intentions, that is, the direct intention of the character who is speaking and the refracted intention of the author, towards Carma and Carminha, not only stresses the gap between the rural people and those living in Lisbon, but also criticizes this situation. Jesuína with her strong voice says that in Lisbon there are

> Gente que já tem luzes... Gente que basta fazer assim com o dedo mindinho, para que todos os instrumentos comecem a fazer o serviço... Gente. Gente que já tem sítio próprio onde dar de corpo sem ser preciso mostrar a vergonha a

> ninguém. Gente que já tem tudo o que nem é possível a gente imaginar (...). E essa gente ainda não estava conformada com o destino. (141-42)

It is interesting to note that she answers herself with a bitter remark: "Aqui é uma tristeza" (143).

For these people the revolution is a mixture of fantasy and reality, because in the end they want to believe in something, as they believe that the soldiers are now visiting all the villages in Portugal in order to "ouvir todas as queixas" (134) and to free them of their misery. When the soldiers arrive, the people of Vilamaninhos scream and shout of joy "porque o espectáculo era o mais arrebatador das suas vidas" (155), but they soon find out "Que se tinham alvoroçado por um nada" (157) since "Esses que aí vieram mostrar-se nem chegaram a ouvir a voz da gente" (157). They did not visit Vilamaninhos to hear the people's stories and complaints, but to bring their own empty discourses, full of ideals but devoid of meaning, for these people. In the end they came, "Mas ninguém compreendeu as palavras" (161), because although they came to speak about freedom, freedom of speech, and unity between all the people, they in fact did not allow the villagers to use their own words. Therefore, the realities of the two groups were too far apart for them to be able to communicate.

This miscommunication, or non-communication, is ironically depicted when one of the soldiers is addressing the community and says, "Oh amigos. Que aquela era a hora dos humilhados e dos oprimidos" (154), and one of the villagers, Manuel Gertrudes, showing his lack of political consciousness asks, "E quem são esses?" (154). The representation of these socially asymmetrical discourses has a strong satirical and political effect, especially if we take into account that the majority of these soldiers were coming from the lower strata of society. What could be understood as differently empowered discourses is in the end a kind of parody of the "official language," because the soldiers are just appropriating another discourse, the discourse of the so-called truth, "Da pura verdade" (134), that in reality is not theirs.

Lídia Jorge seems to want to convey the idea that the revolution "for the people and with the people" was just "(...) ilusão dos sentidos" or "assombração" (162), and she points out the failure of the revolution to transform relations of power. Although these country people might be called "a alavanca dos prodígios" (154), in reality they were and remain impotent after the revolution, and their lives will have to go on as ever before. The title,

O Dia dos Prodígios, when "afinal nada aconteceu," simply reinforces the satirical view of the revolution as a site for the liberation of the oppressed and the fulfilment of their dreams and wishes. The villagers soon find out that the change they were hoping for will not happen because of the snake or a revolution, but it is something that they have to look for inside themselves.

The discursive construction of gender

Bakhtin's sociolinguistic approach to the novel enables us to look into *O Dia dos Prodígios* as a discursive representation of the antagonism not only between the rural "margins" and the urban "center," but also between women and the patriarchal cultural hegemony. Although Bakhtin has been accused of being gender blind and of neglecting the existence of female writers in his work, his theory provides some useful insights for feminist criticism.[12]

I would like to suggest that the struggle or dialogical relation between different voices or particular ways of viewing the world allows for the deconstruction and the undermining of discursive authoritarian practices, founded on binary oppositions, where the category "woman" is always grounded in an essential identity and takes the position of an alien "other."

The narrative sequence built as an entanglement of different stories told by men and women who reveal different ways of perceiving the world shows Lídia Jorge's insistence on the significance of gender. This is well expressed in the chatter between the old couple, Esperança and José Jorge Júnior, in which each of them goes on and on speaking without really listening to each other, "(…) os dois aqui de palestra sem se ouvirem" (33). It is important to remark that while Esperança talks about the thirteen children she had, remembering all the details of when they were born, José, standing on a bench, in a position of superiority as if giving a speech, talks about his ancestors and how brave they were.

Whereas José recalls images of a glorious past, as a form of asserting himself as a man, through the patriarchal history of the family, Esperança's memory is firmly grounded in the materiality of the everyday and is etched in her consciousness as well as in her body, "porque afinal depois de tanta lágrima, nenhuma dor lhe atingia o corpo" (73). José's words can be identified as what Bakhtin calls "the authoritative discourse," because "it is connected with a past that is felt to be hierarchically higher. It is, so to speak, the word of the fathers."[13] Esperança is the stereotyped image of the self-sacrificing, submissive mother and wife, the only role the patriarchal society envisaged for her and to which she must conform. As Sadlier has pointed out, "Their speeches represent an archetypal male and female discourse aimed 'outward,' towards the reader."[14] Therefore, Esperança's double-voiced discourse towards herself and an "absent addressee," or the reader, is subversive because it offers itself to be read in opposition to that official, masculine, phallocentric discourse.

Jesuína Palha: Parody through discourse

According to Holquist, "Heteroglossia is a plurality of relations, not just a cacophony of voices."[15] Lídia Jorge illustrates this with the layout of her narrative, dividing the text into columns to represent unbalanced relations of power. There are two such moments in the narrative—when Jesuína Palha tells Carminha Rosa and her daughter about the snake, and later on about the revolution. Whereas Jesuína Palha's words are on the left column, the column on the right presents gaps to express the silence, the ostracism enforced by the community on Carminha Rosa and Carminha, "(...) banida dentro dos muros da própria vizinhança" (56). The mother is depicted as a sinner and described in terms of moral evaluations, as Carminha is the daughter of a priest, an illegitimate child, "uma condenação" (17). By analogy with her mother, Carminha is also a sinner, expressed by the fact that they have the same name.

Jesuína functions here as the "spokeswoman" of the community and reinforces their marginalized position, calling them "Suas enteadas do diabo" (141) and "gente que sempre foi empedernida e consporcada" (145), supported by a first-person plural voice on the left, "a gente," or the voice of the community, that works like a chorus. Jesuína, making them publicly responsible for the incident with the snake, is just a pretext for "Uma acusação pública e bem testemunhada contra as suas pessoas" (145). She speaks in the name of a community which needs a scapegoat in order to reinforce the cultural rules and the stability of the community.

Although Jesuína is not conscious of her alienated speech, she is a kind of leader of the community, and she identifies with those "virile" women that Kristeva in "The Terror of Power or the Power of Terrorism" identifies as the "guardians of the status quo, the most zealous protectors of the established order."[16] Kristeva argues that even if some women are now in leadership positions in government and industry, the problem of the power structures remains the same. These women end up identifying with the power structures, and instead of a change towards democratization, there is conformism and stabilization.

Jesuína embodies the moral values of Vilamaninhos and by extension of a society that condemns women for threatening the imposed social codes and the stability of the "Law of the Father." By discursively reinforcing the monologic, Jesuína undertakes the role of a centripetal figure in the novel.

Carminha Rosa is a double sinner, because she not only had a child out of wedlock, but also the child of a priest, thus challenging the values and morals of one of the ideological pillars of patriarchal society, the Catholic Church. Jesuína is depicted as a very strong woman: "Nem homem, nem mancebo conseguiu jamais fazer o que fez essa mulher valente." However, she is empowered only by ventriloquizing that same discourse that oppresses her as a woman, the authoritative discourse of patriarchy. She assumes the attitudes usually attributed to men "cospe no chão" (145) and also their language when she incriminates Carminha with the question: "a quantos tu já deste a pinquinha?" (144). Jesuína also accuses Carma and Carminha of opening their door to any man, implying that they are whores, and says, "Mas quem vem nem olha à cara. Nem sequer às pernas. Antes ao fundo delas, para se *aviar* depressa" (144).

Bakhtin relates parody to the tradition of carnival, which he sees as an occasion for temporary inversions of the power hierarchy and "the feast of becoming, change and renewal."[17] The attitude of Jesuína "dez vezes mais varonil que um homem" (156) leading the mob, formed only by women and children, may be associated with carnival rituals. It may be read as a mockery, pointing to the parodic fiction of gender identity as immutable. Jesuína is a "mulher-homem," and so she carnivalizes cultural idealizations of the feminine. Pointing to the fluidity of gender identity, where features of masculinity and femininity are not rigid, it questions the concept of a fixed gender identity. As Bakhtin argues about carnival, "It absolutises nothing, but rather proclaims the joyful relativity of everything."[18] Although Jesuína assumes the dominant role in relation to Carminha Rosa and her daughter, reinforcing the culturally repressive rules defined by patriarchy for "unruly" women, she can only assert her position as a speaking subject by mimicking a masculine discourse. Having internalized a discourse that is not hers, the authoritative discourse of patriarchy, she unconsciously conforms to it as she embodies a masculine attitude and language. If on one hand Jesuína points to the possibility of "renewal" and "change" as she unconsciously debunks cultural mystifications of women's identity, on the other hand she reinforces the established order. Her ambivalent figure points to the ambivalence of carnival itself as a form of liberation. As Herndl suggests when discussing the restricted space of carnival for a true subversion of the structures of power, "Carnival represents an event staged by those with power to subvert any potential power which might be developed by the oppressed."[19]

Branca: a textual strategy of liberation

In her article "Irigarayan Dialogism: Play and Powerplay," Schwab defends Irigaray against accusations of being essentialist. She argues that Irigaray's identification of a certain textual praxis with the morphology of female sexuality has to be read metaphorically and as a dialogical textual strategy. She also contends that "the battle against women's oppression begins at the level of language, of textuality, and will be fought out there."[20] I suggest, then, that Lídia Jorge's writing practice can be identified with Schwab's concept of dialogical textual strategy, which by forcing a dialogue with monologic positions, attempts to disclose and shatter them.

Jorge in a recent interview with Stephanie d' Orey said that

> (...) my novels describe Mediterranean women as powerful, but at the same time apparently submissive. The world of politics is not their concern—their natural arena is the family and the home—about which nonetheless they often complain.[21]

Although this naturalized point of view may be arguable, Lídia Jorge's writing shows what Spivak terms "a strategic use of positivist essentialism" framed "in a scrupulously visible political interest"[22] against patriarchy. Spivak identifies the "subaltern" with the female body, contending that the experience of the female body has to be examined in its cultural and economic context. This is the only way to recover the enormous gap in History concerning women, whose bodies were always taken for granted and exploited. I will argue that although Lídia Jorge in *O Dia dos Prodígios* conveys an essentialist conception of gender, identifying women as victims of patriarchy who conform to their fixed roles as wives and mothers, she introduces the possibility of liberation from the symbolic order through Branca.

Although she complies with sociocultural dictates by becoming a wife and a mother, she always remains skeptical of her role in society. Branca, always "submissa e obediente" (88), is going to assert herself through speech and by the linguistic assimilation and consequent refusal of her role as wife, mother, and "mula." Her husband, Pássaro Volante, always associates her with his lost mule "(…) contra a insolência de uma mula tão louca como a mulher, e como ela perversamente misteriosa e cínica." Pássaro not only calls her a mule, but he also has sex with her as if she were a mule: "Pássaro cavalga. Branca é um dorso macio de aragem pelada" (48). Pássaro uses his wife "para se libertar das forças inúteis do seu corpo" (128), seeing her only as an object and depriving her of her own sexuality, because as "an angel woman," she has no sexuality anyway. She is not only abused, but also deprived of her body and her own voice: "E eu mais do que submissa, acobardada. Caladinha" (88). In Pássaro's mind she is a working-mule, someone who was born only to work for and serve her husband and children. But a mule may also mean someone false or deceitful. Pássaro is both aware and afraid of his wife's subversive potential to deceive him. Ironically, it is through a traditional feminine task used by Branca's husband "para controlar a minha pessoa no próprio espírito" (88), that Branca will start her process of breaking free, embroidering a flying dragon.

Turning her submissiveness and her silence into transgression, because "Um silêncio (…) nunca é bem um silêncio absoluto" (147), she starts what in Bakhtinian terms is a "re-socialization"[23] of an inner conflict.

As Emerson explains, Bakhtin

> does not deny the reality of internal conflicts, but he does socialize them, thus exposing their mechanisms to the light of day. If enough individuals experience the same gap, it is re-socialized: there develops a political underground, and the potential for revolution.[24]

This gap may be understood as the lack of words women have to express their particular experiences within a patriarchal discourse. Branca, recognizing her inevitable place within the patriarchy, creates an alternative position to assert herself, seeing through people and reading their minds. Branca not only speaks out against her oppression, but her discourse, expressing her wishes and powers, can only be expressed in a language no longer defined by masculine meaning. Branca starts to sleep with her eyes open and to hear sounds at a distance, "havia tempo que ouvia os sons à distância" (46), like a premonition. To reinforce the recognition of her role as a woman, as biology is understood as destiny in a patriarchal society, she recalls the first time when she had her period and "se rendera à evidência de uma preparação inexorável para um ciclo" (59). Although her first reaction was "Oh não" (59), Branca knew that after she had had her period, she was ready to accomplish her function as a woman, that is, to marry and have children, according to the same decree that rendered women blind to men's sexual aggressions and that made them accept the authority of fathers and husbands.

Branca never stops thinking about her life: "Ardem-me os olhos dos pensamentos" (87). She dreams of the day when she will be able to free herself and when she will no longer need to "cortar as coleiras que me amarram a língua" (85). When she tells Pássaro about her powers, he says, "Ficou louca" (91) and he does not understand her anymore: "Esta fala latim (...)" (166). The fact that Branca starts to gain consciousness of herself and starts to speak confirms her position as a subject in discourse, in active dialogic relation to others. Branca, asserting herself as a subject, is denying her position as an object to be battered, possessed, silenced, and abused. For Pássaro, this can only mean that she is mad, because she is expressing a reality that is beyond his own discourse and understanding. According to Bakhtin, "The ideological becoming of a human being (...) is the process of selectively assimilating the words of others."[25] Branca's transformation, or "ideological becoming," gradually happens inside herself, by absorbing and then opposing her husband's words, as Pássaro stands for the discourse that she refuses and that oppresses her. Pássaro did not realize that "quanto mais a prendera mais a soltara para um recanto escondido da liberdade" (148). The change that she achieves is inside herself, "eu própria fiz mudança, porque nunca consegui dizer tantas palavras junto de ti (...). Ou seja da noite, da revolução ou de *mim mesma*" (148). But this change is expressed in words, and it occurs through the assimilation of the road sweeper's words as well. The road sweeper states that "Ninguém se liberta se não quiser libertar-se. Empedernidas as pessoas criaram o jeito de olhar a pila como centro do mundo" (91).

Her transformation suggests, then, that identity, like discourse, is constructed in the relationship between speaker and addressee. Unlike Pássaro, who does not feel the need to change because he is "in the center of the world," Branca is tired of being the "escravazinha" (66). Living in a house "onde apenas tinha feito de parideira de meninos machos. E servindo as coisas que serviam as bestas" (88), she realizes that even in a phallocentric world there are ways of contradicting and subverting that same world. Her desire to break free, expressed through gaining powers to predict people's future, is the alternative she finds when she realizes that total freedom is forbidden to her, so she has to create for herself something else as a weapon of survival. Even if Branca is just producing a moment of utopian freedom, it relativizes the authoritative norm, contradicts the idea of the single subject-centered reason, pointing to the need for a reconception of the self. Through Branca, Lídia Jorge found a way to underscore the idea that it is possible to escape the confining dichotomies that ground masculine representations of reality.

Ultimately by reaccentuating the dialects and discourses of the disenfranchised, be they a rural community or women, Lídia Jorge is denouncing authoritarian power structures whether they are fascist, patriarchal, marxist, or Lisbon-centred, and she is making a stand against totalizing concepts of History. *O Dia dos Prodígios* is a struggle of words with words which represents the conditions of existence of those subjects, men and women, who are muted or absent in dominant discourses. Lídia Jorge, in a "breve tempo de uma demonstração" (13), creates a style whereby the relationship between reality and mimesis is problematized, which calls into question the concepts of fiction and truth, and serves to demystify demagogic concepts of fictional truths, such as identity. Even if the acknowledgement of a proteiform concept of female identity is only possible in fiction and through anti-mimetic representations of language, it challenges the institutionalized norm. By defamiliarizing literary and social norms, Lídia Jorge introduces the possibility for women like Branca, "autora de nada"(66), to be the authors of their multiple identity.

Notes

All italicized quotations of *O Dia dos Prodígios* are my emphasis.

[1] Nancy Partner, unpublished paper presented at the 1984 American Historical Association, Chicago, cited in Caroll Smith Rosenberg, "Writing History: Language, Class and Gender," *Feminist Studies/Critical Studies*, ed. Teresa de Lauretis (Bloomington: Indiana University Press, 1986) 31-52, citation from p. 31.

[2] Eduardo Lourenço, "Literatura e Revolução" 13.

[3] Lourenço 15.

[4] Sadlier, *The Question of How* 49.

[5] Wayne C. Booth, "Freedom of Interpretation: Bakhtin and the Challenge of Feminist Criticism," *Bakhtin: Essays and Dialogues on His Work*, ed. Gary Saul Morson (Chicago and London: University of Chicago Press, 1986) 145-75, citation from p. 151.

[6] Diane Price Herndl, "The Dilemmas of a Feminine Dialogic," *Feminism, Bakhtin and The Dialogic*, eds. Dale M. Bauer and Susan Mackinstry (Albany: State University of New York

Press, 1991) 7-24, citation from p. 9.

[7] M. Bakhtin, "Discourse in the Novel," *The Dialogic Imagination: Four Essays by M. M. Bakhtin*, ed. Michael Holquist, trans. Caryl Emerson and Michael Holquist (Austin: University of Texas Press, 1981) 262.

[8] Bahktin, "Discourse in the Novel" 271.

[9] Herndl, "The Dilemmas of a Feminine Dialogic" 7.

[10] Bakhtin, "Discourse in the Novel" 333. Nancy Glazener argues that the importance Bakhtin gives to Dostoevsky is due to his depiction of characters as "ideologues" who "interact with each other, who attempt to persuade each other, who represent certain values for each other" (117). See her article "Dialogic Subversion," *Bakhtin and Cultural Theory*, eds. Ken Hirschkop and David Shepherd (Manchester: Manchester University Press, 1989).

[11] Bahktin, "Discourse in the Novel" 294.

[12] See Denise Heikinen, "Is Bakhtin a Feminist or Just Another Dead White Male? A Celebration of Possibilities in Manuel Puig's Kiss of the Spider Woman," *A Dialogue of Voices: Feminist Literary Theory and Bakhtin*, eds. Karen Hohne and Helen Wussow (Minneapolis: University of Minnesota Press, 1994), 114-27, citation from p. 115. Mary Russo also claims that Bakhtin fails to acknowledge or incorporate the social relations of gender in his analysis. See her article "Female Grotesques: Carnival and Theory," *Feminist Studies/Cultural Studies*, ed. Teresa de Lauretis (Bloomington: Indiana University Press, 1986) 213-27.

[13] Bakhtin, "Discourse in the Novel" 342.

[14] Sadlier 65.

[15] Michael Holquist, *Dialogism* 89.

[16] Julia Kristeva, "Women's Time," *The Kristeva Reader*, ed. Toril Moi (Oxford: Blackwell, 1986) 201.

[17] Peter Stallybrass and Allon White, *The Politics and Poetics of Transgression* (London & Itaca, 1986) 17.

[18] Bakhtin, *Problems of Dostoevsky's Poetics* 125.

[19] Herndl, "The Dilemmas of a Feminine Dialogic" 20. According to Mary Russo, carnival has its limitations and is especially dangerous for women and marginalized groups precisely because of its complicity with the dominant culture. See Mary Russo, "Female Grotesques: Carnival and Theory" 213-27.

[20] Gail M. Scwab, "Irigaryan Dialogism: Play and Powerplay," *Feminism, Bakhtin and the Dialogic*, eds. Dale M. Bauer and Susan Mackinstry (Albany: State University of New York Press, 1991) 57-69, citation from p. 67.

[21] Interview with Stephanie d'Orey, *Cultura* 12.

[22] See Gayatri Chakravorty Spivak, *In Other Worlds* 205.

[23] This is a term used by Caryl Emerson in her article "Outer Word and Inner Speech," *Bakhtin: Essays and Dialogues on His Work*, ed. Gary Saul Morson (Chicago and London: University of Chicago Press, 1986).

[24] Emerson 33.

[25] Bakhtin, "Discourse in the Novel" 341.

Works cited

Bakhtin, M. *Esthétique du Roman*. Trans. Daria Olivier. Paris: Éditions Gallimard, 1978.

———. *The Dialogic Imagination: Four Essays*. Ed. Michael Holquist. Austin: University of Texas Press, 1981.

———. *Problems of Dostoevsky's Poetics*. Ed. and trans. Caryl Emerson. London and Minneapolis: University of Minnesota Press, 1984.

Bauer, Dale M. and Susan Mackinstry, eds. *Feminism, Bakhtin and the Dialogic*. Albany: State University of New York Press, 1991.

———. *Feminist Dialogics: A Theory of Failed Community*. Albany: State University of New York Press, 1988.

De Lauretis, Teresa, ed. *Feminist Studies/Critical Studies*. Bloomington: Indiana University Press, 1986.

d'Orey, Stephanie, *Cultura* 16 (Spring 1998): 12-13

Espírito Santo, Moisés. *A Religião Popular Portuguesa*. Lisboa: Assírio & Alvim, 1990.

Graham, Lawrence and Douglas Wheeler, eds. *In Search of Modern Portugal: The Revolution and its Consequences*. Wisconsin: The University of Wisconsin Press, 1983.

Hirschkop, Ken and David Shepherd, eds. *Bakhtin and Cultural Theory*. Manchester: Manchester University Press, 1989.

Hohne, Karen and Helen Wussow, eds. *A Dialogue of Voices: Feminist Literary Theory and Bakhtin*. Minneapolis: University of Minnesota Press, 1994.

Holquist, Michael. "Answering as Authoring." *Critical Inquiry* 10.2 (December 1983): 307-319.

———. *Dialogism: Bakhtin and his World*. London: Routledge, 1990.

Jameson, Frederic. *The Political Unconscious: Narrative as a Socially Symbolic Act*. London: Methuen, 1981.

Jorge, Lídia, *A Costa dos Murmúrios*. Lisboa: Publicações D. Quixote, 1988.

———. *A Notícia da Cidade Silvestre*. Lisboa: Publicações D. Quixote, 1984.

———. "Escrita e Emancipação." *Revista Crítica de Ciências Sociais* 18/20 (Fevereiro 1986): 57-62.

———. *O Cais das Merendas*. Lisboa: Publicações Europa-América, 1982.

———. *O Dia dos Prodígios*. Lisboa: Publicações Europa-América, 1980.

Lourenço, Eduardo. "Literatura e Revolução." *Colóquio/Letras* 78 (Março 84): 7-16

McHale, Brian. *Postmodernist Fiction*. New York and London: Methuen, 1987.

Medeiros, Paulo de. "Em Nome de Portugal." *Discursos: Estudos de Língua e Cultura Portuguesa* 13 (October 1996): 13-29.

Moi, Toril, ed. *The Kristeva Reader*. Oxford UK and Cambridge USA: Blackwell, 1986.

Morson, Gary Saul, ed. *Bakhtin: Essays and Dialogues on His Work*. Chicago and London: University of Chicago Press, 1986.

Sadlier, Darlene. *The Question of How. Women Writers and New Portuguese Literature*. New York and London: Greenwood Press, 1989.

Seixo, Maria Alzira. *A Palavra do Romance: Ensaios de Genologia e Análise*. Lisboa: Livros Horizonte, 1986.

Spivak, Gayatri Chakravorty. *In Other Worlds: Essays on Cultural Politics*. London and New York: Routledge, 1987.

Stallybrass, Peter and Allon White. *The Politics and Poetics of Transgression*. London: Methuen, 1986.

Sex and Success in *Notícia da Cidade Silvestre*: A Tale of Two Cities

Cláudia Pazos Alonso

In 1972, the publication of *Novas Cartas Portuguesas* marked a watershed in Portuguese women's writing. Ten years later, the literary landscape had changed beyond recognition. Widening the ranks of a select number of already consecrated sisters, unprecedented numbers of talented women writers were making highly acclaimed literary debuts, usually with works of fiction. They included Lídia Jorge, Teolinda Gersão, and Hélia Correia among others. A significant proportion of them, however, rejected the label of "feminist" and feminist militancy,[1] and even the concept of "escrita feminina." For, as Hilary Owen observes, "Many contemporary women writers in Portugal rightly mistrust the inverted sexism and potential ghetthoization that creating an alternative women's canon could imply."[2] This unease notwithstanding, women's fiction does clearly display female-specific traits and concerns.[3]

Among recent women writers, the fiction of Lídia Jorge is exemplary not only for its interrogation of issues such as as history and its re-presentation, common to many post-revolutionary writers, but also for its unmistakable engagement with sexual/textual politics from a woman-centered perspective. The purpose of this paper is to examine her third work, *Notícia da Cidade Silvestre*, awarded the Cidade de Lisboa prize in 1984, in the light of the equality versus difference debate, arguing that through creative practice, Lídia Jorge is able to negotiate, or at least envisage, a conceptual framework that constructs a new and powerful position for women as subjects.

Notícia da Cidade Silvestre[4] is a remarkable work that centers on the profound but increasingly conflictual friendship between two women, Anabela Cravo and Júlia Grei, in the context of their struggle for survival in the inhospitable urban environment of Lisbon in the late 1970s. The novel follows the two women over a period of several years and bears witness to the transformation of the "heroine" Júlia. To that extent, *Notícia* conforms to the pattern of a nineteenth-century *bildungsroman*, as the naive Júlia gradually becomes more streetwise and world weary.[5] Despite Júlia's transformation, literary reviews from the male establishment have tended to center on the figure of Anabela Cravo, described by João Gaspar Simões "a rompante mulher que é essa aventureira dos novos tempos, os tempos da sociedade feminista," "ao pé dela a Júlia Grei não é nada, humanamente falando."[6] Gaspar Simões is fairly scathing in his analysis of the last quarter of the novel, a revealing fact in itself, since it coincides with the time when Júlia, up to then the weakling of the two friends, gradually begins to come into her own.

By contrast, when Lídia Jorge is interviewed by Regina Louro, a rather different emphasis emerges.[7] Lídia Jorge clearly sympathizes with Júlia and passionately defends her character against the (male) misconception that she is a doormat, deserving to be trampled on: "[Anabela] faz mimetismo do homem; Júlia é talvez a personagem por onde a mudança passa realmente" (2). A little later, she elaborates on this point: "Júlia é uma figura reivindicativa, não concorda? Achei que fazê-la de uma forma mansa era mais eficaz do que fazê-la de uma forma revoltada e excessiva [...] Traz em si o desejo de equilíbrio do ser" (3). Indeed, Júlia reaches an unprecedented degree of power and autonomy through the act of writing, given that the novel ends with her about to give up her day job in a bookshop to devote herself to full-time writing. In other words, there is a momentous shift from Júlia's role as passive consumer and guardian of the written word to active productive agent in her own right. In this context, it is significant that the novel is written in the first person in a language akin to what Lídia Jorge describes as "a reprodução livre de uma intimidade falada," enabling the protagonist to tell *herstory*. It is also noteworthy that this "intimidade falada" is addressed, in the first instance, to an anonymous interlocutor whom Júlia, the narrator, meets at a time of great stress, following the suicide attempt of her son Jóia, a point to which we shall return. For, in so doing, the narrative draws attention to the central role of dialogue in the construction of identity and self-definition.

1. Júlia, the Powerless Female

When the novel begins, Júlia, a recently widowed young woman, has to fend for herself and her son and struggles to make ends meet. Therefore, when the strong and determined Anabela comes onto the scene, Júlia soon becomes dependent on her as provider of both emotional and material support. Right from the very opening lines, there is no doubt as to who "wears the trousers," metaphorically speaking: "Se morássemos numa casa com janela na manhã do encontro, eu teria ido por-me no parapeito à espera de Anabela Cravo" (19). Aside from the shocking realization that Júlia's home (which turns out to be her deceased husband's workshop) is devoid of proper windows, making her a prisoner in her own attic, this incipit positions Júlia in the traditional and passive female occupation of waiting at the window for the arrival of a miraculous "prince charming." Júlia lives in a limbo, literally as well as metaphorically, since she is surrounded from all angles by her dead husband's sculptures.

However, by the end of the first chapter, there are already signs that Anabela, far from being a prince charming or even a good fairy who can rescue Júlia from her predicament, is selfish and builds her self-confidence at the expense of her friend. As the friendship develops, Anabela becomes increasingly manipulative. For instance, she persuades her friend to lend her the atelier for illicit sexual encounters with her sugar-daddy, Padrinho. The inequality in the two women's positions is encoded in the fact that Júlia does not even know where Anabela lives, whereas Anabela owns a key to the workshop. The key, a phallic symbol of penetration according to Freud, pinpoints the fact that Anabela can enter Júlia's intimate territory while remaining in complete control of her own space. Anabela rings and visits only when it suits her. As Hilary Owen points out, in time she even takes on characteristics of "the traditional breadwinner" when she compensates for broken promises to Jóia with material goods, such as a "borrowed" television.[8]

Unlike Anabela, the self-effacing and self-abnegating Júlia is a truly caring companion in adversity. When Anabela discovers her unwanted pregnancy, Júlia through sheer intuition manages to locate her friend's dwelling. She handles enquiries to secure a back-street abortion and foots the hefty bill (fourteen contos, a sum nearly equal to her monthly wages). Since abortion was still illegal at the time, Júlia was risking imprisonment. Furthermore, she remains by Anabela's side for a week despite risking dismissal from work (120-37). The roles of carer and provider are thus completely reversed as Anabela temporarily becomes mute, regressing to a childlike state, while Júlia nurses her back to life with unconditional love. This selflessness is all the more admirable given the fact that, in the process of tracking her down, Júlia had discovered that her friend lived under the same roof as her married sugar-daddy figure, Padrinho.[9]

Anabela, initially perceived as a positive, resourceful woman, is therefore soon revealed as simultaneously devious and deceitful. She is a classic example of the predatory woman who uses men sexually on her way to the top, to pay for dental treatment for instance, or to do her articles with a renowned lawyer.[10] Furthermore, she is unable to act any differently in the context of a relationship based on female friendship. She lies shamelessly to Júlia, patronizes and uses her, her atelier and subsequently even her new home, as a part of her self-promoting strategy. More ruthlessly still, when Jóia inadvertently interrupts a particularly important sexual encounter, Anabela abruptly severs all contact with her (195).

Unlike the childless Anabela, who is free to sell her body, Júlia incessantly has to juggle conflicting demands as a single mother with significantly less room for maneuver. In order to secure her and her son's material survival, she works for a pittance in a bookshop. Her lack of qualifications and her precarious financial situation echo that of another widow, Dora Rosário, in Maria Judite de Carvalho's *Os Armários Vazios* (1966). As a result, she has little "quality" time to devote to her son. Whenever there is an unforeseen event, she either has to arrange makeshift childcare or risk leaving Jóia on his own. Because his mother is so busy trying to secure the household's financial survival, Jóia is largely left to his own devices, ultimately with disastrous consequences.

Despite her precarious circumstances, Júlia shuns Anabela's advice of a lucrative marriage with the eligible Saraiva, following her heart instead into a relationship with Artur, the penniless sculptor, footless and free and intent on remaining so. But when Júlia becomes pregnant, he reacts as if it were a curtailment of his freedom. In a desperate bid to save their love, Júlia decides to have an abortion. In telling contrast to Anabela's abortion, Júlia will be entirely by herself, without a shoulder to lean on, since by then Anabela has gone entirely her separate way and Artur is shielded from the grim truth with the explanation of a miscarriage. Even so, Artur eventually leaves her.[11]

2. The New Júlia or What it Takes to Beat Anabela at her Own Game

After she has been abandoned by her nearest and dearest, Júlia decides to become more pragmatic and coldhearted like Anabela, whose success she is able to contemplate from afar. She had tried to survive through the socially acceptable activity of sewing rag dolls, but now, spurred on by the vision of Anabela's success, she adopts a utilitarian view of men. She arranges to meet with Saraiva, a bachelor clearly intent on putting her on a pedestal. Júlia acts as the virginal, demure woman without a past that he longs for, but this role-play places her in an impossible situation because of Jóia's existence, since Saraiva is unable to accept her as a woman with family commitments. Her relationship with Mão Dianjo, a long-standing family friend, also undergoes changes. At a time when she was at her most vulnerable and in need of comfort, they had sex once. Now it just becomes an expedient means to fill the coffers. Eventually Júlia also names her price to her boss, Sr. Assumpção.

Both Mão Dianjo and Sr. Assumpção have incongruously angelical names, since they are in fact lecherous old men who take advantage of Júlia's emotional and financial vulnerability. Saraiva, who shuts Jóia off from their future as a couple, is no better. The name Saraiva "era o mesmo que granizo (...) água congelada caindo em grãos contra a janela" (61), an apt reminder of his lack of humanity behind the façade of his orderly life as an employee in the ironically named insurance company Tranquilidade. Unlike the men in her life, who have both certainty (tranquilidade) and centrality (apótema),[12] Júlia is emphatically condemned to the margins, a fact strikingly brought home when she tries her hand at prostitution for a couple of months (285). She only gives up this degrading but lucrative activity after a close brush with death (in a hallucinatory scene, she is nearly run over by a psychotic male driver), realizing that Jóia needs her alive (286-87).

Sadly, Jóia has become increasingly psychologically disturbed and has problems at school. It will only take one more thing to make him tip over the edge, and this occurs when Saraiva redesigns aloud Júlia's flat in a way such that the boy would be dispossessed of his own room. Saraiva and Júlia go out for a romantic meal, leaving a devasted child behind. The result, predictably, is Jóia's suicide attempt. His death is only narrowly avoided because Júlia, out of sheer instinct, abandons Saraiva in the middle of the meal to rush back to the flat.

Jóia's near death constitutes a turning point in Júlia's life. While in hospital by his bedside, she is overcome by an irrational and all-pervasive need to carry a knife with her (296), a tangible symbol of her pent-up aggression. She also has an uncontrollable urge to write and starts scribbling in her diary. Significantly, we learn that she had been writing for years and it may have been the only way for her to keep her sanity. Earlier in the novel, Júlia had confessed to Mão Dianjo that she was incapable of hatred, an admission of failure by male standards, since Mão Dianjo firmly believes in the need to learn how to hate in order to be free: "Só ele [o ódio] é capaz de defender, de preservar, robustecer a pessoa" (264).

When stating the necessity of hatred, Mão Dianjo had primarily Jóia in mind, implying that in order to survive, it was imperative for the youngster to establish his identity by distinguishing himself from his mother. Certainly, as he lies in his hospital bed mute, powerless and without hair, Jóia reverts back to an infant-like stage. His healing can only occur through successful self-affirmation, a fact that becomes clear when the first words that he writes are his full name "João Mário Matos Grei." His recovery is further ensured by the presence of a "father" figure, Fernando, who gives him a Dalmatian dog. The dog acts as a transitional object, as the (grammatically female) diminutive of Jóia is transferred to the animal, while the boy assumes the more virile name of João Mário.

If hatred becomes profoundly liberating for João Mário, it proves to be equally so for Júlia, in what constitutes a ritual initiation similar to the trajectory of the central female character in Clarice Lispector's story "O Búfalo," from *Laços de Família*. Jóia's suicide attempt constitutes her "epiphany," a point of no return. She starts carrying her knife around, ready for use, and decides to sell her diary. These twin acts gradually transform her, eventually giving her sufficient strength to stand up to the various persons who have used and abused her: Saraiva, Mão Dianjo, Sr. Assumpção and finally Anabela. Her symbolic victory over Mão Dianjo, whom she threatens with the knife (303), boosts her self-confidence[13] and enables her to encounter Anabela to exorcise old ghosts.

In the intervening years, Anabela has made it to the top. She has obtained her law degree, boasts an enviable job, has several people working for her, and owns a luxury flat, which is part of her divorce settlement from her former boss, Atougia Ferraz. Anabela, however, readily acknowledges the emptiness of her life. But, sadly, far from begging Júlia's forgiveness for treating her appallingly throughout their relationship, she carries on in exactly the same vein. This disregard culminates with her humiliation of Júlia by showing her the discarded dolls so patiently sewn by the latter over the years. Anabela had been secretely buying these back as a token of her commitment, as if friendship was no more than a mercenary transaction, an exchange commodity that money can purchase.

In other words, Júlia has been like a rag doll at the hands of the unscrupulous Anabela Cravo, bought and discarded when no longer needed, and never really treasured. As Hilary Owen puts it, "Nothing that Júlia does is undertaken independently of the uterine strings that make her Anabela's puppet. This is finally underlined when she confronts the rag dolls who reflect herself" (422). Therefore, in order to free herself from this stifling umbilical cord, Júlia must throw the knife that she carries with her as a display of (phallic) potency. Again, in Hilary Owen's words, "Júlia must symbolically knife her in order to be free of her, just as Dorian Grey kills his own portrait" (429).

In the lead-up to this climax, Anabela is rather relentlessly caricatured as a tyrannical man who expects "his" submissive "wife" to bring newspapers, cigarettes, drinks, and food at her every call and beckon, and then to sit adoringly at her feet. But at last Júlia can now see through her former friend and is appalled by what she stands for. Anabela is metaphorically sterile, and the mancha negra on her face, which (rather problematically) is attributed to the pill, makes her look as though she had a moustache. She is a mutant, a monstrous creature: "uma nova raça, um outro sexo e uma outra natureza se anunciava em Anabela Cravo como se a terra se movesse para dar à luz uma outra espécie de pessoa" (320). Júlia's rejection of Anabela's model is uncompromising, but it does not force her back into the passive victim role since, by drawing out the knife, she shakes off the yoke and breaks free of this abusive relationship. Her own strength and power do not rely on the same strategy of oppression as Anabela: "Anabela teria de saber que a Terra se move de vários modos" (321).[14] This is confirmed beyond all doubt by Júlia's inner reflections after leaving a terrified Anabela, as she looks at the crowd of night workers on their way to and fro:

> gente baixa, gente gorda, gente negra, gente de poderosas varizes como rios de sangue, gente anã, gente coxa, gente torta carregada de sacos de plástico (...) gente igual a mim, gente minha irmã. Gente ainda por meter medo a alguém pelo menos uma vez na vida. (321)

In other words, despite her newly acquired strength, Júlia's solidarity still lies with the downtrodden.

3. The Subversion of Gender Polarizations

By positing the victory of Júlia over Anabela as the novel draws to a close, and by crowning it with Júlia's complete rejection of the model of power offered by Anabela, *Notícia da Cidade Silvestre* challenges the notion that equal rights feminism is likely ever to solve the problem of women's fundamental inequality in society. Anabela is, of course, a grotesque parody of the liberated woman. She is determined to compete on an equal footing with men, but it is clear that the world that surrounds her is still visibly far removed from a world of equal opportunities. The only way to the top for a woman of her background is to sleep her way up, discarding friendships as soon as they have served their purpose. In order to succeed, she has to be "worse than a man," denying herself any feelings. Finally, being successful and having a child are perceived as wholly and mutually exclusive. Anabela succeeds in reproducing the male pattern of dominance, but only at the expense of utter emotional and physical sterility.

Early on in the novel, Anabela had exploded conventional notions of biological determinism. She had developed a pioneering sexual theory that distinguished between biological sex and inner gender. According to her, the world is divided into two species: those who have knowledge (saber) and those who have (only) intimate understanding (conhecer) (54). These two categories can be roughly approximated to traditional gender polarizations such as (male) reason versus (female) sensitivity. Anabela thus forcefully undermines the preconception that people are gender-bound by virtue of their biological sex. However, in practice, she also reinforces the masculine/feminine hierarchy, by equating "masculine" knowledge and know-how with sought-after power and action. By contrast, it is clear that "feminine" perceptiveness/insightfulness/empathy does not grant any straightforward access to a position of power in the realm of the Symbolic. Anabela, of course, belongs to the former, the law of the Father, whereas Júlia struggles in the latter. Yet, significantly, Júlia seems to come out better than her in the end.[15]

If we apply these categories of "saber" and "conhecer" to the men in Júlia's life, all of them, apart from Artur, have a place in the Symbolic order. As such, like Anabela, they belong to the realm of those who have knowledge and power. Artur is the exception, living like a rebel on the margins of society, and we are repeatedly told that he and Júlia belong to the same "raça interior" and are thus intertwined in an "incesto de almas." There is, however, another momentous exception, Fernando, the only man who remains on the scene at the end of the novel. Arguably, he is the only man who did not use Júlia sexually, even though she offered herself to him as a token of gratitude for his unfailing support of Jóia (299). More importantly, he is the only man who treats Jóia as a real person, giving him his undivided time, love, and attention.

What is remarkable about Fernando is his slow transformation in Júlia's eyes. Much in the same way as Júlia, he was initially positioned as a "loser." At the outset, dwarfed by Artur's physical presence, he was viewed as feminine and almost childlike before gradually coming into his own. By the end, his height is no longer perceived negatively, for his stature has certainly grown in Júlia's eyes. Because Júlia has gained self-confidence, she is arguably better able to revalue the "feminine" Fernando. Through sheer persistence, Fernando has also grown into a talented artist. Halfway through the novel, even Artur applauds one of his works. At the end, when Fernando's exhibition takes place, it is a public success. He has taken to painting mares that seem to fly like the wind. The symbolism of the mares becomes apparent when one of his female co-workers explains to Júlia that, according to an old legend, "na Antiguidade as éguas de Lisboa eram tão velozes que tinham fama de engravidar do vento. Durante a corrida" (306). The legend thus encodes a symbolism of female freedom, as the female animal is not dependent on a male to reproduce. It also re-signifies female identity through the power to give life. Fernando, silently working in the margins, is able to sense and inscribe through allegory the full potential of femaleness.

Therefore, Fernando is an enabling, not a castrating, presence in touch with his "feminine" side. It is thanks to his love and care that Jóia is able to run freely again. His angelic androgyny is arguably difficult to reconcile with the traditional paradigm of "masculinity," but this goes precisely towards showing how difficult it is to explode century-old stereotypes in a "machista" society such as the Portuguese one. In the closing scene, the breakdown of his car, the ultimate symbol of virility, succintly encodes his failure to conform to old models of masculinity. In that light, it may appear doubly ironic that the car in question is a Zephyr, a name that suggests the speed of the wind, since the old banger is hopelessly slow. But the car's name also looks back to the (androgynous) wind which had the power to make mares pregnant and simultaneously calls up the image of Zephyr, the God of the West wind, a powerful image as both wind and west conjure up the idea of change, therefore deconstructing the surface reading which would seem to confirm Fernando's ineffectual masculinity. The novel thus appropriately ends with a new beginning, hinting at the reconstitution of a new family unit. Together, the three "survivors" may be able to build a better future, where the pattern of male dominance would be eschewed in favor of cooperation between the sexes.[16]

4. (Re)-Creating the World through the Act of Naming

As is often the case in Lídia Jorge's novels, names can be interpreted on a variety of symbolic levels. In fact, in the preface, the author herself draws attention to the meaning subjacent to Júlia's name: "Júlia porque é nome de paixão e Grei porque significa gente e povo." The ambiguity of a name that signifies "paixão" is important, since passion signifies both love and suffering. Júlia is undoubtedly both long-suffering and loving. The name of Anabela Dias Cravo is also readily decodable, being inextricably linked with her identity as a *belle dame sans merci*. She is beautiful (bela) but simultaneously as tough as a nail (cravo). Of course, the word "cravo" also means carnation, a symbolically masculine flower, and also, furthermore, the symbol *par excellence* of the "25 de Abril." On a metaphorical level, therefore, as Ana Paula Ferreira incisively speculated, the relationship between Júlia Grei and Anabela Cravo can be interpreted as that of the gradual disenchantment of the Grei with the Cravo, that is, of the people with the Carnation Revolution.[17] The "25 de Abril" promised access to power to all, but in practice equality was slow to come, causing considerable dillisusionment.

The failure of the Revolution to fulfill its promises of equality is even more stark in respect of the position of women in society. The promised land of equality for women, symbolized by Anabela Cravo, turns out to be a mirage and at any rate is certainly not available to Júlia Grei, symbol of the *grei*, the silent majority of working women with childcare responsibilities. Júlia thus rejects the mirage of Anabela Cravo, but in so doing, she is not necessarily forced back into the powerless position of the victim, or only if we do not read her full name. For her full name, Maria Júlia Matos Grei, casts her in a different light, given the significance of her (presumably) maiden name, Matos. Phonetically linked with the verb "to kill," Matos ("mato-os") translates as "I can/will kill them." Júlia's aggression and negative feelings, initially suppressed, eventually surface. But they do so in a liberating, rather than destructive, fashion since she does not allow hatred to take over in the process of self-assertion. Most revealingly, however, the surname "Matos" also evokes a wild, uncultivated field (mato), signaling in no uncertain terms the fact that Júlia, in the end, will not be tamed or co-opted by the existing patriarchal order. Her complete name, therefore, points to the need for self-assertion while embracing love and compassion for others.

Her dramatic transformation, which does not entail her becoming a new Anabela, is marked by the fact that she is willing to surrender her knife to the anonymous person with whom she had been meeting in the (aptly renamed) Bar Together/Tonight. We do not know who this person is, nor do we know whether the person is male or female. Perhaps it doesn't matter. However, contrasting with Anabela/Júlia's friendship, this relationship develops into something above and beyond the immediate financial transaction involved, as the anonymous figure seems to take on the role of a confessor/psychoanalyst in a "talking cure." The potential for abuse of trust is of course enormous, since having bought the *caderno amarelo* containing Júlia's "memories," the mysterious person has effectively bought the "rights" to the story, risking the appropriation of someone else's life-story. However, this person, whoever he or she may be, is scrupulously honest in acknowledging publicly that s/he unilaterally chose to "rewrite" the tale in a way that downplays the *caderno amarelo*. As such, the final result can perhaps still be viewed as collaborative, given that ultimately Júlia is reconfirmed in, not stripped of, her identity as an author:

> [Júlia] haveria de vir a admirar-se que o caderno de capa amarela tivesse tido tão pouco destaque e que, pelo contrário, os papéis que me ia mandando pelo correio, ou por quem calhava, aparecessem com tanta importância. Mas acrescentou que se revia e achava, *por inteiro*. (17, my italics)

In other words, Júlia gives her blessing to the final product, satisfied that it does not falsify her experience. In fact, it could be argued that the occasional diary entries (marked by italic print and separated from the main text) which intersperse the main narrative and chart Jóia's slow progress on the road back to recovery are endowed with a special meaning. In some sense, these diary entries mirror Júlia's own slow surfacing from suicidal silence through the self-defining act of naming/writing in a striking "mise en abyme." Indeed, Júlia had been voiceless and silenced throughout, unlike Anabela, who was as vocal as Tarzan in an early episode. At this early stage, Júlia had been manifestly unable to emulate her (chapter 1). But now, she has access to language in the form of her written memoirs.[18]

It is also crucially important that writing, for Júlia, is posited as the nonviolent alternative to carrying a knife. If the latter was a symbol of male aggression, the pen, by contrast, may be "a metaphorical penis" to recall Gilbert and Gubar's (in)famous definition. But, in a remarkable inversion, attention here shifts to the paper, which is endowed with qualities commonly associated with the feminine: "o papel em branco parece-me um tecido doce, humano e envolvente como uma pele. Passivo, vegetal e outros adjectivos que não vale a pena enumerar" (305). More radically, writing may even break down binary oppositions: "O papel é um tecido doce, humano e envolvente como uma pele. Passivo, activo, e outras qualidades que não preciso de nomear (…) Como se, a partir dessa frágil matéria, sentisse e pudesse dar notícia da outra realidade" (322).

Júlia no longer needs a knife, as she can find autonomy and a voice through the female paradigm of writing her story. Thus, she is now ready to give up the bookshop, where she had been at the receiving end of male-dominated culture and where the printed word was regularly used by Sr. Assumpção to proposition her.[19] Júlia lives to tell her tale or, as she puts it, to "dar notícia da outra realidade" (322). The "outra realidade" is undoubtedly, at least to a large degree, the reality of women so often untold. For the flash of inspiration which signals Júlia's liberating "venue à l'écriture" while her son is lying in his hospital bed is the haunting certainty that beneath the savage reality of the world as we know it lies an uncharted and wild territory full of promises: "experimentava a certeza, ao mesmo tempo alegre e dolorosa, de que a outra margem da rua principal era uma zona silvestre de que este lado era apenas uma lembrança selvagem" (297). According to Lídia Jorge in her aforementioned interview with Regina Louro, "Notícia é a lembrança de um tempo primordial que a vida nesta terra recorda."[20] It is perhaps fitting, therefore, that after moving to her new house and acquiring a room with a view, the sight/site that Júlia can see from her window (presumably when looking at the other side of the main road, "a outra margem da rua principal") is the Church of São Mamede (164). The building becomes the visible embodiment of the "lembrança de um tempo primordial," which she is so actively engaged in re/uncovering. This fact is all the more remarkable considering that São Mamede, like many other Portuguese saints, is androgynous:

> Esta personagem misteriosa (…) parece ser o resultado da masculinização, por acção dos pastores, de uma figura feminina que tanto poderá ter sido a Moira, a Magna-Mater dos antigos, Maria ou ainda Diana (…) A sua masculinização não está ainda completa: Mamede é andrógino, representado como uma mulher viril ou como um homem adulto efeminado, imberbe e de cabelos longos.[21]

The building thus marks the institutional power of a patriarchal Church and points to the "outra realidade," the concealed female signifier buried beneath the surface, which Júlia can begin to restore in her narrative through the act of remembering.

Conclusion

According to Annis Pratt, "The woman's novel asks questions, poses riddles, cries out for restitution, but the synthesis occurs in the mind of the reader, who, having participated in the narrative reenactment, must put its message into effect in her own life."[22] The possibility of reader identification is indeed one of the keys to the success of this novel, since the reader, initially drawn to the strongly delineated Anabela, is likely to feel defrauded when she turns out to be irrecoverable for feminism. Thus, identification with Júlia becomes not merely the only possible, but the only productive, way out.

In choosing to cast Júlia as her unlikely heroine, Lídia Jorge is making a truly outstanding contribution to the ongoing gender debate in Portugal. For approximately a decade after both the publication of *Novas Cartas Portuguesas* and the April Revolution, her novel suggests that the way forward for feminism does not necessarily lie in equality feminism, valuable though that may continue to be, but in a new brand of difference feminism, which must revalue women's role as mothers without ascribing them to silence. Her compelling tale alerts us to the need for change in the structures of society at large and also tentatively takes on board the importance of the de/reconstruction of masculinity. Last but not least, she shows that femininity and masculinity are fluid attributes, available to both sexes, but that as long as they remain locked in a hierarchy of power, the "cidade silvestre" of her title will more readily continue to evoke a urban jungle than a promised city.

Notes

[1] In the case of Spanish America, Debra Castillo explains that fear of feminism stems from its perception as an euphemism for "lesbianism" in *Talking Back: Towards a Latin American Feminist Criticism* (Cornell and London: Ithaca University Press, 1992) 22.

[2] Hilary Owen, "Um Quarto que Seja Seu: The Quest for Camões Sister," *Portuguese Studies* 11 (1995): 179-91, citations from pp. 191 and 186.

[3] Following Isabel Allegro de Magalhães's pioneering work *O Sexo dos Textos* (Lisbon: Caminho, 1995), more recently some of these women writers may be more willing to consider the possibility of "escrita feminina." See article by Hélia Correia, "O Surpreendente Pequeno

Mundo," in *Gender, Ethnicity and Class in Modern Portuguese-Speaking Culture*, ed. Hilary Owen (Lampeter: Edwin Mellen Press, 1996) 49-62.

[4] *Notícia da Cidade Silvestre* (Lisbon: Europa-América, 1984).

[5] As Annis Pratt argues, however, the traditional pattern of the *bildungsroman* is problematic when the heroine is female cf. Annis Pratt, *Archepypal Patterns in Female Fiction* (1981).

[6] João Gaspar Simões, "Os Prodígios de Lídia Jorge," *Diário de Notícias* (24 January 1985): 31.

[7] Regina Louro, "Lídia Jorge: Este 3.° Livro É o Primeiro," *Jornal de Letras, Artes e Ideias* (18-24 December 1984): 2-3.

[8] Hilary Owen, "[W]Rites of Passage," diss., University of Nottingham, 1992, 408.

[9] Padrinho's nameless wife is confined to a wheelchair, a fitting symbol of her victim status under patriarchy (125-26).

[10] In her defense, her ruthless behavior must be contextualized by the fact that, as a thirteen year-old girl, she was raped by Padrinho. In a merciless world, where the law of the jungle prevails, the survival of the fittest required her to turn it to her advantage. Therefore, she demanded that he finance her law studies, the successful completion of which would mark her entry into the Symbolic order. Furthermore, while most of the time Anabela uses men as a means to an end, she claims to be in love with her boss, Atougia Ferraz. Her hopes of a non-abusive relationship are, however, shattered when he demands a kind of sex, sodomy, which she regards as unacceptable in the context of a loving exchange, (which ironically takes place in Morocco, in the city of Rabat, phonetically akin to rabo). Her vulnerability also briefly comes to the fore at the time of the abortion. But thereafter she becomes evermore ruthless, cynically casting aside her romantic ideal in time to resume a profitable liaison with her boss.

[11] Although he may genuinely have loved her, he is ultimately no different from the other men in her life who want her solely for sex and readily edit out of the picture her cumbersome child. He will subsequently beg Júlia again to leave Jóia behind and join him abroad (244), but needless to say this request is unacceptable to her. Artur's attitude is all the more ironic given that his main goal in life is to help liberate those oppressed by capitalist society, yet he is completely unable to recognize that the person he loves is a victim of both class and gender. Ironically, at the end, Artur is reluctantly made to fall into line. He marries Celina, a previous girlfriend, and acquires in the process a neat haircut (symbolizing his castration).

[12] Indeed, Mão Dianjo's workplace is appropriately called Apótema, a word that denotes a mathematical straight line: "the perpendicular from the center to the sides of a regular polygon." In other words, he is firmly at the center, she is "a bit on the side," condemned to remain in the margins.

[13] Immediately after she leaves Mão Dianjo's flat, her "castrating" power is metonimically encoded by the presence in the street of a blind and mutilated man (304).

[14] Critics have accused Lídia Jorge of giving a dismal picture of female friendship. In her interview with Regina Louro, however, Jorge counters the criticism arguing that it stems from the paralyzing (it is implied) "ideia idílica que se tem da amizade feminina." If female solidarity is only part of the picture, ignoring competitive/destructive instincts is ultimately counter-productive. Regina Louro, *op. cit.*, 2.

[15] We may observe, in that connection, that "emotional intelligence" has recently begun to be revalued.

[16] In that light it is also probably not a coincidence that Fernando is a man who is able to work collaboratively. In fact, in a recent interview, Lídia Jorge implicitly pinpoints the need for collaboration between men and women: "Não gosto muito de brandir o tema das diferenças entre os homens e as mulheres. Gosto de brandir o da complementaridade mais do que o da

diferença," in Álvaro Cardoso Gomes, *A Voz Itinerante* (São Paulo: Edusp, 1993) 152.

[17] This interpretation was put forward by Ana Paula Ferreira during the discussion in a parallel session devoted to Lídia Jorge, Congesso da AIL, Oxford, September 1996.

[18] Júlia's close association with the domain of the pre-verbal Semiotic is apparent in the language she uses with Mão Dianjo (153). Her subsequent self-assertion through language gives her access into the Symbolic order.

[19] Admittedly, we do not know how she is going to be able to make a living. We can only hope that through a collaborative relationship with her newfound literary agent she will have "a room of one's own and five hundred a year," to recall the words of Virginia Woolf. The other two possibilities open to her are far bleaker on an individual and collective level. She could be irrevocably silenced, like the Czech poet Milena Jesenská, a victim of the Holocaust, in which case "um tempo muito triste se aproxima do horizonte" (63). Alternatively, she could collude with masculine power by taking up the knife again. In this scenario likewise "um tempo muito violento se aproxima do horizonte (304).

[20] Regina Louro, *op. cit.*, 3.

[21] Moisés Espírito Santo, *A Religião Popular Portuguesa*, 2nd ed. (Lisbon: Assírio & Alvim, 1990) 124.

[22] Annis Pratt, *Archetypal Patterns in Women's Fiction* (1981) 177. By contrast, for the heroine in the novel, the journey very often ends in "disjunction" rather than "reconciliation."

A Costa dos Murmúrios: Uma Ambiguidade Inesperada

Paula Jordão

Desde a sua publicação que *A Costa dos Murmúrios* (a partir de agora referido como *CM*), de Lídia Jorge, tem provocado grande interesse, tanto por parte do público laico, como do literário. Para tal contribui não só o tema tratado neste romance, relacionado com a guerra colonial em Moçambique nos anos 60, como também o modo como esse tema é abordado.

Ao escolher uma estratégia que se pode chamar de metaficcional como enquadramento para *CM*, Lídia Jorge problematiza não só questões textuais e narrativas mas também ideológicas e culturais. Assim, se a Verdade e a História não são consideradas em *CM* mais do que meras "coincidências" ou simples versões susceptíveis de alteração, porque não aceitar, então, o relato de acontecimentos até agora "esquecidos" pela História oficial? Acontecimentos considerados durante muito tempo como tabus do discurso histórico e ideológico da cultura portuguesa, como o massacre de populações moçambicanas por parte de soldados portugueses. Não é, todavia, só a Verdade ou a História que fazem parte desta tentativa de desmistificação em *CM*. Também à Escrita é concedido um lugar na estratégia metaficcional de Lídia Jorge. Um lugar que se traduz no questionar do romance enquanto todo narrativo consistente e enquanto obra de arte.

Considerando os aspectos acima referidos, não é pois de admirar que sejam vários os estudos que abordam *CM* a partir de uma leitura pós-modernista e pós-colonialista.[1] Concordando em grande parte com esses estudos, gostaria de propôr neste artigo algumas linhas de reflexão sobre um aspecto que, até agora, não creio ter sido suficientemente abordado. Este aspecto tem a ver com uma ambiguidade existente na questionação da ordem dominante que Lídia Jorge parece propôr em *CM* e da qual a personagem Evita é um bom exemplo, quer no seu discurso, quer no seu comportamento em relação ao outro.

Vinte anos após os acontecimentos em que participou como personagem Evita, Eva Lopo apresenta a sua própria versão de "Os Gafanhotos." Ao fazê-lo, tem desde o início a preocupação de sublinhar a contingência da Escrita, enquanto representante daquilo que se considera como o real [("Ah, se conta, conte por contar, e é tudo o que vale e fica dessa canseira!" (*CM* 42)]. Desta forma, ela envolve igualmente as suas próprias personagens nessa contingência, deixando-as à mercê de "correspondências." Curiosamente, é Evita uma das primeiras personagens a ser atingida por essa "correspondência," 'perdendo' assim parte da sua coesão como personagem, sendo descrita por Eva Lopo como apenas "um olho": ["Embora eu tivesse descrito Evita como um olho intenso, observando, nada mais que um olho" (*CM* 43)].

Ao 'transformar' (ou minimalizar) Evita, Eva Lopo pretende fazer-nos crer que essa transformação não é mais do que a efectivação de uma cesura na identidade de Eva/Evita.[2] Cesura essa provocada pela passagem do tempo e que, originando um 'divórcio' entre a narradora Eva e a personagem Evita, parece situar Evita num plano de igualdade com as outras personagens. No entanto, se bem que 'divorciadas,' este 'divórcio' tem em si algo de incestuoso. Apesar de Eva Lopo apresentar o seu comentário com uma visão do presente, é a perspectiva de Evita que prevalece em toda a segunda parte de *CM*, quer acerca dos acontecimentos, quer das personagens.

Este privilegiar da perspectiva de Evita, sendo inicialmente um processo narrativo, adquire igualmente um carácter ideológico e político, por ser a tradução dum exercício de poder do Mesmo (o 'par' Eva/Evita) sobre o Outro. Um exercício no decorrer do qual a afirmação do Mesmo significa a inferiorização do Outro, como se irá ver, ainda que este seja um potencial aliado, como é o caso de Helena.

É através da desmontagem desses exercícios de poder que pretendemos chegar neste estudo a uma imagem de Evita que, pela sua ambivalência, se revela bastante diferente da de rebelde contestadora da ordem patriarcal e colonialista, até agora frequentemente apresentada.

Manuseio fácil

A análise da imagem de Evita começa por uma referência ao quotidiano em que está posicionada (o termo é aqui empregue numa adaptação do conceito "located" de Teresa de Lauretis) e que é muito semelhante ao de Helena. Ocidental, burguês e colonizador, localizado na Beira (devido à operação militar em que os respectivos maridos estão envolvidos), este quotidiano é partilhado por grande parte das personagens de *CM*, ligando-se à questão da nação que é sentida como algo omnipresente.

No seu trabalho "Dissemination: time, narrative, and the margins of the modern nation," Homi Bhabha define nação como um conceito que preenche o vazio deixado pelo desenraizamento das populações e seus familiares, originando um sentimento de perda e melancolia. Seguindo a mesma perspectiva, a nação é, então, sentida como algo de longínquo, a representação de um todo coeso pelo qual se anseia.[3]

Relacionando a definição de Bhabha com *CM*, verificamos que também aqui podemos falar de elementos populacionais que, provenientes de um passado diverso, mas igualmente desenraizados da Metrópole, se encontram reunidos na Beira. Experimentando esse vazio resultante do afastamento do seu meio conhecido, eles sentem a nação como um anseio por algo longínquo (inatingível). Um anseio exprimindo-se discursivamente de forma variada, mas apresentando a mesma atitude ideológica e política: uma total inadaptação ao mundo diferente onde se situam. Inadaptação essa à qual cada uma das personagens tenta, de maneira diversa, dar uma resposta. Assim, enquanto alguns tendem a idealizar de uma forma paradisíaca a paisagem africana ou imaginam um futuro utópico de prosperidade luso-moçambicana, outros justificam a presença colonialista portuguesa, através de um discurso bélico repleto de violência e tortura. Para o tenente Luís Alex, o noivo de Evita, a solução parece estar numa glória utópica a atingir por meios heroicamente bélicos, como se pode deduzir do seguinte fragmento:

> A nação estava cheia de gente que nunca assistira a outra cena de combate que não fosse a dum ridículo distúrbio à porta duma taberna, dois bêbedos com dois galos na testa, dois menos bêbedos pegando os outros pelas costas. E de resto, só paz, uma dormente paz. A paz do país, no tempo do general, deveria ter parecido uma pedreira adormecida. (*CM* 58)

E qual é a posição de Evita? Em estudos feitos sobre *CM*, Evita é frequentemente apresentada como tendo uma posição alheia e até mesmo contrária a este tipo de discurso e ideologia. Ela é a que, consciente dos crimes cometidos pelo regime, tenta tomar alguma iniciativa no sentido de os tornar públicos. Observando, no entanto, mais de perto o seu percurso inicial, podemo-nos perguntar se o que determina a sua acção e prática discursiva não é mais uma resultante de uma consciencialização da sua situação privada, do que uma de tipo político. Enquanto que para outros o sentimento de perda e melancolia se liga a uma nação ausente, para Evita esse sentimento liga-se à sua relação com Luís Alex. Uma relação que, ao apresentar-se radicalmente alterada (uma não-relação?) devido à transformação nele operada, de estudante de matemática a fiel seguidor e praticante fervoroso do discurso, ideologia e prática colonialistas, lhe abala por completo o sentimento de segurança pessoal que lhe vem dessa mesma relação. Por outro lado, e de uma forma algo contraditória, é essa relação já completamente alterada que nos fornece ainda elementos reveladores não só da dependência de Evita da ordem hegemónica patriarcal, em que essa relação se integra, como também da sua interiorização dessa mesma ordem.

É principalmente na sua relação com Helena que essa interiorização mais claramente se manifesta. Assim, Evita começa por apresentar Helena num dia de praia, em que os dois casais se encontram juntos. Envolvida numa brincadeira à beira-mar com Forza Leal, o seu comportamento aparece imediatamente reprovado por Evita ["Ela corria à beira, empurrava o bote para fora, saltava e compunha o cabelo, como se naquela simulação de vai não vai no pequeno barco existisse um divertimento exaltante." (*CM* 68)], que vê nele uma demonstração de superficialidade e subordinação sexual. Esta reprovação de Evita não é ocasional, mas obedece à sua intenção de apresentar Helena como o seu contrário negativo. Ao apresentá-la como seguidora obediente da ordem patriarcal vigente, Evita contrapõe-lhe assim a sua própria imagem de inconformista a essa mesma ordem. Uma imagem da qual somos levados a suspeitar perante as expressões que utiliza para descrever quer o casal Helena--Forza ["(...) Helena e Forza tinham uma alegria doméstica triunfante (...). Entraram na porta da casa, fecharam-na, no ar havia harmonia—como um pêndulo bom vai, vem, promete." (*CM* 69)], quer Helena isoladamente:

> Era uma bela mulher, despida lembrava um pombo, como outras lembram uma rã e outras uma baleia. Não era só a voz que lembrava um pombo, a chamar pelo barco, mas era também a perna, o seio, alguma coisa estava espalhada por ela que pertencia à família das columbinas. Talvez o cabelo vermelho, a pele leitosa. (*CM* 68)

Uma das formas de interpretar as descrições acima referidas é através da ironia que lhes é implícita e que faz parte do enquadramento metaficcional que Lídia Jorge pretende dar a *CM*, no qual a ironia é utilizada com a função de subversão do discurso vigente. Tal ironia pode, no entanto, revelar-se inefectiva nessa função subversiva, se considerarmos a ambivalência que nela se esconde. Lembremos a este respeito as palavras de Linda Hutcheon acerca da ambivalência política do pós-modernismo, que, se por um lado critica a ordem dominante, por outro lado também alimenta uma cumplicidade com essa mesma ordem no seio da qual inevitavelmente existe (Hutcheon, "Circling the Downspout of Empire" 130).

Se a descrição que Evita faz de Helena parece, numa primeira instância, traduzir uma subversão da ordem patriarcal, ela acaba por confirmar, numa segunda instância, uma cumplicidade com essa mesma ordem. Ao utilizar palavras como "pombo," "rã" e "baleia" para descrever Helena e as outras mulheres, Evita revela um suspeito manuseio fácil de imagens que, num discurso sexista, são utilizadas para situar as mulheres numa situação de inferioridade. Manuseio fácil esse que leva a considerar a sua interiorização desse mesmo discurso e consequente concordância com a ordem patriarcal a que ele pertence, em lugar de uma subversão. A segunda referência a Helena é feita a partir de um outro encontro entre os dois casais numa marisqueira, no meio de ruidosa azáfama de clientes e empregados, e do diálogo entre Forza Leal e Luís Alex, de teor marcadamente colonialista e bélico. Referindo--se ao alheamento do ambiente que Helena parece mostrar, Evita tenta comunicar com ela, da seguinte forma:

> Por entre o barulho que fazia dentro e fora, perguntei-lhe—"Sabe o que significa o seu nome?"
> Helena de Tróia começou a rir—"Não, não sei."
> "Nunca lhe disseram Haec Helena?"
> "Não, nunca"—disse ela com pestanas inocentes a baterem ao longo dos olhos, afastada agora dos crustáceos e da turquês que lhes quebravam tão bem as eriçadas patas. Quis que Helena soubesse.
> "Dizer Haec Helena é o mesmo que dizer eis a causa do conflito—gosta?" (*CM* 72)

Desta vez Evita não se 'limita' a aprisionar Helena numa imagem estática de superficialidade ou subordinação sexual, mas acrescenta-lhe também ignorância. Ignorância que não tem tanto a ver com a referência a um conhecimento clássico da expressão "Haec Helena," mas que sugere mais uma culpabilização bíblico-patriarcal em que a mulher é a origem de todo o mal do mundo. Ao atribuir indirectamente a Helena 'a causa do conflito,' (atribuição essa que passa já por uma demonstração e transmissão 'superior' de um conhecimento clássico), Evita faz a união metafórica de duas imagens discursivas de inferiorização da mulher. À concepção patriarcal clássica que encara o corpo feminino como causa e justificação de guerra e posse masculina, é aliada a colonialista, segundo a qual o corpo feminino simboliza a Terra conquistada.[4]

Objecto destes dois tipos de dominação, Helena ocupa assim um espaço simbólico comum aos não-europeus e às mulheres. Espaço esse em que, segundo Helen Carr, ambos são vistos como parte da natureza e não da cultura, desfrutando de uma mesma ambivalência. Ambos são considerados como passivos, imaturos, não sofisticados, sem espírito de iniciativa ou de poder intelectual, necessitando de ser guiados e governados. Ou, pelo contrário, são considerados como perigosos, traidores, emocionais, selvagens, inconstantes, imprevizíveis, lascivos e sexualmente aberrantes.[5] Características todas elas que, aplicadas a Helena por Evita, fornecem uma informação bastante esclarecedora acerca da posição ideológica da última. Uma posição que, se à partida aparenta ser de contestação da ordem dominante, acaba finalmente por tornar-se defensora dessa mesma ordem.

Espaço

Dificilmente se pode tentar 'desambiguizar' a posição de Evita quer em relação a Helena quer em relação à ordem vigente, sem focar o papel do espaço nessa 'desambiguização.' Referindo a importância do espaço real como possibilidade de agilidade, movimento e aquisição de conhecimento, Affrica Taylor alerta para uma certa ingenuidade presente nesta concepção de espaço. Segundo ela, há que ter igualmente em conta que assegurar o espaço é um acto político—significando muitas vezes a invasão de territórios, a sua colonização, a apropriação dos bens de outrem—e disciplinador do conhecimento. Por outras palavras: a ocupação do espaço é uma asserção do poder.[6]

Evita e Helena aparentam ter inicialmente uma relação oposta com o espaço em que se inserem. Helena, que desde o início se encontra circunscrita ao espaço limitado de sua casa, parece 'optar' cada vez mais por um maior recolhimento. Se num primeiro momento o faz por não querer (ou não poder) ter outros contactos, mais tarde fá-lo como acto de solidariedade para com Forza Leal, quando este se encontra no Norte de Moçambique, em missão militar. Evita, ao contrário, opta desde logo por uma imagem de rebeldia, que também se reflecte espacialmente, ao recusar sair do Stella Maris e ir morar para uma das casas abandonadas pelos antigos moradores/colonizadores. Seguindo A. Taylor e atribuindo ao espaço um valor positivo de desenvolvimento e aquisição de conhecimento, poder-se-ia assim pensar que a auto-limitação espacial de Helena corresponde igualmente a uma autolimitação de si própria. No caso de Evita, a sua permanência no Stella Maris fornecer-lhe--ia, pelo contrário, um meio de alcançar maior liberdade. Observando, no entanto, a utilização que ambas fazem do espaço, verifica-se que a aparente autolimitação de Helena corresponde afinal não só à afirmação e divulgação de conhecimento—e consequente exercício de poder sobre o Outro que esse conhecimento fornece—mas até à subversão de questões ideológicas.

Tomemos para isso em consideração o episódio em que Helena mostra a Evita as fotografias tiradas durante os massacres em que Alex também participara. Ao fazê-lo, Helena ultrapassa a sua situação de passividade para se metamorfosear na activa divulgadora de uma informação até então desconhecida de Evita (e que lhe dá a posição 'superior' de, ao contrário de Evita, estar a par de segredos militares). Helena vai, no entanto, mais longe no seu papel de informadora. Ao confrontar Evita com as crueldades de que Alex também fora autor, ela transforma o seu espaço num espaço ligado a uma múltipla subversão de valores respeitantes a um sistema patriarcal e colonialista. Assim, ao ser revelada a existência de segredos entre Evita e Alex, é não só a relação matrimonial de ambos que está em causa, mas até o próprio matrimónio como instituição que defende, entre outros, princípios de abertura, franqueza e lealdade entre os dois cônjuges. Paralelamente, ao estabelecer com Evita um contacto de características homoeróticas,[7] Helena subverte ainda o sistema patriarcal, exclusivamente heterossexual. Embora na maioria das vezes partindo da iniciativa de Helena (e recusado por Evita quando Helena tenta seduzi-la sexualmente), não deixa de transparecer nesse contacto uma certa ambiguidade de Evita, ao consenti-lo (e até incentivá-lo?) inicialmente. Finalmente, é ainda através do desmascarar das atrocidades cometidas pelos servidores do regime colonialista, até então ocultadas nas versões oficiais, que assistimos à subversão do sistema ideológico colonialista. Por outras palavras, Helena parece assim utilizar o seu espaço como um espaço de ruptura (sexual e política) no carácter coeso da nação.[8]

Quanto a Evita, se o seu espaço parece ser inicialmente veículo para o alargamento das suas investigações e para uma potencial actividade política, uma análise um pouco mais detalhada mostra que tal não é o caso. Assim, as suas investigações são conseguidas essencialmente através do jornalista Álvaro Sabino, com quem inicia uma relação ambígua. Embora aparentemente de resistência política ao regime colonial, a relação de Evita e Sabino acaba por evidenciar o conformismo e até o comprometimento de ambos com esse mesmo regime. Para Sabino, o seu acto de resistência limita-se à semanal coluna panfletária (inofensiva e "indecifrável," segundo o "jornalista gordo") no *Hinterland*. Para Evita, trata-se apenas da aquisição de um maior conhecimento acerca dos assassínios, não o usando, no entanto, para os denunciar na prática. A este comprometimento político associa-se um comprometimento de ordem sexual, que se verifica através do discurso de Sabino quando este trata Evita por "pomba," palavra de conotação sexista. Ou ainda na relação que Evita tem no exterior com ele, mantendo no Stella Maris o seu estatuto de noiva de Alex, pactuando dessa forma não só com a moral, como também com a ordem política vigente, simbolizada no quotidiano do Stella Maris.

Who's afraid of Helena de Tróia?

A finalizar esta breve análise sobre a ambiguidade em torno de Evita, não pode faltar a referência ao que eu gostaria de referir como "a cena da tentação" entre Evita e Helena, no final de *CM*. Retomemos para isso os acontecimentos que a antecedem.

Depois de uma campanha fracassada (aos olhos do poder) no Norte de Moçambique, Luís Alex e Forza Leal iniciam o seu regresso à Beira. Tanto Evita como Helena têm as suas razões para recearem este regresso. A primeira, ao manter uma relação (ambiguamente platónica) com Sabino, arrisca não só um confronto doméstico mas ainda um escândalo político e social, sendo Sabino mestiço e funcionário no jornal da oposição. A segunda está aterrorizada com a ideia de passar o resto da vida ao lado do tirano Forza Leal, especialmente depois de reconhecer o significado limitado do seu casamento. Esse terror é tão forte que a leva mesmo a considerar a ideia de suicídio, ideia por ela confessada a Evita num dos prévios encontros (por iniciativa de Helena) entre as duas. Assim, pouco antes do regresso de Alex e Forza Leal, Helena pede de novo a Evita que venha a casa dela, e esta, ao chegar lá, encontra-a quase despida em cima da cama.

A descrição que Evita faz do corpo de Helena é marcada por uma distância que o transforma quer num objecto clínico de observação quer até num objecto algo mecânico. Como ilustração leia-se o seguinte trecho:

> Ela [Helena] pôs uma perna fora do lençol. Os músculos gémeos de Helena não se vêem, por mais que Helena comprima o peito do pé. Tenho a perna de Helena na minha mão, peço-lhe que a curve para ver a actuação dos gémeos. A perna apenas toma um pouco mais de volume e engrossa. Passa-se o mesmo com a coxa. Helena abre e fecha a coxa. O seu slip é tão escasso que melhor fora não o ter. Helena puxa os joelhos, senta-se, levanta o assento, retira o slip, escorrega-o pelas pernas sempre unidas, estende-se. (*CM* 223)

Mesmo ao tocá-la, Evita não deixa de observar Helena com o seu olhar clínico, nomeando as várias partes da perna de Helena como se estivesse a efectuar uma fragmentação anatómica num corpo estranho.[9] Evita retira assim ao corpo de Helena a sua dimensão humana e até erótica,[10] afastando igualmente o "perigo" que representa enquanto oferta de uma sexualidade desconhecida e diferente. Depois de Helena tirar o slip e pedir a Evita que tranque a porta, esta deixa de ter qualquer reacção, para passar a uma longa (no texto cerca de duas páginas) série de considerações acerca de Helena. Tomando como ponto de partida a beleza de Helena, Evita tece várias hipóteses (as suas próprias fantasias?) acerca do possível significado sexual do corpo de Helena para o desejo masculino. Por ela são referidos: o caçador de pretos, o capitão, o talhante, o homem do lixo, o coveiro, assim como "os sublimes," isto é, os médicos devotos, os poetas, os prémios da paz, etc.

Ao escolher imagens que simbolizam ideias de sujidade, morte e sangue para exprimir a sexualidade (relacionada com a beleza) feminina, Evita não faz mais do que reproduzir um certo discurso pertencente à ordem patriarcal sexista à qual ela aparentemente se opõe. A imagem de superficialidade, irresponsabilidade e ignorância de Helena fica agora completa com a de promiscuidade e aberração sexual. Recordando o que Durring diz acerca da ligação entre linguagem e identidade ("(...) a choice of language is a choice of identity." 126), Evita revela assim através do seu discurso uma identidade na qual essa ordem está interiorizada. Por isso a única resposta verbal que tem para o "Vamos vingar-nos deles?," de Helena, só pode ser um "Sorry, sorry," denunciador do seu posicionamento privilegiado de classe, sexo e raça.[11] E a única resposta física que encontra é refugiar-se nos braços de Sabino, 'desambiguizando' finalmente não só a sua relação com ele, como a sua própria identidade.

Conclusão

Como nota final, recorde-se uma das afirmações de Foucault referentes à ambiguidade presente no discurso: "(...) [discourse] can be both an instrument and an effect of power, but also a hindrance, a stumbling-block, a point of resistance and a starting point for an opposing strategy."[12]

Também Evita, ao apresentar-se como figura rebelde e contestatária da ordem vigente em que está inserida, não consegue esconder uma cumplicidade com essa mesma ordem, visível na sua relação de poder com o Outro. Nessa relação, o Outro é frequentemente colocado numa posição de inferioridade, através de um discurso—que, ideologicamente, é muito semelhante ao usado na manutenção e reprodução da ordem—, em princípio, por ela contestado. Assim acontece na relação de Evita com Helena, a quem ela aprisiona numa imagem de superficialidade e subordinação, empregando para isso um discurso repleto de imagens e expressões denunciadoras de uma ideologia sexista e colonialista. Mas, se a posição e identidade de Evita se tornam assim 'desambiguizadas,' algo de semelhante acontece em relação a Helena: ao contrário de Evita, ela é libertada da sua imagem de conformista passiva, insurgindo-se de um modo radical contra os tabus políticos e sexuais pertencentes à ordem hegemónica que Evita parece, afinal, ter interiorizado.

Falar de ambiguidade em *A Costa dos Murmúrios* é falar de uma das vias para uma melhor compreensão da problemática variada que a obra encerra, o ponto de resistência e de começo para a estratégia de oposição a que se refere Foucault.

Notas

[1] Alguns desses estudos estão referidos na bibliografia anexa a este artigo para a qual remeto.

[2] Ronald Sousa, no seu artigo "'I Was Evita'or *Ecce Femina*," encontra uma engenhosa fórmula para essa mesma cesura através da palavra "Ev/ita."

[3] Citado em Sally R. Munt, "Sisters in Exile: the Lesbian Nation" 6.

[4] Tradução minha da afirmação de Ania Loomba no seu livro *Colonialism/Post-colonialism*: "Thus, from the beginning of the colonial period till its end (and beyond), female bodies symbolise the conquered land" 152.

[5] Citado em *Colonialism/Postcolonialism* 159-60.

[6] Affrica Taylor, "Lesbian Space: More Than One Imagined Territory" 129-30.

[7] O termo "homoerótico" é usado a partir do termo "homoeroticism" usado por Sally Munt no seu artigo "Sisters in Exile: the Lesbian Nation." Com este termo pretendo definir a relação de erotismo entre Helena e Evita.

[8] Recorde-se o que Homi Bhabha diz a este respeito, ao referir a ideia da nação alienada de si mesma: "We are confronted with the nation split within itself (...). The barred Nation *It/Self*,

alienated from its eternal selfregeneration, becomes a liminal signifying space that is *internally* marked by the discourses of minorities, the heterogeneous histories of contending peoples, antagonistic authorities and tense locations of cultural difference." Citado em Sally Munt, "Sisters in Exile: the Lesbian Nation" 6.

[9] É com base nesta 'fragmentação' do corpo de Helena que discordo de Ronald Sousa quando ele fala de desejo da parte de Evita em relação a Helena, no seu artigo "'I Was Evita' or *Ecce Femina*" (anteriormente citado).

[10] Este meu raciocínio é em parte inspirado em Judith Butler que, referindo algumas ideias de Monique Wittig, afirma: "That penis, vagina, breasts, and so forth, are *named* sexual parts is both a restriction of the erogenous body to those parts and a fragmentation of the body as a whole." Citado de "Subversive Bodily Acts" 112.

[11] Os meus agradecimentos a Ana Paula Ferreira, que me chamou a atenção para este 'pormenor' essencial de classe privilegiada, visível através do uso do inglês.

[12] Citado por Judith Butler em "Imitation and Gender Subordination" 163.

Obras citadas e bibliografia complementar

Braidotti, Rosi. *Nomadic Subjects.* New York: Columbia University Press, 1994.

Butler, Judith. "Subversive Bodily Acts." *Gender Trouble:Feminism and the Subversion of Identity.* New York and London: Routledge, 1990. 79-169.

———. "Imitation and Gender Subordination." *Feminism and Sexuality: A Reader.* Ed. S. Jackson, S. Scott. Edinburgh: Edinburgh University Press, 1996. 162-65.

Cabral, Maria Manuela A. Lacerda. "*A Costa dos Murmúrios* de Lídia Jorge: Inquietação Pós--Moderna." *Revista da Faculdade de Letras do Porto* XIV (1997): 265-87.

De Lauretis, Teresa. *Alice Doesn't.* Bloomington: Indiana University Press, 1984.

Durring, Simon. "Postmodernism or Post-colonialism Today." *The Post-colonial Studies Reader.* Ed. Bill Ashcroft, Gareth Griffiths, Helen Tiffin. New York and London: Routledge, 1995. 125-29.

Ferreira, Ana Paula. "Lídia Jorge's *A Costa dos Murmúrios*: History and the Postmodern She-Wolf." *Revista Hispânica Moderna* XLV, 2. (1992): 268-78.

Hutcheon, Linda. "Circling the Downspout of Empire." *The Post-colonial Studies Reader.* Ed. Bill Ashcroft, Gareth Griffiths, Helen Tiffin. New York and London: Routledge, 1995. 130-35.

Jorge, Lídia. *A Costa dos Murmúrios.* Lisboa: Publicações Dom Quixote, 1988.

Loomba, Ania. *Colonialism/Postcolonialism.* New York and London: Routledge, 1998.

Magalhães, Isabel Allegro de. *O Sexo dos Textos.* Lisboa: Editorial Caminho, 1995.

Munt, Sally R. "Sisters in Exile: the Lesbian Nation." *Space, Bodies and Gender.* Ed. R. Ainly. New York and London: Routledge, 1998. 3-19.

Rimmon-Kenan, Shlomith. *Narrative Fiction. Contemporary Poetics.* London and New York: Routledge, 1989.

Saraiva, Arnaldo. "Os Duplos do Real e os Duplos Romanescos (*A Costa dos Murmúrios*, de Lídia Jorge)." *Arquivos do Centro Cultural Português* (Fundação Calouste Gulbenkian) XXIX (1991): 39-48.

Sousa, Ronald W. "'I Was Evita' or *Ecce Femina.*" (no prelo)

Taylor, Affrica. "Lesbian Space: More Than One Imagined Territory." *Space, Bodies and Gender.* Ed. R. Ainly. New York and London: Routledge, 1998. 129-41.

Memória Infinita

Paulo de Medeiros

> Mémoires, au pluriel. Trop de mémoires.
> (Derrida, *Mémoires pour Paul de Man* 9)

> Evita disse ao noivo que a memória não tinha fim.
> (Lídia Jorge, *A Costa dos Murmúrios* 26)

Não será necessário lembrar a importância que a variada obra de Lídia Jorge tem vindo a assumir quer no campo da literatura portuguesa, onde tem lugar de destaque, quer no campo da literatura contemporânea internacional, não só através dos temas abordados como também das estratégias narrativas em que o experimentalismo formal, nunca gratuito, poderia ser indicado como paradigmático de um profundo vector ético-político na pós-modernidade. Se *O Dia dos Prodígios* merece especial atenção na medida em que incessantemente põe em causa conceitos tradicionais de História e representação, ao mesmo tempo que reconceptualiza o movimento revolucionário e o processo de democratização em Portugal, assim como as diversas estruturas de poder na sociedade portuguesa, tendo sido frequentemente referido como tal em múltiplas abordagens de síntese da literatura portuguesa dos últimos vinte anos, esse mesmo processo de metanarrativa estende-se a todos os seus romances subsequentes. Pode-se referir, a título de exemplo, o espaço terrível da Casa do Leborão, em *A Última Dona*, que tanto significa sítio privilegiado do desejo e da morte, do desejo da morte, como dom da morte a nível pessoal e alegoria nacional. Ou a Casa da Arara à Rua da Tabaqueira d'*O Jardim sem Limites*, com a sua escrita em serpentina alastrando pelas paredes diariamente, sítio de uma utopia comunitária anunciada por um dilúvio que subverte, mesmo que temporariamente, as fronteiras do quotidiano individual, mas que também serve para induzir um processo de entropia extremo, evidenciado pelo Homem Estátua. Só aparentemente é que a narrativa recente de Lídia Jorge se poderia dizer menos experimental. Se se pode apontar sempre para um espaço referencial onde cada romance concentra as tensões da narrativa, e que nas obras da autora vão desde o Albergue ao Stella Maris, é a própria escrita que nos aparece desde o início como lugar de contínua exploração da sociedade, do processo de reinscrição do indivíduo num tempo e espaço colectivos, e do que significa não só escrever mas também ler.

A Costa dos Murmúrios é talvez o romance de Lídia Jorge que, de forma sistemática, mais atenção crítica tem suscitado. Maria Irene Ramalho de Sousa Santos, na sua importante recensão, publicada pouco após o lançamento do romance, preparou de imediato o palco para a crítica seguinte, ao enquadrar o romance numa perspectiva de problemática pós-colonial e de questionamento dos conceitos de História e de representação, peças fundamentais da estética e do pensamento ocidental e, como tal, chaves no processo de domínio hegemónico que o romance contesta. Em comparação com *Percursos*, de Wanda Ramos, e *Corpo Colonial*, de Joana Ruas, a recensão salienta que, apesar de os três romances se servirem do modo autobiográfico, "Lídia Jorge vai mais longe, ao assumir esse recurso estético como deliberada apropriação irónica de um ponto de vista desautorizado, literalmente infiel, que jamais poderia ter acesso à 'verdade' ou ao 'real' ou sequer à 'verosimilhança'" (64). E, no desdobramento do sujeito entre Evita e Eva, Maria Irene Ramalho de Sousa Santos vê precisamente "o cerne mesmo da impossibilidade total da narrativa da história" (65). São estas as coordenadas que têm vindo a ser exploradas numa série de artigos publicados, com uma excepção, fora de Portugal.

Arnaldo Saraiva focou a questão da dualidade que enforma todo o romance, desde a construção formal da narrativa, que inclui "Os Gafanhotos," como texto aparentemente autónomo dentro de si e com o qual mantém correspondência contínua, até à dualidade do sujeito autodiegético e de vários aspectos temáticos. A leitura de Saraiva explora obviamente pontos importantes. Contudo, esta esquematização analítica, ao reduzir a complexidade do discurso de Lídia Jorge a dicotomias, assume uma posição retrógrada em relação à narrativa que subverte simples oposições, optando pela pluralidade de perspectivas, incluindo as que provêm da voz de Eva/Evita, já que um dos efeitos da narrativa é precisamente a fragmentação tanto do discurso como da categoria de sujeito. Efectivamente, alguns dos artigos críticos sobre *A Costa dos Murmúrios* apresentam já uma visão mais próxima da narrativa quando problematizam as oposições em que o texto aparentemente se baseia. Assim, Peter Stolz, embora ainda subscrevendo a noção de que o romance se fundamenta numa estrutura binária, parece já evitar essa atitude redutora ao concluir que o processo dialéctico posto em moção pelo texto não oferece qualquer possibilidade de *sublação*: "Diese Dialektik der antithetischen Dopplung kennt bei Jorge als prozessuale Dynamik kein *tertium*, keine Aufhebung" (88).

Finalmente, como Ana Paula Ferreira afirma, "In one sweeping post-modernist move, Eva Lopo contests then what Jane Flax concisely characterizes as the 'metanarrative' of Enlightenment (...). Nevertheless, the counterclaims she goes on to propose are neither absolute nor transcendental" (271). Este último ponto é especialmente importante, pois é necessário verificar que Lídia Jorge não só recusa a teleologia inerente ao conceito clássico de História como, ao substituí-la por um processo de desdobramento e proliferação das memórias, também não as assume como garante da verdade, mas como um processo de evidência fantasmática. Isto é, Lídia Jorge não transpõe a autoridade da História para o campo individual, expresso pela memória pessoal, mas apresenta-a já como sendo um excesso de memória, "Mémoires au pluriel. Trop de mémoires," ou, nas palavras de Eva Lopo, que tanto afirma: "a verdade é que me lembro de fragmentos. E para quê mais?" (127); como: "Recapitulo tudo (...). Tudo tem ligação com tudo" (201).

Se se pode apontar com certeza para um elo comum entre os vários artigos já publicados sobre *A Costa dos Murmúrios*, é a insistência na História, na relação crítica que a narrativa estabelece com um conceito de História, e com o processo através do qual a subverte, que mais atenção tem suscitado. Embora de modo variado, todos os críticos parecem concordar que este romance, para além de tudo o mais que também ambicione e sem nunca perder de vista o seu carácter de obra de arte, é primordialmente um veículo para desmantelar e reconceptualizar a autoridade do discurso histórico. É assim que, em "History and the Postmodern She-Wolf," Ana Paula Ferreira rigorosamente situa o romance no pós-modernismo e é também assim, se bem que de uma maneira mais diluída, que Helena Kaufman abre e conclui o seu artigo intitulado "Reclaiming the Margins of History": "Most important, however, is to see how different people or incidents coexist to enrich the complex texture of History" (47). Até mesmo o prefácio da tradução americana do romance foca este ponto. Nas palavras de Ronald Sousa: "the novel strikes a postmodern note by casting suspicion on the practices of history writing in general and in fact on any narrative process that seeks to see its results as somehow authoritative" (v-vi). Evidentemente, concordo em parte com estas posições. E, no entanto, parece-me que, ao insistir tanto na História, o que a crítica tem descuidado é uma consideração séria do papel da memória, quer na sua relação com a História quer em termos teóricos. Isto, porque a memória não pode ser encarada como simples meio de re-escrever ou contestar a História.

Lídia Jorge não se limita a apresentar a memória, mesmo que pessoal e múltipla, como simples termo de oposição ao discurso da História. Aliás, a memória tanto pode ser usada para contestar a ideologia dominante como para a reafirmar. Como Jorge Seabra documentou em "O Império e as Memórias do Estado Novo," a memorialização dos "heróis" das campanhas de ocupação de África, no século XIX, era um componente vital da construção mítica da ideia de Portugal. Ao contrário, tal como a afirmação de Ronald Sousa já indica, o que é posto em questão é a possibilidade de qualquer discurso se apresentar como instância de autoridade. As várias afirmações de Eva Lopo são lembranças, recordações, que não pretendem repôr a veracidade dos acontecimentos ou corrigir lacunas de uma qualquer versão, original ou autorizada. Embora seja tentador ver no episódio d'"Os Gafanhotos" um modelo de tal discurso autoritário, em si mesmo ele já é constituído pela (e forma uma instância da) memória. Mesmo que alguns críticos bem intencionados assim vejam o romance, o que se nota é que não há um processo de recuperação nem da história colonial (Kaufman 45) nem do sujeito feminino (Kaufman 44). Também Rui de Azevedo Teixeira, num livro pioneiro intitulado *A Guerra Colonial e o Romance Português*, classifica explicitamente o livro de Lídia Jorge, juntamente com *Os Cus de Judas*, de António Lobo Antunes, e *Percursos*, de Wanda Ramos, como "romances da memória" (135). Mas limita-se a referir a memória como processo narrativo, sem analisar a sua função, preferindo, aliás, interpretar *A Costa dos Murmúrios* como uma forma de jogo metanarrativo: "Jogo é também o termo que melhor define a estrutura de *Murmúrios*, uma vez que a matéria ficcional de *Os Gafanhotos* é ficcionalmente jogada no resto do romance" (135). Embora reconheça a importância do livro de Lídia Jorge, segundo Teixeira existiria no romance, afinal, "uma lacuna capital," já que nele "não há qualquer descrição directa de acções bélicas, qualquer *empiria* da guerra, resultando de uma lei geral—as mulheres não fazem a guerra (...)" (334-35). Ora, tal atitude, para além de evidenciar uma falácia teórica, demonstra uma incompreensão básica do processo de reconceptualização da guerra e da sociedade portuguesa efectuado pelo romance. Neste ponto, uma leitura introdutória da obra de Lídia Jorge, levada a cabo por Renate Heß, e intitulada "Escrever É Recordar--se," se bem que necessariamente limitada, é bem explícita ao encarar a escrita de Lídia Jorge como sendo baseada num processo de memória. Se se quiser aceitar a denúncia que Lídia Jorge, à sua maneira, efectua do processo histórico e da sociedade portuguesa, penso ser necessário aceitá-la na sua extensão sem a aliviar através de uma identificação com pressupostos garantes de um projecto ontológico em que um dos termos—história, colonialismo, masculino—seria simplesmente substituído por outro aparentemente oposto mas em que a estrutura de relacionamento se manteria intacta. Penso, portanto, que Lídia Jorge alcança uma crítica mais contundente ao recusar opor a História à memória. N'*A Costa dos Murmúrios* a memória, embora evoque, nunca memorializa.

E de que memórias deveremos então falar? Antes de mais, as memórias d'*A Costa dos Murmúrios* são memórias de guerra. Guerra colonial, sem dúvida, mas também uma espécie de guerra entre indivíduos, entre homens e mulheres, entre um tempo passado e um tempo presente que, embora inegavelmente constituído pelo passado, não pode evitar recriar continuamente esse mesmo passado. Uma observação de Ana Paula Ferreira pode servir de guia para explorar o modo como o romance de Lídia Jorge trata a questão das memórias de guerra: "*A Costa dos Murmúrios* deconstructs, theorizes and rewrites the traditional war narrative, positing the conditions under which literature can retrieve the past without engaging in what Nancy Armstrong and Leonard Tennenhouse, following Foucault, have termed as 'the violence of representation'" (269). Certamente *A Costa dos Murmúrios* afasta--se de narrativas tradicionais sobre a guerra que, ainda que tenham por objectivo a denúncia ou a oposição, acabam sempre por se reinscrever nesse processo de representação da violência, que é, em si mesmo, inescapavelmente violento. A narrativa de Lídia Jorge certamente desconstrói, num sentido até rigoroso do termo, a narrativa tradicional de guerra, e é por isso que se pode dizer que simultaneamente teoriza e re-escreve o que o acto de escrever sobre a guerra possa significar.

No entanto, é exactamente devido a esse rigor que penso ser impossível ver o romance quer como uma recuperação do passado, quer como estando desligado do processo de violência da representação. E talvez seja isso mesmo que mais distingue este romance de outras narrativas sobre a guerra colonial. O relato "Os Gafanhotos," que até certo ponto Helena Kaufman designa correctamente como discurso de esquecimento ("discourse of forgetting" 46), exemplifica uma atitude tradicional perante a guerra que, ao servir de pano de fundo, é tacitamente assumida como normal. Como já tem sido dito, o ponto de vista predominante neste relato é efectivamente o do opressor (Ferreira 270; Kaufman 42). E, no entanto, também aqui se encontra alguma da ironia que domina o resto da narrativa: "Infelizmente, muito infelizmente, as guerras eram necessárias para equilibrar o excesso de energia que transbordava da alma" (38). Quando, n'"Os Gafanhotos," o marido de Evita corre atrás do jornalista e se ouve um disparo, o cinismo que domina as observações sobre o incidente—"Foi um excesso do alferes, um homem habituado à contra-subversão em terreno" (37)—não só demonstra a atitude racista dos opressores, como simultaneamente a subverte, pois o tiro não atinge o repórter mas, sim, o próprio alferes. Ainda que na continuação da narrativa Eva Lopo apresente uma versão bem diferente de como o marido encontrou a morte, n'"Os Gafanhotos" a morte do alferes não deixa de constituir um exemplo de como o "discurso oficial," longe de ser aceite como normal, se revela desde o início, mesmo para os que dele se utilizam, como falido.

Além dessa falha fundamental, será talvez conveniente lembrar que o relato d'"Os Gafanhotos" abre precisamente com uma citação de Álvaro Sabino, jornalista que aparece no relato sem nome, tal como outras personagens referidas meramente pelo cargo que desempenham, o que sem dúvida contribui para acentuar o carácter alegórico da narrativa. Ao incorporar essa citação, e ao colocar o discurso tradicional sob o signo do discurso que pretende silenciar, o relato "Os Gafanhotos" constitui mais um sintoma do processo de memória que, por mais que evite ou tente cobrir o passado e o reconstrua de forma violenta, não escapa nunca aos traços da memória. Aliás, é precisamente Evita nesta parte do texto, e não Eva Lopo mais tarde, quem afirma ao noivo que "a memória não tinha fim" (26). Impondo um fim arbitrário aos "Gafanhotos," através do uso explícito da palavra "FIM" em maiúsculas, Lídia Jorge demonstra bem a convencionalidade da narrativa, subvertendo-a de imediato, pois esse fim impossível, e imposto, é logo revisitado na página seguinte, quando Eva Lopo se pronuncia sobre o relato em questão: "Esse é um relato encantador. Li-o com cuidado e concluí que nele tudo é exacto e verdadeiro, sobretudo em matéria de cheiro e de som—disse Eva Lopo. Para o escrever desse modo, deve ter feito uma viagem trabalhosa a um tempo onde qualquer outro teria dificuldade em regressar" (41).

O que me interessa sobretudo nesta passagem é, num registo, o modo como a narrativa constrói ironicamente o "relato" como instância de verdade, ao mesmo tempo que o anula completamente; anulando-o já com essa primeira afirmação e continuando a anulá-lo em cada página seguinte, até ao final da narrativa, quando "dos sons restam só os murmúrios, o derradeiro estádio antes do apagamento—disse Eva Lopo, rindo. Devolvendo, anulando 'Os Gafanhotos'" (259). Num outro registo, interessa-me principalmente a forma como Eva Lopo também constrói o relato enquanto processo de memória ("viagem trabalhosa a um tempo onde qualquer outro teria dificuldade em regressar"; "o sentido da sua recordação, atendendo ao que recorda" 41), e como o próprio evento provoca a memória e faz com que Eva Lopo inicie o seu processo de memória, memória deveras sem fim: "Pelo que me diz respeito, o seu relato foi uma espécie de lamparina de álcool que iluminou, durante esta tarde, um local que escurece de semana a semana, dia a dia à velocidade dos anos" (41).

Será necessário voltar ainda a esta questão do "relato" como processo e elemento de instigação da memória, mas por agora penso ser necessário prosseguir com a investigação de como as memórias do romance são memórias de guerra. Numa passagem extensa do romance, Lídia Jorge explora o termo "guerra," o significado de fazer a guerra e como uma situação de guerra colonial se desdobra e atinge todas as actividades civis ou domésticas. Eva Lopo começa por comentar a forma como se apercebeu de que o termo "guerra" não era usado para referir o conflito armado: "Percebia que ninguém falava em guerra com seriedade. O que havia ao Norte era uma revolta e a resposta que se dava era uma contra-revolta. Ou menos do que isso—o que havia era banditismo, e a repressão do banditismo chamava-se contra--subversão" (74). Ora, tem-se já aqui uma explicação do comentário feito no "relato" à acção do alferes, que seria um exagero de quem estava habituado à contra-subversão. No comentário que se segue não restam dúvidas de como Eva Lopo encara este deslize semântico que evita nomear a guerra pelo seu nome preferindo outros nomes aparentemente menos horríficos: revolta, banditismo, subversão. As razões para tal processo são múltiplas, evidentemente, desde o desejo de manter a atitude de que as colónias portuguesas, também elas já com o nome mais inocente de províncias, eram parte integral de Portugal, e assim, qualquer admissão de guerra seria uma admissão de guerra civil, até ao desejo de evitar outra memória bem recente, a da derrota militar na Índia, em 1961.

João Paulo Guerra, no seu livro, com o título significativo de *Memória das Guerras Coloniais*, começa precisamente por problematizar esta questão do nome *guerra* para referir o conflito armado entre as forças militares portuguesas e os movimentos de libertação nacional. No seu prefácio "Guerra é Guerra," a aparente tautologia é uma necessidade absoluta para tentar desfazer o processo de falsificação do discurso oficial. João Paulo Guerra vai direito ao ponto que interessa focar: "Guerra é guerra. Mata-se e morre-se (...). Ganha a guerra quem mais matar e mais destruir" (11), o que nem chega a ser correcto, pois a vitória não depende apenas da quantidade de mortos e da extensão da destruição. Mas o que importa aqui notar é como, ainda em 1994, é necessário chamar a guerra pelo nome de guerra para esconjurar todos os outros nomes que lhe tinham sido atribuídos como disfarce. E se esta *Memória das Guerras*, aliás já no uso do singular, não consegue alcançar o mesmo efeito da narrativa de Lídia Jorge, fixada que está na necessidade de esclarecer factos, esta mesma necessidade deve ser encarada não tanto como uma falha teórica mas como um sintoma de como o processo de memória da guerra é ainda hoje premente.

Basta comparar-se dois estudos recentes, ambos publicados em 1997. Enquanto Norrie MacQueen, em *The Decolonization of Portuguese Africa*, explicitamente se refere aos vários conflitos como guerras, o livro de John P. Cann, *Counterinsurgency in Africa*, como o título demonstra, continua a preferir a evasão ao termo, embora a leitura da obra não deixe dúvidas da extensão do conflito. O prefácio a este segundo livro, da autoria do General Bernard E. Taylor, reforça ainda mais a necessidade que João Paulo Guerra sentiu de chamar guerra à guerra. Depois de elogiar o sucesso que Portugal teve durante treze anos, o General afirma: "Dr. Cann calls attention to this important counterinsurgency campaign, one that was overshadowed by the United States involvement in Vietnam and that is now largely forgotten by non-Portuguese scholars" (xi). As memórias da guerra continuam, portanto, a ser necessárias. Quando João Paulo Guerra afirma que "a iminência da derrota militar, particularmente na Guiné, e de certo modo também em Moçambique, reacendera entre os militares portugueses os traumas da derrota militar na Índia" (12-13), será necessário acrescentar que não foi preciso esperar até ao fim para que essa memória se reacendesse, porque ela esteve sempre presente; só que, como é próprio da memória e do trauma, pode ser invisível. Tal como n'*A Costa dos Murmúrios* só o cego é que via o significado dos quadros da Armada Invencível no salão do Stella Maris. Tal como o "relato" que servia de "lamparina de álcool" para iluminar as memórias de Eva Lopo. Como sempre, na espiral da memória, é uma questão de nomes trocados, de identidades assumidas, esquecidas, enterradas, mas prontas a voltar à superfície, a falar através da aparente inescrutabilidade do passado.

E a guerra? Ao deixar de responder pelo seu nome próprio, a guerra passa a designar toda uma outra série de actividades: "Não guerra. Por isso mesmo, cada operação se chamava uma guerra, e do mesmo modo se entendia, em terra livre, o posto médico, a manutenção, a gerência duma messe, como várias guerras. As próprias mulheres ficavam com a sua guerra, que era a gravidez, a amamentação, algum pequeno emprego pelas horas da fresca" (74). Ao tentar submergir, desviar e anular o sentido próprio da guerra, o discurso oficial só consegue que o termo reprimido venha à superfície por todos os lados, que contamine todas as actividades, mesmo aquelas que mais opostas poderiam parecer à guerra, como o parto ou o amor. Assim, Lídia Jorge também evita cair numa simples dicotomia entre militares e civis, homens e mulheres, criminosos e vítimas. Sem ao mesmo tempo amalgamar tudo e todos, o que seria equivalente a uma abdicação de responsabilidade. Aliás, Eva Lopo é suficientemente lúcida para poder indicar no discurso oficial, na sua tentativa de desvio do sentido do termo guerra, a intenção de confundir as várias categorias, o que, ao suceder, possibilitaria precisamente essa diluição da responsabilidade que é tarefa primordial da memória de resistir: "Para que você saiba—sempre que falar de *guerra*, estes dois sons (...) têm vários sentidos—um deles encapotado na sua desvalorização intermédia e depois absoluta. Um outro tem a ver com a compreensão do capitão pela sua bonita mulher (...). Um terceiro liga-se a momentos genuínos, em que ninguém pronunciava a palavra guerra (...). Lembro-me da preparação e uso a palavra nos vários sentidos. O sentido de guerra colonial não é pois de ninguém, é só nosso" (75).

Mais uma vez a memória ("lembro-me") funciona como ingrediente essencial para evitar quer a submissão ingénua ao processo de desvalorização, contaminação e evasão quer a colaboração plena ou parcial nos mecanismos de repressão. O que dá poder às memórias de Eva Lopo é que, em vez de seleccionarem o que querem mostrar e apagarem o que querem esconder, como é o caso no "relato," elas irrompem por todos os lados, nomeando as várias guerras, lembrando os incidentes como o da mulher do tenente Zurique com o esfíncter rasgado e a criança nado-morta por falta do depósito para a conta da clínica, ou a obliteração da personalidade de Helena por parte do seu marido. Mas as memórias não ficam por aí. Mostram também como no quotidiano as próprias vítimas não se isentavam de vitimar outros, quer se tratasse de Helena, com os seus criados baptizados com nomes de vinhos, quer do jornalista, cujo acto mais directo de revolta para com o poder colonial é afinal mais uma vez a posse de uma mulher e a sua alegorização como nação. No entanto, para além de todas estas formas de guerra, talvez as memórias mais contundentes sejam as dos massacres negados pelo discurso oficial, que não só evita assim chamar guerra à guerra, mas pretende mesmo apagar, varrer da consciência pessoal e nacional, bem como da opinião internacional, as consequências horríficas dessa "não guerra."

Como Maria Irene Ramalho de Sousa Santos já assinalou, parte do processo de uma "aberrante solução pacífica para a guerra [era] o extermínio sistemático dos pretos em África, seja em massacres infames, como o de Wiriamu aqui expressamente evocado, seja por envenenamento ou por esterilização compulsiva (...)" (67). O romance só quase no fim (250) é que nomeia o massacre de Wiriyamu explicitamente, embora não deixe dúvidas sobre a que acontecimentos se refere, quer pela natureza dos actos descritos quer pela referência às fotografias que Helena mostra a Evita e através das quais esta começa a aperceber-se daquilo em que o marido se tornara. É, portanto, como um trabalho de memória e evocação, como Maria Irene Ramalho de Sousa Santos precisamente o classifica, que o romance apresenta esse aspecto mais infame e recôndito da guerra colonial. João Paulo Guerra, num capítulo intitulado "Centenas de Wiriyamus," descreve a reacção oficial à publicação no *Times* (10 de Julho de 1973) de um artigo expondo os massacres em Moçambique: "O governo português desmentiu, no dia seguinte ao da publicação, os factos relatados por *The Times*, afirmando desconhecer qualquer acontecimento, na data e no local dos alegados massacres, que pudesse dar origem às acusações, ou chegando mesmo a insinuar que não existiria em Moçambique qualquer localidade designada Wiriyamu" (290). E quanto às investigações ordenadas pelo governo, João Paulo Guerra observa: "O governo nunca responsabilizou o general Kaúlza de Arriaga pelos acontecimentos de Wiriyamu. O primeiro inquérito militar sobre os acontecimentos foi mandado arquivar pelo próprio general" (292-93).

Talvez seja esta a imagem mais apropriada, a do arquivo, onde o conhecimento da catástrofe poderia ficar seguro e impunemente guardado se não fosse a sua irrupção através das escassas testemunhas e da imprensa estrangeira. E da memória, exteriorizada por relatos como o de João Paulo Guerra ou por narrativas como a de Eva Lopo, que recorda aquilo que fora preservado pelas fotografias do caixote com o rótulo "TO BE DESTROYED" (131), porque "Quando houvesse uma independência branca, aqueles seriam os documentos que haveriam de atestar quem tinha e não tinha ido à guerra" (131). Aliás é a própria Eva Lopo quem aconselha a que se use o arquivo para se ter a noção de como aquilo a que se costuma chamar História se esboroa pelo esquecimento e falta de registo: "Não, eu não invento. Procure no Arquivo Militar" (215). Não só o discurso do "cego triunfal," a anunciar a imortalidade da nação, rodeado pela "imagem dum desastre" (210), mas também as fotografias dos massacres estariam guardados numa espécie de arquivo pessoal: "É assim que me lembro, ainda que para nada—disse de novo Eva Lopo—das caixas e dos envelopes selados que saíram do cofre" (131). A memória dos massacres é sobretudo uma memória visual, tal como outras memórias que nos são apresentadas como imagens, de que são exemplo as fotografias do casamento de Evita com o noivo, o mesmo noivo que Evita reconhece nas fotografias dos massacres, também já elas encaradas como garante necessário da realidade: "se ninguém fotografou nem escreveu, o que aconteceu durante a noite acabou com a madrugada—não chegou a existir" (21). Se Eva Lopo quase não nomeia Wiriyamu não é por colusão com o pretenso esquecimento oficial, mas por não ser preciso insistir num nome próprio para designar o que não foi um acontecimento único e isolado, os "excessos" que, de acordo com a versão oficial, "não ultrapassariam uma dezena pelo meio de 10 mil operações militares" (Guerra 293). Aliás, quando Lídia Jorge finalmente nomeia Wiriyamu, é para insistir na materialidade do sofrimento e horror: "(...) será esse o cheiro que se desprenderá de Wiriamu, Juwau, Mucumbura, será esse o cheiro que se desprenderá dos abatidos, dos queimados, dos que ficaram a arder ainda vivos (...)" (250-51). E, ao mesmo tempo que nomeia, sem ter de nomear, os massacres cometidos em Moçambique, como que para evitar a redução da memória a um símbolo, Lídia Jorge também os relaciona directamente com esses outros acontecimentos banais como o casamento de Evita e Luís Alex no Stella Maris: "a memória não tinha fim."

Será necessário lembrar ainda que as memórias d'*A Costa dos Murmúrios* são as memórias de um trauma imenso, tanto pessoal como nacional? O acesso ao arquivo de Helena certamente proporciona um certo abalo em Evita ao dar-lhe conhecimento do horror da guerra e daquilo em que Luís se transformara. As imagens secretas retiradas do cofre certamente contribuem para que Evita se decida a procurar o jornalista, tente que este divulgue os acontecimentos e se lhe entregue. No próprio momento em que via as fotografias, Evita já tinha consciência de que Helena teria uma razão especial para lhas mostrar: "Via-se nitidamente o pau, a cabeça espetada, mas o soldado que a agitava não era um soldado, era o noivo. (...) Era claro como a manhã que despontava que Helena de Tróia me havia trazido até àquela divisão da casa para que eu visse sobretudo o noivo" (133). Talvez, ao iniciar a amiga no conhecimento, Helena procurasse obter a solidariedade de Evita, convidando--a para ficar em sua casa e oferecendo-se-lhe. Mas, se bem que decisiva, a constatação dos massacres, o assumir da responsabilidade individual, para além de qualquer vaga responsabilidade colectiva, não pode ser indicada como originária. Não é esse o trauma, ou se o é, não é o único nem o primeiro.

Como Eva mais tarde afirma, a barbaridade das acções de Luís não era única, nem original: ele nada mais era do que um elo numa longa cadeia de atrocidades. "Se a Terra tivesse memória, quantos cantos da terra ficariam isentos da lembrança dessas cenas de degola?" (138-139). A maior preocupação de Evita, portanto, é a de compreender como seria possível que o jovem estudante de matemática por quem se apaixonara se tivesse transformado na pessoa que disparava rajadas de metralhadora nas cloacas das galinhas e cortava cabeças com prazer: "o que tentava era achar finalmente o momento, o brilho, a palavra que desencadeava na pessoa o gosto de degolar" (139). Esse brilho é já mencionado n'"Os Gafanhotos": "Evita disse ao noivo—'Não vás!' O noivo, porém, aproximou-se mais do que ninguém daquele diálogo rápido. (...) Tinha casado no dia anterior, mas a Pátria era a Pátria, e o casamento era o casamento. Evita viu—embora a luz fosse esverdeada—aquele brilho que sempre conduz o homem até ao último esforço do músculo (...) brilhar intensamente no olhar do noivo" (36). Embora o noivo pretendesse desligar o casamento da Pátria, é talvez essa conjugação involuntária que mais esclarece o trauma de Eva/Evita, pois "Os Gafanhotos," pouco mais narrando do que esse casamento, ao provocar o colapso temporal em que a morte do noivo se segue quase instantâneamente ao casamento, é eficaz precisamente pelo modo como une o particular e o pessoal ao público, mostrando como a separação dessas esferas nada mais é do que uma ilusão. Tal como a revelação das fotografias pode ser encarada como um estágio inicial de uma tentativa de sedução, o casamento de Evita com Luís é já o início da sua separação. Se o casamento também não pode ser indicado como o momento originário do trauma, embora o processo de narrativa fantástica que domina "Os Gafanhotos" assim o sugira, ele constitui, no entanto, um limiar entre a vida passada de Evita, estudante de História em Lisboa, e a do noivo, estudante de matemática empenhado em conseguir uma solução para um problema abstracto—encontrar "um critério universal para resolver as operações de grau superior a quatro" (47)—, numa pastelaria apropriadamente chamada "Ideal."

A Costa dos Murmúrios explora o modo como o Ideal rapidamente se dissolve, como o Ideal do Império Português, um certo Ideal de nação portuguesa, afinal se esvaiu em sangue e como essa catástrofe não poderá nunca ser resumida a um capítulo da História, a meros números de baixas, balanças de pagamentos, investimentos estrangeiros, quantidades de armamento. Como João Paulo Guerra constata, "pode dizer-se que morreram nas três guerras coloniais, de acordo com os dados oficiais, cerca de oito mil militares portugueses e um número muito superior, indeterminado, de guerrilheiros e de civis da Guiné, de Angola e de Moçambique. Mas não há estatísticas para a solidão, a ansiedade, o medo, o sofrimento, a dor" (11). Aliás, Eva Lopo é bem explícita ao recusar o conceito hegeliano de história e de ideal de um espírito mundial quando afirma logo a seguir ao "relato": "Aconselho-o, porém, a que não se preocupe com a verdade que não se reconstitui (...) estamos longe do tempo em que se acreditava no Universo como uma criação saída dum espírito preocupado com a inteligência e a verdade (...)" (42). As correspondências que Eva oferece como elos de significação são outras, materiais, quotidianas, até banais, mas investidas de um significado intenso. O pessoal, para Eva Lopo, é já sempre o nacional. Por isso, quando Ana Paula Ferreira lança a pergunta "How could an event which has always been in the order of the repressed be (re)constructed through the written word so as to effectively exorcize a national trauma?" (268), penso que a resposta, para além das possibilidades efectivamente abordadas no ensaio, não se refere apenas à guerra propriamente dita, mas terá sempre também de ser procurada ao nível pessoal e do quotidiano. Como Eva Lopo diz, a propósito de Helena, mas com um sentido geral, "Todas as pessoas, mesmo as mais serenas, mesmo as que se comportam na vida como vinhas, guardam na memória o momento dum terramoto (...)" (205). Qual o terramoto, então, de Eva Lopo? Desejo sugerir que, a poder ser indicado, esse terramoto, embora se possa aplicar alegoricamente à nação, é bem pessoal: o sentido de perda de identidade de Evita.

É ainda a respeito de Helena que Eva Lopo afirma: "Cai da cara dela uma torrente de lágrimas. Sei que vai chorar alguém que é só a sua pessoa. Não tenho dúvida que a pessoa chorada é ela mesma perdida no reflexo que teve em alguém" (204-205). Aparentemente esta observação é crítica, imbuída até de um certo cinismo, ao acusar o narcisismo de Helena; no entanto, também é aplicável a Eva Lopo de um modo mais significativo, pois no caso de Eva, o que está em causa não é só a vaidade mas o próprio conceito de sujeito, que, embora problematizado através da questão de identidade sexual—é ao recordar a confrontação com Helena, a sua recusa da oferta de Helena, que Eva, ou mesmo Evita, afirma que entre elas "a identidade é um espelho que nos reflecte e implacavelmente nos isola" (226)—, depende precisamente da memória. Ana Paula Ferreira já apontou como "[a]lthough Eva reiterates her identification with the character Evita, she refuses to be seen as a unitary subject of knowledge who has access to the origins or sources of history" (272). Penso ser necessário ir mais longe e encarar a recusa de Eva em se assumir enquanto sujeito unitário como a recusa mesma da sua identidade prévia. Isto é, Eva Lopo, embora reconheça ter sido Evita e não o disfarce, também necessita de considerá-la como outra personagem, num processo de adaptação ao trauma em que só memórias fragmentárias persistem, ainda que mesmo essas continuamente se diluam.

No "relato", este processo já é indicado em relação ao noivo e encarado de forma negativa, pois o deslocamento para África teria feito com que este deixasse de ser quem era e passasse a ser outro, precisamente por uma falha de memória: "Mas agora parecia haver perdido a memória de tudo isso, ali no pequeno quarto de África. Não fazia mal, alguma vez se perde a memória do que desejámos, e o noivo podia perdê-la já, mas de facto complicava bastante haver-se esquecido assim. Então se nos fôssemos esquecendo do que desejávamos descobrir, e depois de como nos chamávamos, e a seguir de que país éramos (...)?" (47). O noivo recusa violentamente tal possibilidade, sem perceber que a sua recusa é já prova da validade do pensamento de Evita. O que Evita ainda não adivinha é que será ela quem terá de recorrer a esse processo para sobreviver ao trauma que a realidade diária em África na situação colonial continuamente produzia. Susan J. Brison, num ensaio que explora processos de sobrevivência aos efeitos de trauma, demonstra como a reconstrução da personalidade é um elemento fundamental para os sobreviventes. Depois de exemplificar como a noção de sujeito unitário, baseada na correlação ininterrupta da memória pessoal defendida por Locke, é negada nos casos de vítimas de trauma, cuja memória é afectada de maneira drástica, Brison conclui que só admitindo a possibilidade de os sobreviventes se constituirem em outros é que se poderá manter o conceito de sujeito dependente da memória (20).

Um dos exemplos referidos por Brison é particularmente relevante para a compreensão do processo de desdobramento do sujeito no caso de Eva/Evita. Brison cita o caso de Charlotte Delbo, sobrevivente de Auschwitz, que explicitamente se refere a esse processo: "'No doubt, I am very fortunate in not recognizing myself in the self that was in Auschwitz. To return from there was so improbable that it seems to me I was never there at all (...) I live within a twofold being. The Auschwitz double doesn't bother me, doesn't interfere with my life. As though it weren't I at all. Without this split I would not have been able to revive' (1985: 3)" (Brison 20). Mesmo respeitando as diferenças evidentes entre as duas situações, penso ser óbvio que tal como Delbo, também Eva Lopo rejeita, ao mesmo tempo que reconhece, a sua identidade prévia. A necessidade de isolar Evita como um outro eu restrito a um passado e a um lugar específicos pode ser encarada como uma estratégia imprescindível à sua sobrevivência. Talvez seja essa afinal a razão da sua profunda ambivalência para com a memória, considerada simultaneamente como fundamental e ineficaz, vívida e imperfeita. Se a identidade é um espelho, e o passado são fantasmas, se "a memória é uma fraude para iludir o olvido cor de pó" (73), as memórias também serão necessárias para resistir à "funda cova do esquecimento" (225), à morte absoluta.

Helena é capaz de chorar a perda da sua identidade e, através desse processo, continuar a ser quem era, mas Eva não deixa também de a imaginar como tendo chegado ao fim. Tal como Eva diz ao narrador do "relato": "Helena chegou ao fim? Chegou. Tem uma memória boa, o seu rosto chorou bem" (208). Mas é a memória do narrador que é boa, porque a possibilidade de Helena chegar ao fim é devida à sua falta de memória: "Helena é só corpo e voz. Parece não ter espírito nem memória sob o sabão" (201). Ou ainda antes, Helena é já referida como "uma Minerva inocente, sem memória" (93). Eva Lopo frequentemente apresenta o desejo do esquecimento, baseado no conhecimento da futilidade da memória, ou mesmo o imperativo de esquecer para sobreviver: "Que memória histórica, que testemunho? Esqueça de novo, esqueça—disse Eva Lopo" (193), só para afirmar, quase imediatamente, e afirmar-se através da memória: "Agora me lembro (...)" (193). A memória nem sempre sucede, as imagens diluem-se, "se nunca mais evocar esta lembrança à luz duma lâmpada ocasional como a sua, o Stella inteiro (...) acabará aqui" (209). Eva Lopo está bem consciente de como "é impossível suster uma ruína só com a vontade" (108) e de como "[n]ão é porque alguém chama que alguém responde. (...) De nada vale querer que existam nos escombros os fantasmas" (111). Mas Eva Lopo insiste na sua separação de Evita precisamente por causa desses fantasmas que tanto são seus como da nação: "tudo ficou sob sombras. Vejo sombras. (...) evite todas as sombras. Tem-se feito um esforço enorme ao longo destes anos para que nós o tenhamos esquecido. Não se deve deixar passar para o futuro nem a ponta duma cópia, nem a ponta duma sombra" (136). Um esforço enorme, na realidade, e que às vezes parece vencer, suprimir, apagar a memória. No entanto, a supressão da memória não evita as sombras, só permite que nos tornemos nós próprios nos fantasmas que desejaríamos iludir. E, no fim, as memórias são sempre demasiadas, em excesso. A esse respeito, e talvez por ainda não ter necessidade de sobreviver, Evita pode ser lúcida quando diz ao noivo que a memória é infinita.

Obras Citadas

Ambrogi, Marlise Vaz Bridi. "Entrevista com Lídia Jorge." *Estudos Portugueses e Africanos* 5 (1985): 9-12.

Brison, Susan J. "Outliving Oneself: Trauma, Memory, and Personal Identity." *Feminists Rethink the Self.* Ed. Diana Tietjens Meyers. Boulder, CO and London: Westview Press, 1997. 12-39.

Bulger, Laura F. "*O Cais das Merendas* de Lídia Jorge: Uma Identidade Perdida?" *Colóquio/Letras* 82 (1984): 51-57.

Cann, John P. *Counterinsurgency in Africa: The Portuguese Way of War, 1961-1974.* Wesport, CT & London: Greenwood Press, 1997.

Delbo, Charlotte. *Days and Memory.* Trad. de Rosette Lamont. Marlboro, VT: Marlboro Press, 1985.

Derrida, Jacques. *Mémoires pour Paul de Man.* Paris: Galilée, 1988.

Ferreira, Ana Paula. "Lídia Jorge's *A Costa dos Murmúrios*: History and the Postmodern She-Wolf." *Revista Hispánica Moderna* 45.2 (1992): 268-78.

Guerra, João Paulo. *Memória das Guerras Coloniais.* 2.ª ed. Porto: Afrontamento, 1994.

Heß, Renate. "Schreiben heißt: sich errinern. Zum Wek von Lídia Jorge." In *Portugiesische Literatur.* Ed. Henry Thorau. Frankfurt a.M.: Suhrkamp, 1997. 501-20.

Jorge, Lídia. *A Costa dos Murmúrios*. Lisboa: Dom Quixote, 1988.

———. *The Murmuring Coast*. Trad. Natália Costa and Ronald W. Sousa. Minneapolis & London: University of Minnesota Press, 1995.

Kaufman, Helena. "Reclaiming the Margins of History in Lídia Jorge's *A Costa dos Murmúrios*." *Luso-Brazilian Review* 29.1: (1992): 41-49.

MacQueen, Norrie. *The Decolonization of Portuguese Africa: Metropolitan Revolution and the Dissolution of Empire*. London & New York: Longman, 1997.

Martins, Luís Almeida. "A Ficção é o mais sério de tudo." Entrevista com Lídia Jorge. *Jornal de Letras, Artes e Ideias* (29 September, 1992): 8-12.

Moutinho, Isabel. "A Collapsing Empire: Cultural Decay and Personal Transformation in the Recent Work of Portuguese Women Novelists." *Romance Languages Annual* 5 (1993): 484-90.

Saraiva, Arnaldo. "Os Duplos do Real e os Duplos Romanescos (*A Costa dos Murmúrios* de Lídia Jorge)." *Arquivos do Centro Cultural Português* (Fundação Calouste Gulbenkian) XXIX (1991): 39-48.

Seabra, Jorge. "O Império e as Memórias do Estado Novo: os Heróis de Chaimite." *Revista de História das Ideias* 17 (1995): 33-78.

Simões, Manuel. "A Nova Narrativa Portuguesa: de Almeida Faria a Lídia Jorge." *Rassegna Iberistica* 21(1984): 3-15.

Santos, Maria Irene Ramalho de Sousa. "Bondoso Caos: *A Costa dos Murmúrios* de Lídia Jorge." *Colóquio/Letras* 107 (1989): 64-67.

Stolz, Peter. "'(...) nosso Vietnam': Lídia Jorges Geschichten aus Portugals jüngster Zeit." *Germanisch-Romanische Monatsschrift* 44.1 (1994): 87-94.

Teixeira, Rui de Azevedo. *A Guerra Colonial e o Romance Português: Agonia e Catarse*. Lisboa: Editorial Notícias, 1998.

Back to Nietzsche: The Making of an Intellectual/Woman Lídia Jorge's *A Costa dos Murmúrios*[1]

Hilary Owen

> Moçambique está para a África Austral como a Península Ibérica está para Europa—estão ambas como a bainha está para as calças. E a culpa? E a culpa? perguntou o major também já sentado.[2]

Introduction

A Costa dos Murmúrios, first published in 1988, remains one of Lídia Jorge's best known and most successful novels. It confirmed her reputation among the leading writers of the post-revolutionary period and became closely associated with the remembrance and collective exorcism of the guilt and trauma surrounding Portugal's Colonial War in Mozambique (1964-1974/5). The novel contains two separate narratives of the same "events." The first narrative, "Os Gafanhotos," is a sentimental obscurantist short story that relates the suicide of a newly married lieutenant in the Portuguese forces in the late 1960s. The second account, the main body of the novel, is a conscious corrective to "Os Gafanhotos," told twenty years later by the lieutenant's bride, Eva Lopo, who refers to herself in her youth as one of the protagonists, Evita. She adds various items of new information, notably her realization that her husband has been transformed by his participation in a cruel and barbaric "dirty war." Closer to home, she also uncovers evidence of a campaign to poison the native black male population by planting methyl alcohol supplies in conventional bottles and containers. Most critical readings of this text work, at some level, from Eva's ostensible motivation to de-authorize the first telling, as her corrective text undermines and complexifies History as monolithic and "official." Somewhat more contestable, however, is the extent to which this de-authorization involves "setting the record straight."[3] Helena Kaufman, for example, claims that:

> The dual structure sustains a polemic view of History dependent on the subject who constructs it, the prevalent ideology, and the type of narration. The full story emerges only after the reading of both parts. (41)

While the type of narration and the prevalent ideology are certainly relevant factors in the "de-authorizing" project, it is debatable whether it is the "full story" that emerges from reading both parts, or merely a denser one. Eva's narrative is certainly more detailed and more deconstructively incisive than "Os Gafanhotos," but it is barely more stable than the text it displaces. Although Eva's text serves to interpellate Eva herself as a more authoritative narrator, as Ana Paula Ferreira asserts in her conclusions to "History and the Postmodern She-Wolf," she does not "replace one gender-based truth with another" (276). As a result, the novel's apparent appeal to meaningful collective remembrance and national expiation is paradoxically enjoined through an anti-historicist exploration of narrativity, aesthetics, and, to employ Hayden White's term, "emplotment."[4] I argue that this paradox is constitutive of the novel's attempt to map out various problems and possibilities in the transition from a Portuguese "post-colonial" consciousness responding to the moment of immediate historical crisis to a tentative of "post-coloniality" as a mode of theoretical reflection. The tension between Jorge's historical inscription of women in wartime and her assertion of the "feminine" as deconstructive figure affords my point of entry to the text.[5]

I

In his review for *Jornal de Letras* in 1988, António Bahia describes *A Costa dos Murmúrios* as "o romance da nossa culpa" (5) relating "a história de uma certa África no feminino," but also "a imaturidade de um povo colonizador, que não será somente o português, mas antes [de] uma raça, a raça branca despótica e verde" (5). However, the narrative deviates significantly from the constructions of collective identity, the "nossa" which characterizes other post-revolutionary novels such as Olga Gonçalves's *Ora Esguardae* and Teolinda Gersão's *Paisagem com Mulher e Mar ao Fundo*. The first-person plural subject of "culpa" in *A Costa* proves labile and unfixable. In an interview with the Mozambican journal *Lua Nova*, conducted during a visit to Mozambique in 1994, Jorge herself defined her task as to show:

> (...) a forma como as pessoas mais pacíficas são capazes de se transformar em seres agressivos perante circunstâncias agressivas, mas também como as

> mulheres são cúmplices daquilo que se pensa ser apenas a natureza violenta dos homens. Não. As mulheres, à sua maneira são cúmplices da mesma forma. (9)

Jorge's pronouncement contains an interesting note of ambivalence, "à sua maneira" against "da mesma forma." Rather less ambivalent, however, is Bahia's view of woman as historical scapegoat, who slides seamlessly into the time-honored role of "representing" the guilt of a whole generation, a function potentially enhanced by the postmodernist eschewal of historical determinism to which he refers:

> Essa "guerra" também foi feita pelas mulheres (...) que se queriam arredadas, não intervenientes, submissas (...) Mulheres que poderão *pura e simplesmente representar o silêncio cúmplice de toda uma geração*: a geração da guerra colonial portuguesa, embora já se saiba, não tenham sido objectivos da autora imprimir uma espécie de determinismo histórico ao romance. (5, my emphases)

In her contribution to *Men in Feminism* Rosi Braidotti argues, echoing traditional feminist distrust of postmodernism, that the feminine is symptomatic of dissolution and decline in anti-humanist philosophies, in a manner suspiciously continuous with woman's age-old scapegoat function in phallocentric epistemology.[6] According to Braidotti:

> Ever since Nietzsche, passing through every major European philosopher, the question of woman has accompanied the decline of the classical view of human subjectivity. The problematic of the "feminine" thus outlined is nothing more than a very elaborate metaphor, a symptom, of the profound illness of Western culture and of its phallologocentric logic. (...) My argument is that this "feminine" bears no direct or even necessary relationship to real-life women. In some ways, it even perpetuates the century-old mental habit which consists in assigning to the "feminine" disorders or insufficiencies pertaining to the male of the species. (236)[7]

Jorge's inscription of Braidotti's "real-life" women into war history, in the form of the officers' wives who inhabit the Stella Maris promises to work, then, in creative tension with the inscription of Woman as figuratively symptomatic of the decline of classical human subjectivity in philosophy. Eva and Helena, as figures, symptomatize History as teleology, Helen of Troy being the archetypal end of a civilization and Eve the beginning of the history of man's sufferings on earth.[8] *A Costa*, therefore, traces a shifting and contingent frontier between the figure of the feminine in deconstructive (or as Braidotti more broadly implies anti-humanist) criticism and what Gayatri Spivak terms woman's "minimal predication as indeterminate [which] is already available to the phallocentric tradition" (82). As we will see, the historical invisibility of women's minor or insignificant war experiences thus functions as cover story for interrogating humanist historical emplotment in terms of the exclusions of phallocentricity. In precise, formal terms, this means that Eva's critical rewriting of "Os Gafanhotos" questions the nature of the relationship between the singular event, the "smallness" of history as a minimal unit here emblematized by women, and the general conceptual framework or, in Hayden White's terms, "metahistory" to which the singular event relates.

This historiographic focus on the relationship between event and concept echoes the preoccupations of New Historicist criticism as exemplified by Joel Fineman in *The Subjectivity Effect in Western Literary Tradition* where he poses the question how:

> to find some way to introduce into the ahistorical historicality of Hegelian philosophy of history some break or interruption of the fullness and repletion of the Spirit's self-reflection, so as thereby to introduce to history the temporality of time. (57)

This sense of "ahistorical historicality" in *A Costa* is arguably common to both Christian Imperialism and, by extension, Marxist-Leninism as the teleological discourse of progress and "civilization" which succeeded colonialism in the Lusophone African context.[9] When Eva ironically describes as "progress" the image of a black woman framed by the window of a half-built, already crumbling apartment block, she could equally be referring subtextually to post-independence Mozambique in the late 1980s when the Marxist-Leninist government, beleaguered by destabilization and war, was spiraling into crisis:

> Lembrava um postal que ilustrasse uma ideia especial de progresso, de abraço entre as raças, feito nos andaimes duma casa a construir já em escombros. O tempo falava por si com uma veemência enorme de princípio e fim em simultâneo. Nada melhor para ilustrar a sociedade sem tempo. (174)

According to Joel Fineman, the specific narrative form of the anecdote as "historeme, i.e., as the smallest minimal unit of the historiographic fact," (67) enables it to act as a device for reintroducing the temporality of time to history. It is:

> the literary form that uniquely *lets history happen* by virtue of the way it introduces an opening into the teleological, and therefore timeless, narration of beginning, middle, and end. The anecdote produces the effect of the real, the occurrence of contingency, by establishing an event as an event within and yet without the framing context of historical successivity, i.e., it does so only in so far as its narration both comprises and refracts the narration it reports. (72)

The women, the children, and the black Mozambican servants in the "espaço eunuco" (85) of the Stella Maris protagonize a series of minute, singular events for which Eva is at pains to find an appropriate narrative description, as she remarks:

> Quando não chegavam a ser episódios com seu drama, sua intriga, seu enigma, e desfecho, havia pelo menos descrição de caracteres, ou sinuosidades deles com os nomes, as anecdotas, as gargalhadas. (108)

An example of how anecdotes operate in the text occurs with the death by methyl alcohol poisoning of Bernardo, the hotel's black receptionist and switchboard operator. He occupies a central, symbolic position within the closed history of divinely inspired conquest. One could see:

> como nele vinham confluir as vontades indomáveis dos Príncipes de Avis, com sua mãe severa, seus retratos trocados, seus barretes polémicos, empurrando os barcos até ao último ponto da esfericidade da Terra. Lá, no último porto, fora encontrado o Bernardo. O Bernardo podia representar sozinho a conquista que, a partir desse impulso uníssono duma só família, tinha sido perpetrada através da História, precisamente para que os povos entendessem que a salvação estava além da História, se acaso rezassem. (86)

The metaphor of the "impulso uníssono" connects the telephone network to the national foundational "impulse" of the "ínclita geração," making

Bernardo's switchboard the symbol *par excellence* of teleological connectivity. Bernardo's story is thus *within* imperial history as a dynastically inspired totality, but also *without* it when the singular event of his unexpected death becomes the material of anecdote, placing him outside the "framing context of historical successivity" (Fineman 72). When asked whether Bernardo's death had any consequences, Eva replies with reference to the narrative of "Os Gafanhotos," "Teve, mas nada que fira o som duma palavra da sua narrativa tão conforme. Coisa simples que durou dois dias" (88).[10]

The anecdotal articulation of a "within and yet without" seems to provide the narrative format *par excellence* for locating the Stella Maris women's insignificant, personalized histories on the margins of war. The problem with the anecdote, however, as Robert J. C. Young puts it in his critique of Fineman, is that it is apt to spill over into "the metonymic status of the example (...) in which the relation of the part is to illustrate and comprise the whole" (173).[11] This is demonstrated in *A Costa* when the birth of Zurique's child goes unexpectedly wrong, his wife's anal sphincter is torn in a miscarriage and the child subsequently dies. Rather than remaining disruptively anecdotal, the event becomes exemplary of the stereotypical colonial fiction of "native incompetence" at the hospital and also metafictionally illustrative of the narrative organization of history in terms of cause, effect, and explanation. Eva announces didactically, "Agora explico-lhe finalmente como os músculos invisíveis podem ter um desempenho especial na organização dos factos históricos" (189). From being a contingent event the anecdote becomes an illustrative micro-teleology or "teiazinha," with the power to "comprise the whole" of the larger, metahistorical schema, or "teia." Eva is thus able to predict:

> A imagem desses anéis rotos e inchados é tudo o que sobeja dessa viagem quando se vê o tenente Zurique [...] Triste, não é? Só que nesse momento ainda nenhuma parte dessa teiazinha entrou na teia da História. Mas entrará. (185)

Just as the anecdote is formally reassimilable to teleology by way of the non-contingent "exemplary," so too are the events in the women's lives, always liable to re-appropriation by History. The very instability of the anecdotal format "within and yet without," the framework of historical successivity, marks their capacity to be re-enmeshed in Historicist totalities under certain exemplary rubrics and conditions. Living under the sign of the Virgin Madonna at the Stella Maris, the officers' wives embody precisely those roles that are traditionally available to patriotic women in wartime. According to Elisabetta Addis et al., in their sociohistorical study of women soldiers, the patriotic woman might be:

> a mother prepared to bear sons and sacrifice them to the motherland, or a housewife prepared to follow her military husband in his various shifts of location, maintaining his honour through grace, fidelity, order and other domestic virtues. (...) Despite historical exclusion from regular armies, it is incorrect to assert that armed conflict was alien to women and that women had no part in wars. (xvi-xvii)

The women of the Stella Maris do not, therefore, emerge from Eva's re-telling as empowered agents of their own history or as subjects of resistance to a particular version of history as hegemonic. Indeed the conclusion of the novel reduces them to an undifferentiated "sebe de costas" (257), affording a pun on the novel's title. Rather, they serve to highlight the formal terms on which certain traditional inclusions of the feminine in war history are already negotiated. The semi-permeable membrane which the anecdote/exemplum slippage sets up between "teiazinha" and "teia" mirrors Jorge's ambivalent description of female complicity in war, compared to male, in terms of "à sua maneira" but "da mesma forma" (*Lua Nova* 9). It also provides the alibi for a more fundamental, epistemological analysis of Woman at the level of metahistory.

II

Distancing herself from the sacrificial "mothers" of the Stella Maris, Eva gradually assumes discursive authority in relation to the "fathers" of the western philosophical tradition, which is grounded in the negation of Woman (Eve and Helen of Troy) and which, in Hayden White's terms, furnishes the conceptual frameworks and narrative emplotments of history. As Ana Paula Ferreira has suggested,[12] a case might be made here for analyzing Eva according to Jane Gallop's hypothesis of the daughter's seduction.[13] Gallop's readings of Julia Kristeva in "The Phallic Mother. A Freudian Analysis" are certainly apposite as regards Ev/ita's self-imposed "exile" from patriotic society. According to Gallop, "A woman theoretician is already an exile; expatriated from her *langue maternelle*, she speaks a paternal language; she presumes to a fraudulent power" (126-27). Eva self-consciously represents herself on several occasions as being still a daughter, unable to identify with the other women's birth experiences. Although she seems set to re-enact a classic narrative cliché of colonialism, that of the inexperienced European woman who explores her sexuality in the relative freedom of the tropics, her journey from "naiveté" to "promiscuity" is more intellectual than sexual.[14] The power of knowledge in the novel is circulated and negotiated in terms of Evita's ambivalent sexual identifications and the undecidable physical encounters these produce. Helena's homologic, narcissistic position leads to silence and mortality while, in a move which retraces Kristeva's gestures to normalize heterosexuality even in her more radicalized invocations of it,[15] Evita does not pursue the possibility of lesbian revenge.[16] Although the relationship between the two women proffers the fantasy of a radical feminist variant on the traditional ploy of disrupting the patriarchal military economy by heterosexual adultery, its force is effectively re-territorialized and diverted in the direction of Eva's self-constitution as a philosophical woman who exerts narrative authority over the author of "Os Gafanhotos." Through her complicit conversations with the journalist (who treats cross-racial paternity as a form of genetic revolution) and her responses to the author of "Os Gafanhotos" (whose textual paternity rights are systematically undermined), Ev/ita is afforded a series of intertextual dialogues with the "fathers" of western philosophy, most significantly with Platonic mimeticism and the subversive counter-pull of Nietzschean anti-humanism. Her most common self-identification initially, however, is with cynicism, here restored to its narrow sense in ancient Greek philosophy.

Ev/ita and the journalist repeatedly strike the detached pose of the cynic. On various occasions Ev/ita describes herself as a dog, recalling the etymology of the word cynic in the Greek for dog, and affording a humorous resonance with the Latin "Cave Canes" sign on Helena's house ("Beware the dog" or "Beware the cynic"?) which has been left abandoned by Italians (78).[17] Helena, on the other hand, is the ultra self-caressive, narcissistic woman, the "narciso com uma mosca no meio" (223), traditionally associated with the female sexual economy.[18] Ev/ita's stock response to Helena's melodramatic, over-mimetic posturings is correspondingly over-intellectualized as she watches Helena and thinks, "Eu receava esquecer o que aprendia, e tudo o que tinha no momento era vontade de fixar e aprender" (97). Although Helen exaggerates her role to the point of parody, it is significant that she does not do so knowingly.[19] Rather, she is an oxymoronic "Minerva inocente, sem memória" (93). As Gallop puts it, "Knowingly, lucidly to exercise *and* criticize power is to dephallicize, to assume the phallus and unveil that assumption as presumption, as fraud" (122).[20] The concentric circles which Helena draws around herself are themselves encircled and appropriated by the gaze of Eva, whose assumption of the phallus is a potentially disruptive unveiling because it is lucid.[21] However, Gallop's call for woman to "exercise *and* criticize power" (122) necessitates, in Kristeva's formulation, an "impossible dialectic of two terms" (121). Kristeva's privileging of woman as *uniquely* appropriate to command this "dialectic of self and self-loss, of identity and heterogeneity" (122) risks re-erecting woman, so Gallop argues, into the role of the "phallic mother." This is the constant risk of Eva's project wherever her comparative intellectual lucidity attains a commanding height that is cynical without the self-irony that would divide this phallic uniqueness against itself. As Gallop claims, "Any position can become assimilated into the symbolic order as a codified, fixed representation. No 'experience' or 'identity' can guarantee one's dissidence" (123).

According to Gallop, Evita's dialectic of "self and self-loss, of identity and heterogeneity" (122) is played out through her oscillation between Helena and the journalist. Her rejection of Helena is bound up with desire for the (binary) oppositional mortality of heterogeneity as she says/thinks, "O que amo em ti não tem enterro nem aspiro a isso. Os homens sim, fazem-me feliz porque me enterram e me tornam mortal. Quero que um homem se ponha em cima de mim para me sentir mortal" (226). Evita's subsequent meeting with the journalist leads to a sexual encounter underwritten by the promise of phallic uniqueness. Expressing her desire to seduce the journalist, Evita thinks, "Espero sentir sob o robe o inchaço do seu quinto membro. Com essa vela içada, ele pode conduzir-me onde eu sozinha não posso entrar" (227). She echoes her own valedictory words/thoughts to Helena as "o jornalista desnudou-se e fez-me mortal" (227). Evita thus re-enters the cycle of life and death, asserting a self in self-loss that re-affirms the symbolic order. If Helena is the principle of a decadent, sterile morbidity of sameness, Evita's desire for heterogeneity as "mortality" principle is effectively a life-affirming gesture in which both she and her masculine "other," the journalist, enjoy the play of dephallicization and the power of shared laughter. The dominant narrative tense of Eva's text is the present. The journalist's survival is paramount to her aesthetic project as the following citation with its focus on performative speech indicates:

> Gosto que o jornalista, vinte anos depois, *se declare sobrevivente* duma cadeira vermelha. A teoria tem uma força vital que ultrapassa a vida. A teoria e o conto. (258, my emphasis)

Eva's critique of "Os Gafanhotos" in terms of a celebration of life evokes the Nietzschean call for a life-serving historical consciousness that clearly informs the novel's anti-mimeticist, anti-humanist poetics.[22] According to Hayden White's reading of Nietzschean anti-historicism in *Metahistory*:

> Nietzsche's interpretation of the spirit of Tragedy (...) consists of a conflation of the conventional conception of Tragedy with that of Comedy, so that the two truths separately taught by each of these are now combined into a single multiplex acceptance of life and death. (345)

In its resolutely anti-mimetic aesthetic, *A Costa* reveals events proper to the horror of tragedy, but Ev/ita and the journalist are "comediantes" (97). He refers to her as "sua farsante" (126), and their complicity is most commonly expressed through laughter. According to White, Nietzsche's original Greek Tragic spirit reacts against the morality and mimeticism of the Platonic in favor of a truly Tragic art which is both "realistically illusionist" and "creatively destructive of its own illusions" (338). Ev/ita recalls her mother's Platonic entreaties as the voice of morality, but Ev/ita is not a woman who listens to mother. Who was the mother of Eve, anyway? "Lembrava-se da mãe, da fina voz da mãe—'As almas boas são atraídas pelas paisagens grandiosas, como os grandes prados, os grandes rios, porque são grandiosas como elas!'" (138). As Evita reacts to the photographs of atrocities which Helen has shown her, she remarks, "Não se deve deixar passar para o futuro nem a ponta de uma cópia, nem a ponta duma sombra" (136). The concept of constructive erasure affords Eva's most direct engagement with Nietzsche in terms of his dialectic of remembering and forgetting, contrasting animal incapacity for memory with human inability to forget. Ev/ita ponders, with a hint of wistful longing for the impossible, the burning of the library at Alexandria: "estimo os países de vocação metafísica total, os que não investem na fixação de nada" (131).[23]

Nietzsche's life-serving historical consciousness turns on the notion that history must become a life-serving form of art which would place an emphasis on objectivity in Nietzsche's specific sense of the term (cited from *The Use and Abuse of History*) as "'composition' in its highest form, of which the result will be an artistically, but not historically, true picture" (White 352). Eva's commentary on "Os Gafanhotos" constantly draws attention to competing conceptualizations of "artistic objectivity," opposing to the author's reliance on "verdade" and the illusionism of "verosimilhança" (42) her own aesthetics of reality, or "correpondência," the non-specular sense experience of "o cheiro e o som" (42). Reflecting on the horrific events which she has just "witnessed" via Helena's purloined photographs, Ev/ita thinks relativistically, "Entre o bem e o mal uma mortalha de papel de seda" (141), concluding, or apparently concluding, "'Sendo assim, tanto faz—tudo é idêntico a tudo'—pensou transitoriamente" (141). The discontinuity of this "transitoriamente" (141) is the defining poetic mode of Eva's intellectual counter-odyssey. Uncoupling cause and effect in a process recalling Nietzsche's set of "retroactive confiscations" (White 363), Eva draws instead on densely interwoven patterns of metaphor that echo Nietzsche's "return of historical thought to the Metaphorical mode [which] will permit liberation from all efforts to find any definitive meaning in history" (White 372).

The process of deserting the various "housings" of metahistorical consciousness which Eva's narrative undertakes belongs to a systematic intellectual clearance programme borne out through the novel's dominant metaphorical patternings in terms of space and spatial interrelations. From the beginning of the novel, it is evident that "locations" are less permanent than their occupants might believe them to be. The Stella Maris is described by the Luís Alex as an "acampamento de ciganos sem burro" (77). Ev/ita foresees the hotel's immanent ruin as the war ends, the Europeans flee, and nature reasserts itself. The monuments to an era will be reclaimed by matter and space. We learn that as a young history student Evita had abandoned her course because her concept of time as relative was arrogantly dismissed by a Salazarist clerical professor who believed only in the absolute time of God. Dislodged from the academic foundation, her subsequent play with philosophical intertexts and dialogues constitutes a string of nomadic "camp-cites." She distances herself from the Stella Maris, refusing to live in Helena's house by the sea, refusing to escape and go to live with the journalist, meeting him only in places that are more and more remote and finally being exiled entirely from the community of wives, who "faziam uma sebe de costas no meio do hall" (257). One of Evita's favorite spaces for philosophical dialogue and reflection turns out to be the bathroom. Almost at the end of the novel, to the mocking chorus of a Sebastianic intertext, "é agora," Evita wonders when to reveal her affair, only for Eva to interrupt with the curious observation, "sim, sempre foram importantes as banheiras" (239). This brings full circle Eva's assertion in the first chapter of her text, "claro que teve a sua importância, a banheira" (45). Metaphors of water and washing, fluidity, and flow accumulate throughout the novel, evoking the ablution of guilt in terms of dirt or matter that may be dissolved temporarily, only to be transported and deposited somewhere else. Evita's decision to discuss the poisonings with the journalist follows a fluid metaphorical route that meanders through her consideration of African and Euopean civilizations in terms of relative sedimentation:

> O choque das nossas civilizações parecia tão banal e tão lento quanto o feito pela sedimentação dum rio. (...) Era bom e definitivo imaginar que tudo iria embrulhado no novelo escorregadio do esquecimento—Essa é uma ideia onde se mergulha como num banho tépido para passar os dias. Há momentos, porém, que agitam o banho tépido como uma vaga. (164)

Bathrooms, hosepipes, rivers, tears, canals, estuaries and, of course, the sea, are connected through metaphor in a process whereby flow is regulated, cut off, re-distributed, and decanted as Evita thinks, listens, and talks to people by rivers and seashores, in bathrooms and under showers, developing significant correspondences between water and sound/silence, between dispersal and return (108, 137-38, 144, 201, 216, 219). Following the return of the soldiers, she remarks, "Mas depois dos banhos e de todas as águas correntes, do rumor intenso do regresso, o Stella Maris mergulhou no silêncio" (243).

These cumulative, metaphorical patterns of connecting and disconnecting flow are resonant with the Nietzschean-inspired poetics of radical displacement and deterritorialization of desire[24] propagated by Gilles Deleuze and Félix Guattari and subsequently popularized in Euro-American academia via various reinterpretations of their concept of the "nomadic subject" as the ultimate symbol of "displacement and dispersion" (Kaplan 87). Deleuze and Guattari's theories of deterritorializing and reterritorializing desire as a force for destabilizing oedipalized institutions such as family, the army, the State, and the church, have been debated and contested by feminist and post-colonial schools of criticism alike.[25] I choose here to focus on the latter, as it relates to subjective interest investments, through Gayatri Spivak's classic engagement with *Anti-Oedipus* in "Can the Subaltern Speak?". Spivak argues that Deleuze and Guattari's failure "to consider the relations between desire, power and subjectivity renders them incapable of articulating a theory of interests" (68). The western radical intellectual, whose "sovereign subject" (66) is not so easily banished or dispersed through the choice of "becoming minor" from the hierarchically empowered center, is called upon by Spivak to examine more effectively the investments implicit in her/his own intellectual positioning. The task is all the more urgent where a western radical philosophy seeks euphorically to dissolve an unexamined subjectivity, which continues none the less to depend on Othering in the very constitution of the "nomadic" movement it declares.

Re-considering *A Costa* in light of Spivak's pronouncements, what are the implications of Eva's poetics of "displacement and dispersion" for the evocation of "nossa culpa" which furnished the point of entry to my analysis? The closing lines of the novel suggest a sense of gradual erasure:

> A pouco e pouco as palavras isolam-se dos objectos que designam, depois das palavras só se desprendem sons, e dos sons restam só os murmúrios, o derradeiro estádio antes do apagamento.

However, Eva's disruptive laughter in the closing lines also implies a circling of the text and a gesture of return: "disse Eva Lopo rindo. Devolvendo e anulando 'Os Gafanhotos'" (259). "Anular" here means to annul, but it is also cognate with anular, suggesting a ring or circle. The conclusion of the novel is dialectically poised between dissolution of history as narrative (mimetic) emplotment and the circularity of an anular (or anal?) return, the irreducibility of material suffering to narrative emplotment, such that the material and the somatic have a peculiar capacity to remain. The novel's gesture toward "collectivity" is not therefore represented in terms of the conscious or the reflective. Rather, it is metaphorized in terms of the endurance of physical matter. Thus, the universalization of fear as transhistorical human commonality is ushered in through images of corporeal flow, linking the anal tear of Zurique's wife to the journalist's loss of anal control in the Russian roulette game, to the terror of the Wiriyamu victims whose monument should be a "caldeirão de fezes reais" (251), to the ultimate, human incarnation of Christ in the garden of Gethsemane who "sentiu que os esfíncteres do seu corpo se delassavam e saía, pelo seu ânus carnal, a matéria que define o nosso medo" (251). Although this movingly demonstrates that the absence of definitive historical *meaning* can never eradicate suffering as definitive historical *experience*, the metaphors of materiality risk merging the particular dirt of "a nossa culpa" into the universal "dirt" of "o nosso medo" (251), effectively levelling the relations between "desire, power and subjectivity" (68) which in Spivak's terms would allow for a theory of interests. Perhaps, as Spivak claims, "It is when signifiers are left to look after themselves that verbal slippages happen" (70). But how far are the signifiers of *A Costa* left to look after themselves?

Caren Kaplan's review of nomadism productively reformulates one of Spivak's central prevarications as follows:

> In making recourse to the metaphors of marginality and displacement, Deleuze and Guattari attempt to displace the sedimented bulk of European humanist traditions. Their antihistoricism seeks to deconstruct classical lineages even as it may tend to homogenize or blur the kinds of differences upon which contemporary identity politics insist. (88)

And yet a central contradiction of *A Costa* is that this antihistoricist deconstruction of "classical lineages" does not wholly homogenize "the kinds of differences upon which contemporary identity politics insist" (88). Through the specificity of Portuguese colonial historical referencing in relation to an international context,[26] Jorge effectively draws attention to semiperipherality as a distinct geopolitical and cultural concept which is none the less not quite reducible to the categories of difference privileged by identity politics. Boaventura de Sousa Santos[27] provides a classic working definition of semiperipherality in the Portuguese context:

> Since the demise of the empire in 1974, Portugal has been renegotiating its position in the world system. It seems that a semiperipheral position of some kind will be maintained, this time based on the terms of Portugal's integration in the European Economic Community and on its privileged social relations with Portuguese-speaking Africa. (34)[28]

Caren Kaplan's distinctions between the free choices implicit in a romanticized nomadism and the enforced dislocations of migrancy become particularly relevant in the context of semiperipherality as the basis for new modes of "identity formation." Kaplan objects to the conflation of modernity and postmodernity[29] into "undifferentiated cultures" such that:

> European gypsies and Third World immigants share the same theoretical space not through structural relations of historically specific diasporas but through a kind of generalized poetics of displacement. (87-88)

The key to *A Costa* is that it does not pursue a totally *generalized* poetics of displacement. Historically indexed referents (the Wiriyamu massacre, the war zones of the Nó Górdio campaign, Eduardo and Janet Mondlane, the Moulin Rouge club in Beira, and the Portuguese exodus from Mozambique) and the dominant discourses of Portuguese colonialism (the Fifth Empire, lusotropicalism, miscegenation, the war propaganda) inflect the transhistorical generalizations of displacement poetics with the specifics of Portuguese empire and its collapse. Thus, returning to Spivak's phrase, the signifiers are not entirely left to look after themselves. Kaplan claims that Deleuze and Guattari's "mappings" make "the Third World function[s] as a metaphorical margin for European oppositional strategies, an imaginary space rather than a location of theoretical production itself" (88). I would argue that *A Costa* does not resolve, but does significantly complexify, the oppositional duality behind Kaplan's critique. The feminine identity dialectic which structures the novel may be taken to configure the double movement of Portuguese semiperipherality between *migration* from "Third World" metaphorical margin (of Europe) to a European oppositional strategy which would be differently predicated as a result, and the possibility of a *nomadic* dispersion that would not feel uniquely (phallically) positioned to avoid projecting oppositional European strategy onto the real Third World as metaphorical margin.[30] As *A Costa* effectively asks, how does the "bainha" of Europe's trousers set about unstitching itself?

Notes

[1] I am indebted to Till Geiger for his comments on this article and for affording some very productive debate on historiography.

[2] *A Costa dos Murmúrios* (Lisboa: Publicações Dom Quixote, 1988) 28. All subsequent references are to this edition and are abbreviated to *A Costa.*

[3] As Ronald W. Sousa points out, "Criticism written on *Costa* has uniformly seen the interaction between its two constituent parts and the gesture of negation in the text's concluding pages as a composite critique of traditional history: critique, that is, of the notion that there somehow is a single 'history' to be revealed" ("The Critique of History" 135). See also Ferreira

270n for references to the debate in Portugal concerning the uncertainty and undecidability of history in *A Costa*.

[4] According to Hayden White, "Emplotment is the way by which a sequence of events fashioned into a story is gradually revealed to be a story of a particular kind" (*Metahistory* 7).

[5] See Isabel Moutinho, "A Collapsing Empire: Cultural Decay and Personal Transformation in the Recent Work of Portuguese Women Novelists," *Romance Languages Annual* 5 (1993): 484-90. Moutinho considers *A Costa* alongside female-authored colonial war novels by Wanda Ramos and Joana Ruas. For a similar feminist angle, see Isabel Allegro de Magalhães, *O Sexo dos Textos e Outras Leituras* (Lisboa: Caminho, 1995) 29 and 33-35. For a Foucauldian feminist reading of *A Costa*, see Ana Paula Ferreira, "Lídia Jorge's *A Costa dos Murmúrios*: History and the Postmodern She-Wolf."

[6] Ana Paula Ferreira refers to "a number of critics [who] have denounced the phallocentric bent of postmodernism" (274), though her own "History and the Postmodern She-Wolf" argues persuasively that Eva's "deconstruction of the myths that have sustained the will to know and represent a univocal historical truth perhaps did not need any intellectual 'Fathers,' after all" (276). My reading is indebted to Ferreira, who develops the concept of Eva as "reader, critic and theorist" (270) who sweeps away the "metanarrative" of Enlightenment (271) so that "*A Costa dos Murmúrios* invites also a critical consideration of 'the postmodern turn' not only within the conjuncture of contemporary Portugal, but specifically in relation to women's writing" (272).

[7] See also Gayatri Spivak's comparison of the subaltern and the feminine as "deconstructive figures." "The 'subject' implied by the texts of insurgency can only serve as a counterpossibility for the narrative sanctions granted to the colonial subject in the dominant groups. (…) It is well known that the notion of the feminine (rather than the subaltern of imperialism) has been used in a similar way within deconstructive criticism and within certain varieties of feminist criticism. In the former case, a figure of "woman" is at issue, one whose minimal predication as indeterminate is already available to the phallocentric tradition. Subaltern historiography raises questions of method that would prevent it from using such a ruse" (82).

[8] Ferreira describes woman, following Eve, as traditionally held "responsible for the beginning of History" in the Judeo-Christian sense "conceptualized as the teleological process of Man's struggle and sufferance" (274).

[9] In his critique of Marxism's implication in Enlightenment processes, Robert Young contends that "the dominant force of opposition to capitalism, Marxism, as a body of knowledge itself remains complicit with, and even extends, the system to which it is opposed" (1990, 3).

[10] The concept of sequentiality is constantly parodied in *A Costa* with punning on the words "liga/ligar" (variously evoking links, garters, leagues, etc.) and their failure to hold fixed "ligações" in place. See, for example, 63, 67, 83 and 88-89.

[11] Robert J. C. Young usefully elaborates on this as follows: "(…) its somewhat precarious status as anecdote—[which] lasts only so long as it avoids sliding into the metonymic status of the example (…) in which the relation of the part is to illustrate and comprise the whole. For Fineman, the anecdote must work in a non-metonymic excessive relation to a history formulated as a historicist totality" (1996, 173).

[12] See Ferreira, 272n.

[13] António Bahia tellingly refers to History itself as being "seduced" by the novel. "E se o romance não se rende à História, esta deixa-se seduzir indubitavelmente pelo livro" (5).

[14] Mineke Schipper describes the continued importance of this trope in anglophone post-colonial African novels. "The Western woman is depicted in African novels by male

writers—especially those set in colonial times—as the dangerous, frivolous, adulterous type (European marriages are generally unhappy and infidelity is more of a rule than an exception)" (42).

[15] Eva refuses the temptation of lesbian revenge, with the justification that it is not the Church fathers who have instilled this taboo, but rather it occurred at some point in the process of separation from the mother: "Seria necessário voltar à mamada inicial para corrigir este defeito" (226). This is interestingly resonant with Jane Gallop's critique of Kristeva's "Sorcières" and "Des Chinoises" in which she claims that homosexuality appears on occasion to be treated as "a defense, a short-circuiting of the relation to heterogeneity, a 'safety belt' (...) a rigid, fragile phallic stand on identity, a fearful refusal of the mother, the vagina and the semiotic" (128).

[16] See Ronald W. Sousa, "'I was Evita,'" for an insightful, close reading which uses Evita's highly ambivalent encounters with Helena to interrogate Laura Mulvey's "canonical gaze paradigm." Sousa complexifies Mulvey's rather rigid framework whereby the object of the gaze is feminine, the desiring/possessing subject masculine, and the identifying subject feminine.

[17] For example, Eva remarks, "A minha mãe me pôs no mundo tendo-me dado por invólucro um cueiro de cinismo. Ela não teve culpa de me oferecer esse babeiro de cachorro com o qual revesti o rosto" (101).

[18] Gallop describes this self-referential economy as follows: "According to the classic psychoanalytic view, female sexuality is narcissistic. (...) Female sexuality can be characterized by continual reference to the self and the body, a continual drawing attention back to the body/self, an economy that Grunberger [in *Female Sexuality: New Psychoanalytic Views*] calls concentric" (118-19). See Ferreira, for an enlightening discussion of the sexual connotations of "pomba" and "pombinha" which Eva uses with reference to Helena, and which the journalist adopts as a nickname for Evita (275n).

[19] Similarly, Sousa suggests that "while Helen plays her role when it is necessary and does otherwise when it is not, Ev/ita is fascinated by Helen as a sign of her-self (Ev/ita) and is involved simultaneously in both the role-playing *and its examination*" ("'I was Evita,'" my emphasis 21).

[20] The exhortation to movement and oscillation is central to Jane Gallop's transformative synthesis of Kristeva and Irigaray, which calls on women to "exercise *and* criticize the power" (121) to avoid "the paralysis of an infantile, oceanic passivity" in the former case and to stave off "the opposite paralysis of a rigid identity" in the latter (121).

[21] The journalist, significantly, initiates Eva into the usurption and corruption of the paternal symbolic when they are stranded near a church in the middle of a rainstorm, and the priest "expels" them (from paradise?) thinking they are young lovers engaged in sexual misdemeanors. "O jornalista diz que é assim mesmo, que nas sociedades disfarçadas todo o entendimento é um crime, se possível um crime sexual. (...) o sexo é como Deus—o sítio secreto da expressão secreta a que se atribui tudo o que não tem explicação. (...) Sob aquela intensa chuva, o jornalista acha que qualquer entendimento pode ser entendido como um crime" (146). Having unveiled as fraud the "sítio secreto da expressão secreta" which typifies "veiled" societies or "sociedades disfarçadas," their motor car, the aptly named "fiat" of divine creation, stalls and refuses to move forward. "O Fiat não anda" (146).

[22] The affinity with Nietzschean, or more specifically Foucauldian, concepts of history in *A Costa* has been commented upon by Ana Paula Ferreira, with reference to Foucault's "Nietzsche, Genealogy, History." She remarks, "Proposing an alternate, non-humanist concept of History, such an advice [Eva's to the author of "Os Gafanhotos"] reveals a close affinity to Nietzschean or, in any case, Foucauldian thought" (272).

[23] On Nietzsche's dialectic of remembering and forgetting, see Hayden White, 356.

[24] Mark Seem usefully summarizes deterritorialization in his introduction to *Anti-Oedipus*: "Against the Oedipal and oedipalized territorialities (Family, Church, School, Nation, Party), and especially the territoriality of the individual, Anti-Oedipus seeks to discover the "deterritorialized" flows that have not been reduced to the Oedipal codes and the neuroticized territorialities, the *desiring-machines* that escape such codes as lines of escape leading elsewhere" (xvii). See Caren Kaplan, *Questions of Travel: Postmodern Discourses of Displacement*, for a recent and detailed discussion of Deleuze and Guattari's collaborative work and the challenges it poses for a politics of location.

[25] For a feminist critique of Deleuze and Guattari, see Rosi Braidotti, "Discontinuous Becomings: Deleuze on the Becoming-Woman of Philosophy," *Nomadic Subjects*, 111-23. Her attempt to synthezise a feminist politics with the Deleuzian position on "becoming-woman" leads her to contend that "what is at stake is how to make 'woman' the referent of the intensity of becoming of all, but especially of women and not the necessarily self-effacing servant at the banquet of the Socratic club. For me it is unthinkable that the question of the deconstruction of phallogocentrism could be disconnected from the concrete changes taking place in women's lives" (115).

[26] For further discussion of the international contextualization of the events in *A Costa*, see Sapega, "No Longer Alone and Proud," 182. Sapega reviews this work and other post-revolutionary novels in the context of a move beyond discourses of Portuguese historical uniqueness, typified by Eduardo Lourenço and the concept of "hyperidentity."

[27] Immanuel Wallerstein's concept of "semiperipherality," originally developed in the context of world system theory, was the starting point for Boaventura de Sousa Santos's detailed reworking of the term in relation to Portugal. See "State and Society in Portugal," *After the Revolution. Twenty Years of Portuguese Literature, 1974-1994*. Eds. Helena Kaufman and Anna Klobucka (Lewisburg: Bucknell University Press, 1997) 31-72.

[28] Responding to Fredric Jameson's categorizations of First and Third World literature in "Third-World Literature in the Era of Multinational Capitalism," *Social Text* 15 (Fall 1986): 65-88, and drawing on Boaventura de Sousa Santos's analyses of the Portuguese semiperipheric, Maria Irene Ramalho de Sousa Santos asks, "se, nos países 'centrais' se perdeu o sentido social, político e nacional na representação estética, e se, pelo contrário, nos países 'periféricos', alegoria e a sátira políticas são, designadamente no romance, o modo de representação privilegiado, que se poderá esperar encontrar nas culturas 'semiperiféricas?'" (65)

[29] For discussion of location and Portuguese national identity in relation to modernity/postmodernity tensions, see Sapega and Lacerda Cabral.

[30] Margarida Ribeiro places Portuguese colonial war novels, including *A Costa*, at an historical and epistemological crossroads, as "importantes elementos de reflexão sobre o modo europeu/português de estar em África (particularmente no crepúsculo do império) e simultaneamente peças indispensáveis para entender o modo de estar hoje em Portugal. Que Portugal se pode imaginar a partir daqui?" (149)

Works Cited

Addis, Elisabetta, Valeria E. Russo and Lorenza Sebesta, eds. *Women Soldiers. Images and Realities*. Houndmills and New York: The Macmillan Press and St. Martin's Press, 1994.

Bahia, António. "O Romance da Nossa Culpa." *Jornal de Letras, Artes e Ideias* (16 March 1988): 5.

Braidotti, Rosi. *Nomadic Subjects. Embodiment and Sexual Difference in Contemporary Feminist Theory*. New York: Columbia University Press, 1994.

Cabral, Maria Manuela A. Lacerda. "*A Costa dos Murmúrios* de Lídia Jorge: Inquietação Pós--Moderna." *Línguas e Literaturas. Revista da Faculdade de Letras do Porto* XIV (1997): 265-87.

Deleuze, Gilles and Félix Guattari. *Anti-Oedipus. Capitalism and Schizophrenia*. Preface by Michel Foucault. Trans. Robert Hurley, Mark Seem and Helen R. Lane. London: Athlone, 1983.

Ferreira, Ana Paula. "Lídia Jorge's *A Costa dos Murmúrios*: History and the Postmodern She-Wolf." *Revista Hispánica Moderna* XLV 2 (December 1992): 268-78.

Fineman, Joel. *The Subjectivity Effect in Western Literary Tradition. Essays Toward the Release of Shakespeare's Will*. Cambridge, Mass.: MIT, 1991.

Gallop, Jane. *Feminism and Psychoanalysis. The Daughter's Seduction*. London and Basingstoke: Macmillan Press, 1982.

Hutcheon, Linda. *A Poetics of Postmodernism: History, Theory, Fiction*. London: Routledge, 1988.

Jardine, Alice and Paul Smith. *Men in Feminism*. New York and London: Methuen, 1987.

Jorge, Lídia. *A Costa dos Murmúrios*. Lisbon: Publicações Dom Quixote, 1988.

———. "A Literatura É Só Uma." *Lua Nova* (Março de 1994): 8-9.

Kaplan, Caren. *Questions of Travel. Postmodern Discourses of Displacement*. Durham and London: Duke University Press, 1996.

Kaufman, Helena. "Reclaiming the Margins of History in Lídia Jorge's *A Costa dos Murmúrios*." *Luso-Brazilian Review* 29.1 (Summer 1992): 41-49.

Kristeva, Julia. "About Chinese Women." *The Kristeva Reader*. Ed. Toril Moi. Oxford: Blackwell, 1986. 138-59.

Ribeiro, Margarida. "Percursos Africanos: A Guerra Colonial na Literatura Pós-25 de Abril." *Portuguese Literary and Cultural Studies* 1 (Fall 1998): 125-52.

Santos, Boaventura de Sousa. "State and Society in Portugal." *After the Revolution. Twenty Years of Portuguese Literature, 1974-1994*. Eds. Helena Kaufman and Anna Klobucka. Lewisburg: Bucknell University Press, 1997. 31-72.

Santos, Maria Irene Ramalho de Sousa. "Bondoso Caos: '*A Costa dos Murmúrios*' de Lídia Jorge." *Colóquio/Letras* 107 (January-February 1989): 64-67.

Sapega, Ellen. "No Longer Alone and Proud: Notes on the Rediscovery of the Nation in Contemporary Portuguese Fiction." *After the Revolution. Twenty Years of Portuguese Literature, 1974-1994*. Eds. Helena Kaufman and Anna Klobucka. Lewisburg: Bucknell University Press, 1997. 168-86.

Schipper, Mineke. "Mother Africa on a Pedestal: The Male Heritage in African Literature and Criticism." *Women in African Literature Today*. Eds. Eldred Durosimi Jones, Eustace Palmer and Marjorie Jones. London and Trenton, NJ: James Currey and Africa World Press, 1987. 35-54.

Sousa, Ronald W. "'I Was Evita,' or *Ecce Femina*" forthcoming. Page references are to the unpublished manuscript version.

———. "The Critique of History in Lídia Jorge's *A Costa dos Murmúrios* or Helen of Beira Meets Luís of Troy." *Cincinnati Romance Review* 16 (1997): 135-43.

Spivak, Gayatri Chakravorty. "Can the Subaltern Speak?" *Colonial Discourse and Post-Colonial Theory. A Reader*. Eds. and introd. Patrick Williams and Laura Chrisman. New York: Harvester Wheatsheaf, 1993. 66-111.

Young, Robert. *White Mythologies: Writing History and the West.* London: Routledge, 1990.

Young, Robert J. C. *Torn Halves. Political Conflict in Literary and Cultural Theory*. Manchester and New York: Manchester University Press, 1996.

White, Hayden. *Metahistory. The Historical Imagination in Nineteenth-Century Europe.* Baltimore and London: The Johns Hopkins University Press, 1973.

Donning the "Gift" of Representation: Lídia Jorge's *A Instrumentalina*

Ana Paula Ferreira

> Nothing is more difficult than to accept a gift.[1]

Among the writers of fiction who emerged during the period following the "revolution not of the gun, but of the word,"[2] otherwise known as the "Carnations Revolution," Lídia Jorge is perhaps the one most in tune with what post-structuralist thought has variously denounced as the "violence of representation" (Armstrong). Ostensibly drawn from her life experiences as a self-fashioned writer, each of the author's prose works published to date evokes contemporary realities with more or less localized historical, social, and geo-cultural specificity.[3] Whether by means of allegory or, as is increasingly the case starting with *Notícia da Cidade Silvestre* (1984), through simulacra of "private" realities predicated especially on cinematic, metonymical images, such fictional scenarios resist enclosure in the "effect of the real" (Barthes).[4] They problematize representation by calling attention to its complicity with power and by insisting on the provisional, discursively contingent, and overdetermined status of all figurations of history, community, identity, and otherness.[5] Oscillating between the questioning of any truth claim bearing the imprint of the metaphysical, humanist logos and a renewed political and ethical imperative of referentials, Jorge's fictions, somewhere between John Dewey's philosophy of "instrumentalism" and Richard Rorty's "pragmatism," put into play ideas as tools for living within a postmodern episteme. In this manner, they pay back, further incur, in and bring the reader to bear witness to the debt of representation crystallized by the April 1974 revolution's "greatest gift"—language freed from censorship.[6]

Any writer's work is always something more or something other than what any given pretense of interpretive mastery can take it to be. Far from what would amount to a sweeping gesture of signification, the foregoing is but an attempt to poise the short story *A Instrumentalina* (1992) on the philosophical, aesthetic, and political pragmatics proper to but exceeding the open-ended textuality, or *écriture*, practiced by Lídia Jorge. As Maria Alzira Seixo has suggested, the author's short stories "may be considered arguments of a more extensive fiction," that neither "describes" nor "recreates" the real, but "cites" it. In all their brevity and expressive force, these narratives are eminently citational, inciting the reader to take part in the "textual dialogue" or "interdiscursive passage" that they enact (Seixo 1998; emphasis in the original; my translation). The density of meaning commanded by such an art of intertextual and intratextual "in-citation" is particularly exhibited in *A Instrumentalina*, arguably the best example of the meta-representational dimension of Jorge's fiction. Hence its "instrumentality" for refracting the salient theoretical-practical features of the greater textual corpus, published before as well as after it. In fact, Jorge's latest novel, *O Vale da Paixão* (1998), continuously "cites" the setting, figures, narrative threats, and themes first presented in the short story, so much so that what may be said about the latter may function as an introduction to the longer text.[7]

Notably, Seixo's review of *Marido e Outros Contos* (1997) does not mention *A Instrumentalina*, published separately in 1992 although also included in this volume. As the imaginary bicycle of its title, the forty-one page story is both too grand and too delicate, too fleeting to easily stand a swift, even if interpretative, productive "in-citational" reading as just one story among others. Its original publication the same year as that of *A Última Dona* is in itself indicative of a uniqueness demanding a more pondered, special treatment. And this is obviously not just due to the status of the book as an editorial investment in an "isolated piece, endowed with its own autonomy and with a fascination that the reader will not forget."[8]

Similarly, to a precious, intractable gift enveloped in layers of superimposed tissues (or texts), *A Instrumentalina* occupies a privileged position among Jorge's other "writerly" attempts at figuring representation as an impossibility, as nothing else than a "gift [that] is *not*," a "poisonous" gift.[9] This position, as will be subsequently demonstrated through a series of detailed analytical un-wrappings, is one that momentarily suspends the circle of economic exchange in which every "gift" of representation, including every means to that end, is implicated. While nonetheless offering historical, political and aesthetic testimonies of such ("poisonous") deadly exchange, the preciosity (if you will) of *A Instrumentalina* shines through those textual folds and contours, pointing to a liberating ontological and ethical elsewhere: a genesis-like stance of writing not as representation or reproduction, but as semiotic productivity. This anti-idealist (and anti-humanist) stance parallels Jorge's other thematizations of writing, as evinced, for example, in *Notícia da Cidade Silvestre*; *A Costa dos Murmúrios*; *O Jardim sem Limites*; and, most particularly, in *O Vale da Paixão*. Writing is thus shown to emerge—to use the author's own deliberately vague, though citational formula—from that margin of the margin "where the writer finds himself" waiting in silence and circumspection to be saved by "the angel of language" (Jorge 1994: 93; my translation).[10]

That such an evasive, life-saving margin is closely associated to the childhood world of dream, a world still relatively innocent of utilitarian, logocentric thought, is first of all suggested by the contrapuntal relation established between *A Última Dona* and *A Instrumentalina*. Calderón de la Barca's renowned Baroque drama, *La vida es sueño*, constitutes an appropriate intertextual framing (explicitly, in one case, and implicitly, in the other) for both texts, and thereby bringing to light the polarity of their respective dream worlds. If the novel attests to the annulment of the humanist Cartesian subject in a world reduced to simulacra and simulations (Baudrillard), the short story points to a vital, non-specularized and, therefore, non-objectified beyond; a space that may be said to revisit a generative, pre-symbolic locus of "*signifiance*."[11]

Bearing the historical and philosophical lesson of Seguismundo's existential dilemma in the form of an epigraph—"Não me despertes se durmo e, se estou acordado, não me adormeças,"[12] *A Última Dona* can be described as a postmodern thriller, an obscenely sinister nightmare staged by omnipresent image-making interests. Death, in the form of suicide by soporifics—that of Ana Palma, alias, Anita Starlet—becomes the ultimate sign of "life" in this all-too-cinematically planned charade of empty figures and depthless images; of intricate, though flat background scenarios; and of successive cuts. The intrigue lies precisely on the degree to which the latter occur because neither the figures nor the space they inhabit necessarily fulfills the director's expectations—as if some remnant of human agency and of natural forces disturb the order of the shiny, uni-dimensional screen.[13] Symptomatically so, the Engineer is the first to find himself impotent to perform; he is literally taken by the ludicrous but ultimately tragic picture that he only apparently directs, confident that his buying power can fulfill his libidinal capitalist fantasies. Thus the gift he buys himself, for his would-be sexual delight, (the image of) a woman richly donned in a white wool coat and whom he calls "Anita Starlet," cannot but turn out to be a sacrificial offer (gift/"*don[a]*") made to a world devoid of transcendental values, and where the only guide for living are cinematic referentials.[14]

A Instrumentalina provides a direct contrast to this adult, eerie dream world reminiscent of a post-modern "late picture show," engulfing all in the ubiquitous fateful reign of representation—a scenario more complexly developed in *O Jardim sem Limites* (1995). As a glimpse of light rising above the image-making machinations going in *A Última Dona*'s "Casa do Leborão" (the prototype of which may be Calderón's Baroque palace/prison), the short story evokes a time-space of childhood innocence carved in the imprisoning "long nightmare" of Portugal's dictatorship. Such a time-space is created through a representation—the homonymous bicycle of the story's title—that is an instrument of freedom but also of emotional maturing resulting from trauma, from loss of a dream. Neither bought nor sold and destined nowhere, it is only in retrospect that such a privileged event is recognized as possessing the quality of a gift of knowledge, one bearing a kind of supernatural grace escaping the economics of exchange.[15]

The text opens with an epigraph that may not be as much a justification for its minute dimensions as it is a hermeneutic appeal: "Um conto breve faz um sonho longo." Capturing the reader from the start in the lingering vital dimension of that dream, or gift, whose apparition the text re-presents, *A Instrumentalina* compels the interpretative articulation of those other representations (and instruments thereof) dictating over the nightmarish historical world against the odds of which the liberating dream/gift emerges.

A fictional autobiographical memoir, the narrative presents itself as an intimate, affective re-collection of a distant fragment from the past prompted by an incidental trip turned narrative "voyage" (9) through personal and collective time.[16] Waiting at the bar of the Royal York Hotel in Toronto for an uncle whom she has not seen in thirty years, the narrator-protagonist finds herself in a position of geographical, temporal, and ontological distance. Suspended in disbelief, she evokes the uncle's bicycle, "*A Instrumentalina*," bringing together into a nostalgic new metaphorical whole—"o simulacro duma imagem que foi mas o tempo já fez vã" (10)—the part images which had previously sheltered her from confronting a lost plenitude of being.[17] Her narrative enfolds, then, as a recuperative (and therapeutic) transit between the present, fragmented subject that she is, sitting in the dimly lit bar of the Royal York, and that foundational imaginary scene, whereupon an ideal "I" had been transported and constructed by the uncle's bike, his words, his picture-taking.

The objective is not to mis-recognize herself in the cinematic frozen frame of the little girl sitting in a field of daisies and interpellated as "Greta Garbo," a fantasy image of the uncle's "proof" or "gift" of love, subsequently shattered by the disappearance of both vehicle and owner.[18] Rather than an alienating monument to a love gained and lost, the narrative (re)invention of "*A Instrumentalina*" becomes a practical instrument of discursive quest through which the subject looks for her whereabouts not as a temporally continuous individual, but as a signifier-symptom of the transindividual experience that constitutes it in language heteronomically through the workings of the unconscious.[19] In other words, the "I" that recollects here—as that reappearing in *O Vale da Paixão*—is nothing other than a necessarily transitory pretext (a signifier) through which emerge those other texts (signifiers) that determine its position in social discourse. This is eminently the discourse of a people, a nation, metonymically displaced across space and time due to the symbolic, dictatorial power of perpetuating representations that let no beyond-the-frame, no "outra margem do tempo" (12) be phantomed. The glimpse of this "other margin"—as the other side of the city in *Notícia da Cidade Silvestre*—is the (non-symbolized) gift moving the narrative towards the scene where memory-writing delivers life to the endless flux of signification.

Although no precise chronological references are given and the only mention of the spatial location of diegesis is an ambiguous "ao sul do meu país" (13), later recalled as "terra da poeira" (40), the narrative "in-cites" (Seixo) an allegorical historical reading. The grandfather's house, where women and children are deposited by sons who emigrate is, obviously, a picture reminiscent of the collective experience of those "guarded"—or confined—in the Portugal of an increasingly moribund, but still standing, dictatorship. That something is about to instill a "desiquilíbrio inevitável" in this "tragédia obscura" (13) is sensed only subliminally. Only much later would the source and means of such a political "imbalance" be recognized, in association with a symbolic vehicle of flight. Meanwhile, mothers go on miming the traditional, atemporal domestic gestures commanded by the paternalistic-fascist ideology of "happiness in the hearth": they cook, sew, write letters to absent husbands, sing and dance to the sound of the phonograph but, underneath it all, they secretly cry their solitude, their abandonment (14). In contrast to the women's resigned obedience to the family and national law emblematized by the figure of the old, symptomatically invalid, patriarch, their children run freely, "como uma matilha indomável, sem dono" (12). And, although ordered to continue the old man's role as master of the family's estate, the only young man left in the house rides around on a bike, apparently with no other objective than to escape his father's dictum.

It is no wonder that his vehicle of flight, derogatorily called "*A Instrumentalina*" by the enraged patriarch impotent to stop it (17), becomes an extension of the rebellious son. Both he and his bike represent that space of freedom, play, and dream barred to those who, either for moral or economic reasons, are obliged to and further reproduce the old father's dictates—the women who stay and write letters, and the workers with fantasies of leaving (33). Thus, the children, particularly the female ones, devote a "fanatic" fascination to the cyclist (19-20); and thus the "instrument" poses an increasing threat to the adults who see it as a means of undermining the social order. As mothers write longer and longer letters and as the patriarch goes on asserting his authority, sitting immobile in his own prison (18), uncle and children take flight in "*A Instrumentalina.*" Their destination, if any at all, is unimportant; what matters is that they go, that they displace themselves—even if only by touching part images of the bike (19).

Interestingly so, two distinct paradigms of representation and their consequent historical, political, and aesthetic implications are contrasted in this scenario. On the one hand, linguistic expression is shown to support and reproduce what exists by virtue of its representation: the signifier of Law, or the family-nation abandoned to the lasting agony of a paternalistic regime frozen in time. This circular movement is, on the other hand, halted by the continuous eruption of non-mimetic representations that allow for fluid, non-binding imaginary identifications.

As suggested before, mothers not only occupy the center stage of the representational space of hearth but, in effect, they are the guardians of its self-reflecting, unchanging image. Their songs echo (i.e. reproduce) those they hear in the phonograph; their partners of dance are none other than themselves; the letters they write seem to have no response. Such representations of "voice," movement, and self-recreation where, in reality, there are none constitute not only testaments to the women's emotional and physical devastation, but, principally, to their complicity in upholding the frail, decrepit representation of the fascist institution of "the Portuguese home." It is logical, then, that as instruments-executors of the patriarch's word, the women-mothers are expected to suppress any threat, any sign of disorder in a home (-nation) left to wreckage or "ruin" (33) by the men-fathers who had abandoned it. This explains why the old man first approaches the little girl in love with her uncle—the miniature of a would-be wife-mother—with a gold coin in exchange for the bike's disappearance (27-29). And that is why then he offers a generous dowry to any young woman who would snatch the cyclist uncle to marriage (31-32). One never knows what and if he pays the daughters-in-law for hiding and ensuring the destruction of the uncle's bicycle (34-36)—the symbolic vehicle of resistance against the seemingly eternal order which their reproduction of domesticity guarantees.

Against this model of representation, the narrative suggests what may be a non-mimetic, perpetually unstable way of (re)presenting not what is but what is not, or in other words, what can only be inferred as a liberating, utopian time-space. Named by a figure reminiscent of god-the-father, giver of all names, the bicycle "*A Instrumentalina*" in actuality backtracks the "poison" incurred in the "gift" of its name. Thus the anger and confusion that leads the shaken patriarch to name his son's transgressive vehicle fall upon none other than himself, delivering the present of a signifier-image that escapes symbolic fixation.[20] Remaining "indiferente a terras e mulheres," uncle Fernando is only "prisoner" of the bike (34), of its supernatural quality as gift outside the market of exchange. In this way, "*A Instrumentalina*" cuts through the "realism" of the allegorical narrative outlined above. As a perpetually moving signifier, it—both the bike and the uncle—point to the outside of its signifying frame. At this level, both the instruments and the ways of representation become denaturalized; they no longer serve any other objective than playing up the mobility of the signifier, its necessarily absent anchoring point.

Conjoining the linguistic and ontological free play put into motion by the uncle/bike, two mediums of representation highlight and, in a way, take further the narrative's liberating scene of signification postulated by "*A Instrumentalina.*" They are the uncle's only other prized possessions: a Kodak camera and a typewriter. Instead of taking on the responsibilities of the family's estate as a *paterfamilias*, which would be tantamount to upholding the reigning patriarchal law, the uncle bicyclist is an *amateur* photographer; and he pounds away at his typewriter throughout the night (26). No identified purpose for his writing is given until after the uncle sees his bike destroyed; from then on he appears to write letters in desperation to leave, to run away (36). Like "*A Instrumentalina*," the Kodak and the typewriter are, then, used against their functional purposes; they may be considered artistic mediums of imaginary leaps to a sublime world devoid of the rule of reference.

In this regard, the scene in which the little girl, who had silently and subserviently demanded to be recognized by the absolute, fascinating Other, receives from him the gift of a "voyage" to a field of daisies, is emblematic. Here, posing for his Kodak and transfigured by his words, she is not only made to feel like a "queen"; she is led to visualize herself in the image of Greta Garbo: "uma mulher divina cujo olhar tirava o sono a quem a visse. Um dia, também eu haveria de vê-la e aprender com ela a fixar o olhar numa coisa distante que não havia" (25). Despite the "destino inevitável" that awaits her at the grandfather's house, where eight cousins dispute the *transporting* figure of the uncle/bike, the protagonist is forever touched by the "mágica das fotografias" (37). A non-verbal, non-rationalized feeling that compounds knowledge about the self as Other with the liberating, transforming power of non-mimetic representations, that "pressentimento" reemerges thirty years later as a shield against the pretense of quotidian or representational language: "[A]quelas surpreendentes linhas não me pareciam ser verdade," she notes in response to the handwritten message in which the uncles evokes their past affect in order to summon their present encounter (40). His former interpellation—"Isso, isso, não te mexas, Greta Garbo" (25)—appears, thus, not only to stand in direct opposition to the written message but, in fact, to have deflected (for the protagonist) any symbolic mandate of order-bound identification. The turn away from "real" reference to a cinematic one, of which the protagonist is originally unaware, is what constitutes the pictures' lasting "magic." Its memory may be understood as the "instrumentalina" that the protagonist herself rides as she constructs from literal and figurative shadows an uncle who, perhaps, *never was*: "Acaso o dono d'*A Instrumentalina* não teria sido um sonho destinado apenas a fazer crescer pessoas indefesas?" (40-41).

The doubt overtaking the narrator about the very physical existence of her object of representation is, of course, the most concrete proof of the pure, non-exchange value of the gift that he had unwittingly granted her. This is, in part, because the donor's photographs, words, and gaze evade the ploy of verisimilitude; their fantastic meaning, if any, cannot be intelligible but as a presentiment. In addition, the uncle, as will also happen with the almost mythic father-uncle who draws births and constantly displaces himself in *O Vale da Paixão*, does not follow the path of any other representative of the socio-economic and political order that dictates the exile of thousands of Portuguese. The uncle does leave the patriarch's home-nation as a characteristic clandestine, aided by an automobile rider go-between (38). Yet, he does not settle in any one particular place as his emigrant brothers do; he simply "disappears." All that is subsequently known about his whereabouts is limited to hearsay, and thus "[o] nosso tio fora-se transformando assim numa figura dispersa pela Terra como um espírito." Presumably moving from city to city and continent to continent, he dies, "tal qual um Deus que se não mostra" (39). Escaping representation, with no wife, children, or possessing affects to imprison him to the demand for recognition and return (i.e. exchange), the uncle is transformed in an idea abstracted from corporeal materiality as well as from the contingencies of time and place. This idea may be conceived as the very spirit of resistance to the Father's (any Father's) representational mandate. Nevertheless, its analogy with the lake (Ontario) that the protagonist faces with a cold and skeptical heart as she brings up the uncle's presence (41) is suggestive of the mimetic trap built into that idea-turned-representation.

Invoked through the written word, such a presence threatens to kill the short story's "long dream." For when the uncle fashioned out of the ashes of memory returns to address the mature woman waiting upon/writing the "gift" that the narrative recovers, he personifies the very "poison" of reference. The middle-aged, well-garbed figure who rushes through the (symptomatically) "transparent" glass door can, at best, speak as though he has just dismounted from a common "bicicleta": "'Cresceste, miúda, cresceste. Mas a tua cara é ainda a mesma...'" (41). In other words, the "long dream" mentioned in the epigraph, the non-congealing, fleeting meaning of "*A Instrumentalina*" as a vehicle of transport to "uma coisa distante que não havia" (25) is, in the end, destroyed by the fate of language. The lines on the card and, subsequently, the uncle's words impose sameness, continuity, and identity where (for there to be the flux of life) there should be none. Here is the "destino inevitável" (op. cit.) that the marginal and detached, but still desiring, memorialist's "heart" must face.

Closely related to the confining trap and, simultaneously, the redeeming, emancipatory potential of representation, Lídia Jorge's skepticism with the question of sexual difference in her writing finds here an "instrumental" illustration.[21] In tune with a deconstructive notion of "femininity" in its possible linkage to the condition of "gift" (in the sense that femininity as well as the gift respond to *what is not*), the story suggests how destructive is the temptation to name, to categorize, what should remain unsymbolized.[22] To use language for the purposes of pinning down the flux of time and of identity is the work of those who are (or become, like the mature uncle) the instruments of the pervasively dictatorial, logocentric, socio-cultural order. Or, to recognize the "miúda" of yesteryear in the face of the woman voyaging through the necessarily foreign, marginal space of writing-memory, is tantamount to withhold from her the discovering, productive stance that constitutes her textually.[23] Thus, the narrative riding on a kind of "instrumentalina," the process of writing as begetting the infinite mobility of self, others, the world, thrives on the eminent threat of objectifying, falsifying and ultimately killing the movement of life that it is due to (re)create.

This impasse of representation is fully dramatized in *O Vale da Paixão*, following the evocation or, better, "convocation" of a female autobiographical narrator who bears the unsettling reminder of a father who *is not*. Overwritten with other memories, other voices, all profusely referenced spatially and temporally, the protagonist pieces together the textualized fragments of her father's memory, incorporating and, at the same time othering herself along with them. The movement back and forth from the "I" of enunciation to the "she" of the *enoncé* (as also happens, for example, in Eva Lopo's narrative in *A Costa dos Murmúrios*) emphasizes the fragmentation and discontinuity that the narrative in vain tries to foil. More importantly, however, that process of constant doubling and displacement gestures towards the gift of sorts that the father represents for the writer of the memoir, ultimately because what he gives her remains (for him) an unfulfilled promise, a debt: "'Tanto que te devo!'" (22). This paradox is the ideal condition rendering possible the "gift" of representation that the narrator indeed beholds—the father's drawings, originally enmeshed in the duplicitous interchange of donnees (her mother and uncle/stepfather) who assign her an ambiguous place in the social order (23). From these drawings, or the ontological and socio-cultural margin that their tracings entail, the narrator can at will call upon "O filme de Walter Dias…um filme onde ninguém entrava nem saía que não fosse por vontade dela" (25).

Just like the amateur uncle photographer of *A Instrumentalina*, the father roams around, delivering himself to the "ocupação inútil" (234) of drawing birds as an escape from the authoritarian, reproductive environment commanded by a land-owning patriarch who administers his estate as Salazar is known to have administered the nation.[24] Subsequently, the father may ride boats, trains, and automobiles, but he goes on sending home drawings of whatever species of birds he finds abroad. Such literal and metaphorical traces recalling previous traces (as opposed to the representational memory of the man himself) are, however, repeatedly tainted by others' narratives, and especially by "cartas envenenadas" sent by the father's siblings to inform the family back home of his doings and whereabouts (191). Like missiles, these missives insist on representing, on endowing with "realist" physical materiality, and demonized at that, what amounts to an emblem of unconventional or artistic flight from the deadly submission to socio-cultural referents.

In the face, then, of an over-represented, spoiled memory on the mirror of which she finds herself, the writer-protagonist must at once honor the father as open, polyvalent text and kill its possible "reality" in order to survive:

> Ela queria visitar o interior de Walter. Queria assaltá-lo por dentro, sem ruído...destruir-lhe a pessoa, conspurcando-o, transformando a doçura da sua imaterialidade evanescente numa parábola de natureza carnal para que desaparecesse (210-11).

Having become increasingly identified and recognized by others as a direct descendant of the man, the thirty-year-old woman thus coldly converts the memory of her father in a "caso interessante," treating and analyzing it as if it were a corpse. Her aim is to throw upon such a textual corpus/corpse the "rede da aranha explicativa" with the intention of capturing, of smashing, and thus of freeing herself from the lingering phantom-signifier "Walter" (212). One never knows what are the contents of the three narratives that she hands to her reluctant father in his shady Buenos Aires dancing hall, not surprisingly named "Bar los Pájaros." What the daughter, and the reader, is given to know is how futile, if not dangerous, representation in fact is in a political atmosphere commanding reproduction and representational terror: "Sí, sí, no necesito dibujarlos para encontrarlos. Los pájaros..." (220). While the mature man has learned to free the birds from his own fixing gaze, the daughter's narrative, in the end, may accomplish just the opposite. Walter finally dies, leaving her his last, sole possession—the soldier's blanket whereupon he had presumably delivered himself to the "useless" activity of drawing births (235). Accompanying this testamentary monument to his life and works, he leaves his daughter the grace, or "miracle," of a handwritten card that ultimately recovers the image of "a inocência da criança, quando a criança estende as palmas das mãos para mostrar a inocência" (237). On and all, and with perfect circularity, the novel captures and inscribes this depthless, virtually cinematic show of innocence, rehabilitating the father's gift from all "poisoned" representations to the domain of fantasy—this running counter to and ironically commenting on the simulacra of historicism propelling the narrative movement.

Notwithstanding the metatextual *tour de force* of *O Vale da Paixão*, it is all there already in the "short story that makes a long dream," *A Instrumentalina*. This text indeed may be considered Lídia Jorge's most "instrumentalist" reflection of her creative investment in the complex issue of representation through the apparently unpretentious narrative form of a parable. As a simple story relating an ordinary occurrence of greater philosophical (and pedagogical) appeal, the text is exemplary in terms of the author's alleged "survival through [the art of] writing."[25] At the same that it illuminates both earlier and later novels' representational arrests, it plays up that margin of the margin—to use Jorge's formulation once again—where "the angel of language" saves the flux of life through the written word. This double movement of evoking or, if you will, citing the multi-layered and multi-voiced texts that go by the name of socio-cultural, local, and historical "reality" and, simultaneously, of hinting at something else, at a beyond the frame of symbolic reference constitutes the irrecuperable "gift" of the author's works. If these don the Revolution's "greatest gift," they also consistently engage figurations of "gifts" of representation that can only be *not*, lest the economics of exchange give way to yet another mere simulacrum of utopia.

Notes

[1] Derrida, in Kamuf 410. I wish to express my gratitude to Lídia Jorge for giving me *A Instrumentalina* in the Summer of 1994, with the dedication, "Para que o mar que separa, una, através de cais imaginados." Coincidentally, a first draft of the present paper was presented at the Royal York Hotel in Toronto (an "imaginary pier" featured in *A Instrumentalina*), where the Annual Convention of the MLA was held in December of that year.

[2] Riegelhaupt 3.

[3] Throughout numerous interviews and public presentations about her work, Lídia Jorge

often recalls how writing has been for her a form of survival since she was a child. "Não imagino sobreviver sem ser através da escrita," she affirms with respect to her novel *A Costa dos Murmúrios*, adding the self-explanatory note, "África é um mapa de *recordações ligadas à escrita nas minhas experiências da vida*" (in Vitorino 23, my italics). For the early formative years of Jorge's "writerly" life experiences, see especially Ambrogi 9-10; for a broader panorama of the author's persistence to go on writing against all personal and political odds, to write as a form of (feminine) survival, see particularly Luís Almeida Martins.

[4] *Notícia da Cidade Silvestre* (1984) may be considered the point of transition from the allegorical mode exploited in *O Dia dos Prodígios* (1980) and *O Cais das Merendas* (1982) to the shiny, "more real than real" part-image characteristic of postmodern culture and aesthetics in their eminently cinematic underpinnings. This latter tendency, as well as its social and ethical implications, comes obviously to the fore in *O Jardim sem Limites* (1995). *A Última Dona* (1992) is, however, in my view, an emblematic narrative about the literally suicidal precipice faced by the subject-turned-surface, cinematic image by what Fredric Jameson calls the "cultural logic of late capitalism."

[5] I have demonstrated this at length elsewhere. See especially my "Lídia Jorge's *A Costa dos Murmúrios.*"

[6] The phrase "a grande dádiva" to describe the freedom of expression brought about by the April 25, 1974 Revolution appears in a 1983 interview of Lídia Jorge as part of the post-revolutionary scene encouraging the emergence of new prose writers and the more general yearly increase of publications in prose. See Valdemar 12.

[7] For reasons of space, I will limit myself here to point out briefly at the end of this study how the latter narrative text echoes the representational impasse sketched in *A Instrumentalina.* I focus on *O Vale da Paixão* in a separate study currently in progress.

[8] I quote from the editorial blurb on the book's back cover; my translation.

[9] Here I use Derrida's argument about the gift analogously, by bringing it to bear on the issue (or the "gift") of representation as something that "*is not.* One cannot ask, 'what is a gift?'; yet, it is only on that condition that there *will have been*, by that name or another, a gift" (in Kamuf 410; italics in the original). Derrida's concept of the gift draws on the suggestion that the German homonym for "gift" is the adjective "poisonous." The same can be said about the "gift" of free representation in the context of post-revolutionary Portugal.

[10] Typically ambivalent with regard to the gender specificity of her writing, in a paper delivered in the congress "Le scritture delle donne nelle culture iberiche," held in Venice in Jan. 25-27, 1993, Lídia Jorge ends up by defending the ontological marginality that commands the genesis of any writing (Jorge 1994). Although, of course, no mention of theoretical sources is made, Jorge's formula echoes in part Hélène Cixous's concept of the writer as an "exile" (12) and Deleuze and Guatari's arguments about the nomadic or gypsy-like position that "minority" writers occupy in a dominant literary language (18-21).

[11] I use the term here in a Kristevean sense to mean the infinite generational and combinatorial play of meaning characteristic of textuality, as opposed to a quotidian, representational use of language. See, in this regard, Ducrot 356-59.

[12] The quote is extracted from *La vida es sueño*, Act III, Scene IV, when Seguismundo, who has learned a lesson in humility and skepticism, responds cautiously to the soldiers who go to his prison to hail him as their master and Prince: "A reinar, fortuna, vamos; / no me despiertes si duermo, / y si es verdad, no me duermas. / Mas sea verdad o sueño, / obrar bien es lo que importa;. . ." (Calderón de la Barca 158).

[13] In this analyis, I loosely follow Jameson's concept of postmodern space.

[14] When asked about the filmic references present in her work, especially visible in *O Jardim*

sem Limites (1995), Lídia Jorge explained that her use of cinema obeys a non-premeditated "impulso" in following "os sinais do presente." She states, "Não é no cinema que encontramos o pensamento, mas é nele que encontramos *os pontos de referência que balizam a nossa vida*" (in Maria João Martins 15, my italics).

[15] As Derrida states, "A gift, if there is one, does not destine itself" (Kamuf 507).

[16] This "voyage" has all the characteristics of a therapeutic psychoanalytical narrative, as the following reading will suggest. Whether deliberately or not, Lídia Jorge's texts owe much to a Lacanian concept of the subject in language, that is, the subject of desire. See, in this respect, my study of *O Cais das Merendas*, "Lídia Jorge's 'Strategies of Navigation.'"

[17] Lacan associates the metaphor to the question of being and the metonym to its irrecoverable loss—what he calls the "manque à etre" throwing the subject in endless (narrative) displacements through the defiles of the signifier. See, for example, Lacan, 174-75.

[18] What characterizes the little girl's demand for the uncle's attention and recognition, that is, for his unconditional love, is the illusion that the Other (the uncle) possesses "the 'privilege' of satisfying needs, that is to say, the power of depriving them of that alone by which they are satisfied. This privilege of the Other thus outlines the radical form of the gift of that which the Other does not have, namely, its love." In this way, "The very satisfactions that [demand] obtains for need are reduced to the level of being no more than the *crushing of the demand for love*" (Lacan 286, my italics).

[19] I here follow Lacan's concept of the unconscious as "that part of the concrete discourse, in so far as it is transindividual, that is not at the disposal of the subject in reestablishing the continuity of his conscious discourse" (49).

[20] Here I follow Derrida's famous argument in "Des Tours de Babel" regarding the origin of language in God's name and its consequent dismemberment in tongues, sowing confusion among men, and poisoning the gift of language (Kamuf 246).

[21] Jorge's standing on the question of sexual difference may be read in Louro, 1984; Ambrogi, 1985; and, especially, in the author's own essay, "Sobre o género," about Greenway's adaptation of Virginia Woolf's *Orlando* to cinema.

[22] In "Choreographies," Derrida briefly addresses the "im-pertinence" of the question of sexual difference in relating it to the condition of "gift" (Kamuf 446-47).

[23] In this respect, see also Jorge, 1994: 93, mentioned in note 10 above.

[24] "O dono de Vamares achava que a sua casa era uma empresa sólida, uma unidade de produção à semelhança de um estado, dirigindo-a como um governador poupado gere o estado" (46).

[25] See note 3 above.

Da *Performance* Como Retórica (e Vice-Versa)

Maria Lúcia Lepecki

Para Maria Fernanda Henriques

Raphael—(...) there's no room at Court for philosophy.
Morus—There's certainly no room for the academic variety, which says what it thinks irrespective of circumstances. But there is a more civilized form of philosophy which knows the dramatic context, so to speak, tries to fit in with it, and plays an appropriate part in the current performance. That's the sort you should go in for. Otherwise it would be like interrupting some comedy by Plautus, in which a lot of slaves were fooling about, by rushing on to the stage dressed up as a philosopher, and spouting a bit of that scene in the Octavia, where Seneca is arguing with Nero. Surely it would be better to keep your mouth shut altogether than to turn the thing into a tragicomedy by interpolating lines from a different play? For, even if your contribution were an improvement on what had gone before, the effect would be so incongruous that you'd ruin the whole show. No, do the best you can to make the present production a success — don't spoil the entire play just because you happen to think of another one that you'd enjoy rather more.

Thomas More, *Utopia**

Este texto pretende descrever o que considero ser a dimensão filosófica de *O Jardim sem Limites*,[1] de Lídia Jorge. Para isso entenderei que "toda língua natural é susceptível de produzir filosofia,"[2] o que considero insofismável, embora tenha de precisar que, para produzir filosofia—ou ter mínima natureza filosofante—é preciso que a língua natural se organize em discurso com duas ou três características obrigatórias.

A primeira dessas características é o *uso repetido*, sobre o qual diz Lausberg a seguinte e interessante coisa:

> O discurso de uso repetido é um discurso que é pronunciado pelo mesmo orador, ou por oradores que respectivamente se alternam, em situações típicas (festivas) que se repetem periodicamente ou não periodicamente (...). Cada sociedade de suficiente *intensidade social* conhece esses discursos de uso repetido, os quais são um instrumento para *manter conscientes a complexidade e a continuidade da ordem social e, frequentemente, o carácter forçosamente social da existência humana em geral* (...). Do uso repetido resulta a necessidade de se conservarem os discursos pela escrita ou, então, na memória de uma classe de funcionários disso mesmo incumbidos. Desta conservação nasce uma 'tradição de discursos de uso repetido' que, no tocante à literatura e à poesia, aparece como 'tradição literária.'[3]

Essencial à literatura, o discurso de uso repetido é imprescindível também à filosofia.[4] Tanto a literatura quanto a filosofia precisam, para existir, daquilo que se chama "circulação alargada" no espaço e no tempo. A circulação alargada propicia o surgimento de novos discursos exegéticos e hermenêuticos, que enriquecem, por complexificação de vários tipos, a proposta do discurso inicial. A cadeia de discursos que a partir de um primeiro se produzem é de natureza histórica e de formulação metonímica, tornando contíguo o meu pensamento com o pensamento alheio, sobre o qual me debruço, entro em processo de diérese, abertura (que tende ao infinito) das evidências e das subjacências da palavra de outros. Escusado será dizer, mas sempre se vai dizendo, ser a metonímia o princípio retórico essencial da complexificação do pensamento. Ela permite não apenas a compatibilização dos incompatíveis[5] mas também, o que tem mais fundo interesse, a criação de incompatíveis artificiosos, lugares possíveis do exercício de todas as re-escritas daquilo que foi posto em texto como quase forma do absurdo.[6] Nessa perspectiva, a circulação alargada, de cuja existência dependem a literatura e a filosofia, é soleira—ou será uma realização?—do infinito. Mais ainda, a circulação alargada, implicando a infinitude do discurso, faz com que todo labor exegético e, sobretudo, toda prática hermenêutica sejam sempre próximos do encontro com o sagrado. Talvez sejam mesmo qualquer coisa muito próxima da mística.

Suspeitas e intranquilidades

Diérese e infinitização do pensamento que interpreta textos (mundos e Mundo) são incompatíveis com o entendimento literal da palavra. Filosofia e literatura dependem da intranquilidade e da suspeita. Nascem quando a palavra se constitui não como "veículo de ideia" mas enquanto "problema para se entender a ideia que apesar de tudo se aponta." Já a ironia socrática encena o drama do homem com a palavra—e toda a cultura ocidental tem repetidamente posto em palco, pelos séculos fora, a mesma história que, aliás, goza de particular visibilidade nos discursos filosófico, teológico e literário.

Junto com o discurso de uso repetido, a metonímia e as posturas exegética e hermenêutica, um outro traço é necessário para a produção de discurso filosófico: a definição clara de um tema. Sem esse recorte da área de interesse, sem uma fronteira que defina o campo de preocupações onde me movimento, torna-se impraticável qualquer observação, qualquer ponderação lúcida de um problema. Torna-se, aliás, impossível a existência de problema. A observação (necessariamente demorada), levantando a epiderme do discurso, constrói a única via para a suspeição sem a qual não existe postura especulativa. Para olhos ingénuos, toda a palavra é translúcida e todo discurso diz o que parece querer dizer. Só quando paramos e olhamos é que damos tempo ao verbo pulsar, propiciando aberturas de horizontes de entendimento e indagação.

Realizam-se na obra literária os traços da escrita filosófica que acima apontei, mas realizam-se intimamente associados com o ficcionar, de tal maneira que a filosofia cabe no literário não porque se arranje um lugar para ela estar, mas porque a filosofia acontece naturalmente, pelo modo como as questões se põem e o binómio metonímia-complexificação (alargamento de horizontes) toma existência. O jeito de a filosofia estar no literário tem de ser, assim, natural, casual e necessário.[7]

Barbara Hardy define o modo de ser da ficção nos seguintes termos: "The novel is an affective form. Not wholly so, or simply so. While it expresses, shapes and analyses feelings and passions, *it also expresses, shapes and analyses ideas and arguments* (...). At its best, the novel uses emotion to investigate emotion."[8] Reconhecendo na narrativa a capacidade de "conformar e analisar ideias e argumentos," Barbara Hardy aponta o lugar preciso onde aquele tipo de discurso se encontra com a filosofia, o lugar preciso onde a metonímia e a hermenêutica se fundem para criar discursos complexos e problemáticos. Parece, ainda (ou poderá parecer) que, em havendo perfeito equilíbrio entre conformar e analisar sentimentos e conformar e analisar ideias, a ficção narrativa poderá constituir, para além da concretização diegética, e como correlato natural da discursividade filosófica, uma dimensão alegórica. Será preciosa (ou simplesmente precisa, necessária?) a alegoria para reforço do teor suspeitoso, problemático, do texto, e isso porque enquanto representação de um universal, a alegoria contradita as suas próprias representações dos particulares, permitindo-nos ver a esses últimos em diálogo com um pano de fundo que tanto os enquadra quanto lhes confere existência no campo das categorias.[9]

Lisboa, à beira-Tejo

O Jardim sem Limites conta a história de um grupo de pessoas que, por razões várias, vai viver para quartos alugados numa casa à beira-Tejo, em Lisboa. Os donos da casa também estão lá, embora preservem com certo cuidado as distâncias que devem existir entre locatários e locadores, mormente em situações que poderiam tornar-se constrangedoras.

Quase todos os moradores da casa à beira-rio se ligam à problemática da representação, em algum tipo de texto, daquilo que costumamos chamar "realidade." O cineasta representa a realidade em filmes, o fotógrafo em fotografias, o dono da casa em escrita contabilística (já que outros vôos, infelizmente, lhe estão vedados). Enquanto isso, a narradora[10] vai colocando em texto literário o que se passa à volta, dando especial atenção a um *performer*, o que plenamente se justifica, pois nele a questão do representar/parecer e a questão do ser poriam problemas sérios a qualquer intérprete e, por maiores e mais ponderáveis razões, àquela lúcida intérprete que nos conta a história, questionando obsessivamente os modos de a contar—e os modos do contar em geral.

Espero ter ficado claro, a partir da pequeníssima descrição que acabo de fazer, que *O Jardim sem Limites* coloca reiteradamente o tema da representação, desde logo circunscrevendo, para personagens e leitor, um espaço de potencial reflexão filosófica. Essa reflexão faz-se, contudo, e é fundamental que isso se diga, dentro do mais estrito critério de necessidade e de naturalidade. Quero eu dizer que, sendo a representação uma preocupação (e uma vivência a todos os títulos dramática) das personagens, natural e necessário se torna que a narradora, sujeito de observação dos vários dramas (inclusivamente do seu próprio), acabe por ser conduzida a pensar organizadamente sobre o que é "representar." Até aqui temos, então, dois dos aspectos que apontei no início da exposição como necessários a uma escrita filosófica: circunscrição nítida de objecto a ser observado (o objecto é a *representação de realidades*) e revisitação (por desmultiplicação das personagens ocupadas em *representar*) do mesmo objecto em perspectivas diferentes e mutuamente enriquecedoras. Circunscrição e revisitação necessitam absolutamente de uma retórica de repetições, mais exactas ou mais abrandadas.[11] As repetições concentram o nosso olhar sobre o mesmo problema que já exigiu concentração por parte da narradora. Elas educam-nos para o ritmo compassado e paciente que toda reflexão deve ter. Não consta que se faça filosofia a correr, nem parece ter jamais constado que o pensamento de natureza filosófica se possa constituir sem retorno a pontos fulcrais de irradiação de sentidos e de novas questões. O discurso filosófico é eminentemente revisitativo, porque substancialmente hermenêutico. Hermenêutico e revisitativo é todo o discurso ficcional de Lídia Jorge, não apenas o que encontramos em *O Jardim sem Limites.*

Todas as personagens que, nesse romance, se ocupam de representações, sabem que o "mundo concreto" a trasladar para discurso é *um sistema*, sem dúvida, mas é, sobretudo, *um sistema com subsistemas dentro*. Essa espécie de dupla sistemática inextricável, a que todos no romance são sensíveis, configura um outro tema a ser filosoficamente tratado. Esse tema é o do mundo enquanto espectáculo de sintaxe.

Apercebendo-se de que o mundo a ser representado em qualquer tipo de texto ou discurso é espectáculo de sintaxe, é ordem consistente (embora não necessariamente apreensível, na sua lógica de fundo, a um primeiro olhar), as personagens preocupam-se com o modo de transportar a "realidade do mundo" (em retórica se dirá *res*) para o meio que a representa e certamente—como todos no livro sabem—lhe confere autonomia de existência. Os modos de transportar (que, para a narradora, são modos verbais) têm de ser tão consistentes quanto consistente é a realidade transportada: as muitas conversas entre as várias personagens, incidindo sobre as diferentes artes que praticam, documentam a preocupação com o que se costuma chamar verosimilhança. Obcecados pelo modo de representar, todas as personagens de *O Jardim sem Limites* estão construindo uma arte poética, numa linha de informações que se vai aos poucos adensando, até que o poético (no cinema, na fotografia, na escrita, na performance) se torna o assunto fundamental do romance—e de tal maneira assim é que podemos entender (sem prejuízo de outras interpretações) ser a arte, qualquer arte, *o jardim sem limites*.

Persona, história e pensamento

Representar a realidade é, assim, a tópica onde mais claramente se vê a dimensão filosofante do romance de Lídia Jorge. Faz-se a reflexão sistemática, aqui, por personificação e por historicização: isto é, o texto vai pensando enquanto conta a história ou, o que é ainda melhor, o próprio jeito de contar a história e de traçar as personagens é um jeito de pensar. Personificação e modos de representação aparecem nitidamente relacionados com a tópica da inexpressabilidade, mas ao contrário do que afirma Barbara Hardy.[12] No livro de Lídia Jorge, as realidades são sempre expressáveis, embora não seja fácil expressá-las. Assinale-se que a confiança na expressabilidade sinaliza entendimento positivo das relações homem-mundo, enquanto a dificuldade no expressar aponta para a necessidade de trabalho consciente e árduo para conseguir dizer.

Sendo difícil, porém possível, dizer, a expressão pertinente tem de ser procurada em vários tipos de linguagem, ou em territórios diferentes da mesma linguagem, tendo ainda de ser procurada na *confluência* de muitas linguagens — que é precisamente o que o romance nos ensina dever existir. Procurar a expressão apropriada em muitos tipos de linguagem, em confluências de linguagens, põe em campo com a maior clareza a dinâmica metonímica do discurso, dinâmica compatibilizadora de diferentes elementos e produtora da necessária nitidez que, num discurso, pode criar a consistência filosófica. Desmultiplicando as personagens que se servem de variados modos de representar, reunindo-as nas conversas em que falam do assunto e reunindo-as, sobretudo, na fala da narradora que as conta, *O Jardim sem Limites* complexifica o seu próprio campo de observação filosófica, sem perder a disciplina de olhar nem rarefazer o objecto específico de questionamento.

Diz-se a confiança na expressabilidade pela confiança na possibilidade de transpor conteúdos, o que equivale a dizer pela confiança na tradução, que é o modo como os conteúdos do mundo tomam forma (repetem-se, diria J. Hillis Miller[13]), transformando-se em discursos (em quaisquer linguagens, não apenas na verbal) susceptíveis de excitar, de modo sistemático e adequado, a inteligência do interlocutor. O tema da tradução — recurso retórico chamado repetição abrandada — enquadra todo o texto de *O Jardim sem Limites*, em cuja abertura e fecho nos informam estar tudo sendo dito (e poder ser infinitamente de novo dito) "por outras palavras."

Exibindo a ficção enquanto retomada/tradução de uma realidade também existente em si mesma,[14] a repetição é ainda responsável pela dimensão filosofante do discurso, pois só repetindo se constitui a espiral de retornos sistemáticos aos mesmos tópicos, assim se colocando, naquela espécie de palco textual onde se concentram os olhares dos leitores, a *biografia* de uma filosofia em conformação. Sempre que as informações retornam—e talvez muito particularmente as informações sobre a narradora e o *performer* mais a sua companheira—complexifica-se o tecido informativo geral e muda de qualidade a exigência em relação a nós, intérpretes.

A primeira vez que uma informação aparece, ela *indica*, ensina a retórica. Repetida, a informação *afirma*—o que devemos entender como "torna firme, consistente,"—assim fazendo problemática e cada vez mais problemática—a realidade cuja denominação/exibição se reitera. Ao conferir natureza de problema ao que se diz, a repetição nos encaminha para o aprofundamento do nível escritural do texto, e somos compelidos a perguntar-nos por que razões se escreve assim. Simultaneamente, a repetição obriga-nos a enriquecer o nível proposicional do mesmo texto: tanto mais somos compelidos a interpretar quanto mais insistem em nos dar, com maiores ou menores variantes, as mesmas informações.[15]

Uma última observação deve ser feita sobre o princípio repetitivo-tradutivo em *O Jardim sem Limites*. Da tradução-repetição pode dizer-se o mesmo que dizia Calvino da metáfora: é uma acomodação do incompreensível às limitações da nossa inteligência. Acomodar à inteligência é preocupação dominante em Lídia Jorge e isso tem a ver com a *superioridade* das questões pelo seu romance colocadas. Relembra Alister E. McGrath[16] ser a acomodação o princípio geral que parece subjazer à natureza da linguagem teológica. Evoca a sugestão de Orígenes de que "God faced much the same problems in addressing sinful humanity as those experienced by a human father trying to communicate to small children. God condescends and comes down to us, accomodating to our weakness, like a schoolmaster talking 'a little language' to his children, or like a father caring for his own children and adopting their ways (...). This approach was taken up (...) by John Calvino who developed the theory usually refered to by the term 'accomodation' (…) that here means 'adjusting or adapting to meet the needs of the situation to the human hability to comprehend it.' In revelation, Calvino argues, God accomodates to the capacities of the human heart and mind."

Parece obrigatório alargar a qualquer discurso e a qualquer campo retórico a ideia da acomodação: não existe comunicação verbal que não traduza, para as capacidades do interlocutor, aquilo que se está querendo fazer chegar a ele.[17]

Em *O Jardim sem Limites* muitas acomodações, sempre ligadas ao paradigma repetitivo, reiteram a preocupação de tornar o que se diz apreensível, tangível e concreto. Dessas acomodações, duas são crucialmente importantes: a que se faz por antropomorfização — quando se "transformam" ideias e questões em personagens, dentro do espírito do que observa Barbara Hardy — e aquela que nos chega por materializações outras, sempre, porém, ligadas ao campo de acção e aos modos de comportamento das personagens. Estão nesse último caso todos os artefactos produzidos pelos moradores da casa à beira-rio (fotografia, filme, texto narrativo) e está neste caso muito particularmente o *performer*, em cujo corpo de pessoa se pode corporificar outra realidade.[18]

Corporificando e antropomorfizando, *O Jardim sem Limites* põe questões do foro da estética não apenas literária mas também de outras artes, tratando ainda reiteradamente o modo como nos apropriamos, por meio dos sentidos, do concreto à nossa volta. Corporificando e antropomorfizando, manipulando-nos sentidos e inteligência, *O Jardim sem Limites* propicia o nosso entendimento e a nossa interpretação de coisas a que acedemos pela palavra narrativa, mas que nos chegam como se delas tivéssemos apreensão imediata, como acontece no mundo real onde vivemos e sobre o qual Lídia Jorge nos quer ensinar a pensar e a agir.

O manto diáfano

Parece perfeitamente legítimo dizer-se que, em *O Jardim sem Limites*, Lídia Jorge realiza, sob diáfana capa ficcional, uma reflexão sistemática sobre aquilo que, com R. Howard Bloch, podemos (e talvez mesmo devamos) entender como a perda da universalidade da ideia inseparável da expressão da mesma ideia.[19] É essa a paradoxal conjuntura a partir da qual—e a despeito da qual—tem de nascer o discurso, nomeadamente aqueles dois discursos que denominamos "ficcional" e "filosófico."

A narradora de Lídia Jorge sabe que não tem hipóteses de testemunhar sobre o seu mundo sem o auxílio da palavra, e sabe também, perfeitamente, quão perigosa a palavra é e quão capaz é de esconder em vez de mostrar, de perturbar em vez de esclarecer. Revisitando o *topos* da palavra *traiçoeira*, Lídia Jorge incursiona em campo simbólico interessantíssimo na nossa tradição: aquele onde a retórica — que é o próprio discurso verbal, como diz Paolo Valesio[20] — se iguala, nos seus "perigos" e "mentiras," ao feminino.

Pensando sempre sobre quaisquer modos de representação da realidade, a narradora de *O Jardim sem Limites* pensa talvez, sobretudo, na problemática da representação por palavras. Temas de retórica discursiva aparecem então, permanentemente, como os verdadeiros antagonistas da narradora e dos personagens e é, de facto, na sua relação com a palavra enquanto problema que a narradora de Lídia Jorge assume a categoria de pessoa ficcional e de pessoa *tout court*.

Um primeiro tópico retórico sobre o qual se debruça—pensando por interpostas concretizações dramáticas—a nossa contadora de histórias é o da credibilidade do seu próprio discurso. Essa credibilidade é procurada de duas maneiras. Primeiro, pelas reiteradas garantias de que tudo o que nos está sendo dito aconteceu mesmo, sendo a narradora testemunha directa dos factos. A credibilidade aqui é, então, conferida pelo facto (que aceitamos no pacto de leitura) de a narradora nos garantir que está *repetindo* a realidade para que nós a conheçamos. Sendo a natureza documental o primeiro suporte da credibilidade discursiva nesse romance, outra fonte de credibilização há e mais importante: a configuração discursiva do texto, o modo como a retórica da narrativa dá consistência a questões estéticas que são questões humanas, o modo como as sensibilidades das personagens transformam questões estéticas em questões pessoalmente assumidas enquanto existenciais, e muito particularmente o modo como os problemas da *res*, da *elocutio*, da *inventio* e da *dispositio* se constituem como as alteridades com e contra as quais a narradora constitui o próprio percurso dramático.

A esse propósito é interessante evocar o que diz Lausberg sobre as categorias retóricas acima arroladas. A *elocutio*, diz ele, "traslada al lenguaje las ideas halladas en la inventio y ordenadas en la dispositio."[21] Enquanto isso, a *inventio* "es un proceso productivo-creador; consiste en extraer las posibilidades de desarrollo de las ideas contenidas más o menos ocultamente en la res."[22] A *res* que, diz Lausberg, é "conteúdo conceptual," apreende-se pelo processo da *intellectio*. Finalmente, a *dispositio* é a escolha e ordenação dos elementos da *res* e dos meios verbais que a podem veicular.[23]

Qualquer leitor atento de *O Jardim sem Limites* se dá conta de que, embora contracene com as outras personagens no plano intelectivo, afectivo e mesmo na partilha de preocupações estéticas, a narradora, na verdade, entra em contraposição dramática não com as pessoas que tem à volta, mas com as categorias retóricas da *res*, da *elocutio*, da *inventio* e da *dispositio*. Com elas tem a narradora problemas éticos[24] a resolver, problemas sobre como actuar para as coisas serem como devem ser: ordenadas em verbo narrativo e, por isso mesmo, capazes de se nos mostrarem como o corpo vivo de uma alteridade apreensível, acomodada ao entendimento.

Trazendo a retórica para a boca de cena do paradigma reflexivo e filosófico do romance de Lídia Jorge, a exploração sistemática do tópico do "como expressar" carreia outras tópicas: como observar-captar-compreender para pôr em discurso, como interpretar o discurso que se fez e como utilizar a interpretação que se vai fazendo para novas interpretações a vir. Num quadro como esse, de desafios à verbalização de uma realidade e de maiores desafios à compreensão desta mesma realidade tem de surgir, é fatal, a problemática do feminino. Retórica como palavra e discurso verbal, retórica como organização discursiva de imagens e corpos humanos (fotografia, cinema e *performance*) e feminino estão, com efeito, tão ligadas em *O Jardim sem Limites* que, sentindo embora existir relação metafórica entre uma e outra, é difícil ao leitor decidir se é a retórica que metaforiza o feminino ou se as coisas se passam ao contrário—e, nesse caso, o feminino metaforizaria o retórico. Talvez seja de fugir a ambas as soluções, optando por uma terceira: retórica e feminino se metaforizam mútua e simultaneamente, o que faz , nesse livro, que a dinâmica de transposição da realidade seja tão substancial como inextricável nos seus muitos meandros. Se for assim, todo o imaginário de Lídia Jorge, em *O Jardim sem Limites*, assenta no entendimento do mundo como diferenciação e variedade—e a noção da diferença e da variedade fundamenta o princípio metafórico, tanto quanto, aliás, constrói alicerces para todo o discurso de natureza histórica, o que também o romance é.

Falar da equivalência entre retórica e feminino é mergulhar de cabeça em tempos remotos da nossa cultura . Podemos fazer isso com o auxílio de R. Howard Bloch, no livro que já citei. Comentando a "Dissuasão de Valério a Rufino o Filósofo," onde Walter Map enuncia, em discurso cheio de manhas, as inconveniências do casamento por serem as mulheres falsas e enganosas, assinala Bloch que "the author tries to do to his interlocutor precisely what he accuses women of doing: to deceive with words, to provoke contradiction, and to seduce with that which is defined as the essence of the feminine, the ruses of rhetoric."[25] Ora, argumentara antes Bloch, "if woman is defined as verbal transgression, indiscretion and contradiction, then Walter Map, indeed any writer, can only be defined as a woman."[26] Dentro desse quadro, assinala ainda Bloch a ligação entre mulher e matéria, mulher e sensorialidade, mulher e superficialidade dos sinais captados pelos sentidos, tudo fundamentos, argumenta Bloch—e não há razão para duvidarmos—da identificação radical entre o feminino e o literário. Para o que me interessa aqui, ainda uma citação é necessária: "The seductiveness of the feminine is for the medieval Christian West virtually synonymous with delusiveness of language embodied in rhetoric, whose seduction, that of 'mere words, worse than that of empty noises' (Augustine) recapitulates the original sin — that 'she,' in the words of John Chrysostom, 'believed in the one who professed mere words, and nothing else.'"[27]

Em *O Jardim sem Limites*, o problema de dar corpo à ideia é crucial e se liga, como não podia deixar de ser na nossa tradição, à tópica do feminino. Para além da narradora do romance, duas personagens são particularmente importantes para compreendermos a questão: refiro-me à inseparável dupla constituída por Paulina e o *performer*. Esse último encena, em grau máximo, a mesma questão da corporificação da ideia, que a narradora encena com o seu próprio corpo, assentado ao canto de um quarto, escrevendo, com as suas mãos a baterem no teclado de uma máquina um texto, e este último é o corpo que ela vai produzindo e que nos chegará sob a forma de livro.

Se o caso da narradora-escritora já nos poria por si só, e com clareza, a tópica da constituição da ideia em corpo (textual), o caso do *performer* ainda é mais interessante. Ele é um homem, mas o seu trabalho é produzir uma mensagem *com o corpo*, através de meios (em arte verbal falaríamos de "recursos retóricos") muito precisos: a postura, a expressão, a caracterização. Transformado em texto,vai o *performer* oferecer-se ao seu público, *desejando fasciná-lo*, como fascinar desejam as mulheres e o escritor, com a preciosa ajuda das "artimanhas" verbais para as quais alerta Walter Map. Deseja, ainda, o *performer* em acção, ser objecto do discurso hermenêutico dos seus espectadores. É esse mais um aspecto, e importantíssimo, da sua convergência na tópica do feminino: tomaremos consciência disso se nos lembrarmos ter sido a mulher, na nossa tradição cultural, o primeiro desafio à interpretação e o mais permanente, ao longo dos séculos, objecto de discurso hermenêutico sistemático.[28]

Escrevendo mensagem com o seu próprio corpo, o *performer* transforma em ícone—e rigorosamente em "estátua"—a tópica da linguagem como construção e como engano. Mas trata-se de um engano muito especial, conatural de toda criação artística, um engano sem o qual não podemos representar o mundo. Sendo ao mesmo tempo verdadeiro porque existe e enganoso porque está por outra coisa (está por uma interpretação do mundo), o corpo *performativo* do *performer* é realidade e ilusão, verdade e mentira, frontalidade e manha. Ele encarna a natureza de qualquer arte—está lá, num canto da rua Augusta, oferecendo-se para ser visto e apreciado mas, mais ainda, para ser indagado e interpretado. Por todos esses aspectos—e, sobretudo, por ser materialização de ideia e desafio à interpretação (porque a perda de universalidade de uma ideia materializada pode e deve ser anulada pelo discurso hermenêutico)—o corpo-retórica do *performer* metaforiza a própria natureza do feminino.

Uma natureza feminina tem de provir, ao que parece (ou ao menos ao que propõe o romance de Lídia Jorge), de outra natureza feminina. E assim acontece, efectivamente, com o nosso *performer*. Ele nasce para a *performance* com a ajuda de Paulina, a mulher que o treina e lhe transforma o corpo em espectáculo de discurso, de retórica, de manhas e subterfúgios imprescindíveis para se constituir, pela interpretação, um tipo superior de saber. Criando o texto-homem ou o homem-texto, provocando com ele o olhar, a indagação e o pensamento de outros, Paulina espelha, de modo muito claro, a figura da narradora de *O Jardim sem Limites*, com ela inteiramente partilhando as preocupações quanto aos modos de dar forma textual à realidade e de apontar onde, naquilo que se representa e se (re)constrói em arte, podemos encontrar um dos rostos possíveis da verdade.

Notas

*Cito da tradução de Paul Turner (Londres: Penguin Books, Penguin Classics, 1965) 63.

[1] Lisboa: Publicações Dom Quixote, 1995.

[2] "Toda língua natural é susceptível de produzir filosofia. No seu entender, em que tipos de texto melhor se produz filosofia na literatura portuguesa contemporânea?" foi o tema que me propôs o Professor Joaquim Cerqueira Gonçalves, da Faculdade de Letras de Lisboa, para um seminário que conduzi numa sua turma de Mestrado em Filosofia.

[3] H. Lausberg, *Elementos de Retórica Literária*, trad. port. de Raul Miguel Rosado Fernandes, 2.ª ed. (Lisboa, Fundação Calouste Gulbenkian, 1972) 14-17, itálicos meus. Extraordinariamente interessantes as implicações epistemológicas e, mais geralmente, antropológicas, das palavras de Lausberg. O discurso de uso repetido surge sempre que uma sociedade tem "suficiente

intensidade social," suficiente "complexidade de ordem social" e, ainda, consciência tanto da intensidade quanto da complexidade. O discurso de uso repetido funciona, então, como discurso de sistematização das relações grupais, porque constitui um corpo estável de referências onde se vai buscar desde a memória colectiva (a história) até as configurações simbólicas (religião, literatura, filosofia), passando por tópicos preferenciais para observação científica do mundo.

4 E, naturalmente, à ciência.

5 É pela diérese do pensamento—pela metonímia—que podemos, por exemplo, explicitar discursivamente o processo de dupla sinédoque necessário à formulação da metáfora que, sendo tropos de salto, junta o que não deveria ser juntado, exactamente o incompatível: o divino com o humano em "essa menina é um anjo," ou o animado com o que não tem alma, caso de "essa menina é uma flor."

6 Os incompatíveis artificiosos—as mais das vezes metáforas, mas frequentemente também oxímoros—acabam por ser nítidas provocações ao filosófico e a eles só se pode responder por discursos com satisfatória sistematização.

7 Já pode o leitor ver a razão da epígrafe deste texto.

8 Barbara Hardy, *Forms of Feeling in Victorian Fiction* (London: Methuen & Co., 1985) 19, itálicos meus.

9 Parece lógico referir alegoria a propósito de filosofia na ficção narrativa—e muito especificamente na de Lídia Jorge. Figura de pensamento, a alegoria exige formulação complexa e discursivamente extensa. Tal como a filosofia e a ficção, a alegoria pede-nos actuação hermenêutica, pois não prescinde do aprofundamento de sentidos dos sinais que a conformam, por recurso a intertextualidades de vário tipo. Trabalha a alegoria sobre estruturas alargadas de sentido, assim se afastando da metáfora que manipula unidades semântico-discursivas isoladas ou muito reduzidas. Para além disso, a alegoria se encena claramente como discurso narrativo-interpretativo, podendo ainda funcionar na interpretação de outro texto, alegórico ou não, tal como se vê na hermenêutica cristã e, sobretudo, na judaica.

10 Quando apresentei a primeira versão deste trabalho, num seminário do grupo de investigação sobre Filosofia e Feminino (Faculdade de Letras de Lisboa), informou Lídia Jorge que tinha sido sua intenção não fornecer quaisquer indicações sobre o género do sujeito de narração em *O Jardim sem Limites*. O facto é, contudo, que dois adjectivos ("exausta" e "culpada," respectivamente nas páginas 21 e 375) põem uma mulher como narradora. Não se trata de um descuido, no meu entender, mas de uma daquelas situações em que a pena foge para a verdade: todo o clima discursivo de *O Jardim sem Limites* é feminino—e muito da feminilidade do texto se deve, como tentarei pelo menos sugerir, à obsessiva encenação do tema da representação.

11 A *repetição* serve, ensina a retórica, à *amplificação* afectiva, pois "detém o fluir da informação," dando "tempo para que se 'saboreie' afectivamente a informação apresentada como importante" (Lausberg. *Elementos* 241). É preciso notar-se, contudo, não ser a amplificação afectiva a única função (e o único efeito) da repetição. Interrompendo o fluir da informação, a palavra ou expressão repetidas também propiciam o aprofundamento da intelecção: surgem assim condições para construir pensamento, naquela dinâmica espiralada em que todo pensar se faz. Sobre os tipos de repetição lembre-se que a *exacta* retoma precisamente o que já foi dito, a *abrandada* retoma-o com modificações. O romance de Lídia Jorge abre-se justamente sob o signo da tradução, que é repetição abrandada. As primeiras palavras que lemos são justamente "Ou por outras palavras."

12 "Personification and the topos of inexpressibility are twin aspects of a mimetic representation of emotional crisis, conflict and continuity" (Hardy, *op. cit.* 13).

13 A repetição integra plenamente o modo de ser narrativo (não apenas o poético, como frequentemente somos levados a pensar), justamente por causa do pensar por antropomorfização/dramatização (cf. Barbara Hardy) e, ainda, por causa da *amplificatio* sem a

qual não se faz pensamento. Sobre a repetição na narrativa veja-se J. Hillis Miller, *Fiction and Repetition. Seven English Novels* (Cambridge, MA: Harvard University Press).

[14] Esta existência, no romance de Lídia Jorge, ultrapassa os muros de uma casa de quartos em Lisboa, e alarga-se para a experiência histórica portuguesa ao longo, pelo menos, do período fascista.

[15] O mais evidente exemplo da obrigatória convivência, repetição—interpretação (abertura dos horizontes do texto para outros horizontes, sobretudo para os horizontes interiores do leitor) é o texto poético. Nessa perspectiva, uma leitura apropriada da poesia equivale a exercício de pedagogia de intertextualidade e de interdiscursividade. Mas no romance também é essencial a intertextualização e a interdiscursividade: o ponto está em que nem sempre a ficção narrativa encena, com a mesma força que o faz a poesia, os mecanismos repetitivos.

[16] Alister McGrath, *Christian Theologyy. An Introduction* (Oxford, Cambridge, MA: Blackwell, 1994) 139-40.

[17] O caso da ironia é, nessa perspectiva, interessante: uma ironia acomodada, traduzida, perde quase tudo do seu valor. A "tradução" do enunciado em valor irónico deve, então, ser potenciada por índices discretos, mesmo correndo o risco de esses mesmos índices escaparem ao leitor ou interlocutor oral menos treinado. Caso para se dizer que não apenas o produtor do discurso deve preocupar-se com acomodações, mas que também o consumidor do discurso deve saber adaptar-se—por prática sistemática de observação de artefactos verbais—àquilo que é costume, numa tradição cultural e literária, tomar existência discursiva. Por outro lado, a escrita hermética traduz para o leitor a impossibilidade (ou a falta de vontade) de traduzir, criando um paradoxo comunicativo em si mesmo irónico, e ironicamente sempre susceptível de ser de algum modo traduzido.

[18] As muitas e obsessivas corporificações (em pessoas ou em artefactos) que perpassam por todo *O Jardim sem Limites* têm um efeito interessantíssimo: fazem-nos ler *presencialmente*, como se tudo o que nos é contado estivesse ao alcance da mão e da vista. Isso coloca o livro de Lídia Jorge sob o signo da *percepção*, isto é, da experiência física material das coisas, única situação que permite, realmente, observar. Sobre *percepção*, cf. Jean Pierre Changeux, *O Homem Neuronal*, trad. de A. J. Pires Monteiro (Lisboa: Publicações Dom Quixote, 1985). Sobretudo capítulos IV e V.

[19] R. Howard Bloch, *Medieval Misogyny and the Invention of Western Romantic Love* (Chicago: The University of Chicago Press, 1991) 109 e *passim*. Muita da argumentação que vai a partir daqui até o final deste ensaio foi inspirada pelo trabalho notável de Bloch.

[20] Muito deste meu texto, como aliás muitíssimo da minha prática crítica, deve a Paolo Valesio, *Ascoltare il silenzio. La retorica come teoria* (Bologna: Il Mulino, 1986).

[21] H. Lausberg, *Manual de retórica literaria. Fundamentos de una ciencia de la literatura* (Madrid: Editorial Gredos, Biblioteca Románica Hispánica, 1983) 453.

[22] H. Lausberg 260.

[23] H. Lausberg, *Elementos de retórica literária* 46.

[24] Não resisto a colocar aqui a mais pertinente definição de ética que jamais me caiu nas mãos, e cujo autor completamente esqueci: "A ética vê uma diferença entre o que é e o que deveria ser. Essa diferença constitui um espaço e dentro dele o sujeito actua."

[25] R. Howard Bloch 57-58.

[26] R. Howard Bloch 56.

[27] R. Howard Bloch 49.

[28] Sobre a mulher como objecto privilegiado de interpretação, cf. Howard Bloch, *op. cit. passim.*

Contingency and Loss in *Marido e Outros Contos*

Ellen W. Sapega

In the fall of 1997, Lídia Jorge published a volume of collected short stories under the title *Marido e Outros Contos*. Bringing together seven brief narratives that had been previously published in magazines, anthologies, or independently as individual stories, this collection was welcomed by Jorge's readers who saw it as providing a new opportunity to partake of the author's imaginative process and, perhaps, to find new approaches to assessing her previous work. Indeed, much of this volume's initial critical reception focused on the manner in which these stories could be understood as complements to the novels that have made Jorge's literary reputation or as a practice ground for future literary endeavors. In a review published in the weekly newspaper *Expresso*, José Nobre da Silveira offered such general observations as "o conto é, de facto, (...) lugar de acumulação de tentativas que, de uma ou de outra forma, ilumina a obra maior do romancista," and that "ele será, na maior parte das circunstâncias, o espelho da obra do romancista." Maria Alzira Seixo, on the other hand, commented in the *Jornal de Letras* that the incidents captured in the author's short stories seemed to beg for treatment in lengthier, more fully developed fictional forms: "Por um lado, Lídia Jorge escreve contos que podem considerar-se *argumentos* de uma ficção mais extensa, sem que por isso tenhamos que lamentar a sua brevidade" (24).

In seeking to interpret these stories as comments on Jorge's fictional universe, as reflections of her novels, or as experimental terrain for future projects, these approaches to Lídia Jorge's short stories move beyond a simple comparison of specific texts written by a single author to participate in a conceptual exercise that focuses on the difference between or hierarchy of genres. More specifically, these critics, like many before them, implicitly privilege the novel genre over that of the short story. In an essay entitled "The

Short Story: The Long and the Short of It," Mary Louise Pratt has pointed out that "both the conception and the practice of the short story are conditioned by its relation to the novel, as the smaller and lesser genre" (181). While practitioners of short story theory and criticism traditionally attempted to distinguish the shorter narrative form as an autonomous genre, Pratt's objective was to approach the modern short story as a "dependent countergenre to the novel" (185). This, in turn, led her to outline a series of propositions regarding short fiction that are based on the assumption of an asymmetrical relationship between the novel and the short story.

I shall refer to several of these propositions as I now briefly describe the contents of *Marido e Outros Contos*. Pratt's first three propositions highlight the fragmentary or incomplete nature of the short story's contents.[1] As opposed to the novel, this shorter genre typically does not attempt to narrate a full-length life, and often it does not even pretend to capture the psychological complexities of an individual character's personality. Thus, we come to expect that the "novel tells a life, [while] the short story tells a fragment of a life" (182), or that the short story deals with "a single thing, the novel with many things" (184). In *Marido e Outros Contos*, several of the stories do focus on a single, defining moment in the characters' lives—"A prova dos pássaros" narrates a Professor's quest to prove or disprove God's existence by means of a simple exercise of counting birds in flight; "Espuma da Tarde" is the tale of an unnecessary death which comes about by the characters' desire for something (anything) to happen to change the course of their mundane lives; and "O conto do nadador" describes the near drowning of a young woman and the response of the anonymous onlooker who attempts to save her.

In a slight variation on the short story that captures a fragment or the excerpt of a life, "Marido," "A Instrumentalina," and "Testemunha" are short stories that seem to fulfill Poe's requirement of a "*single effect* to be wrought" (Pratt 184). The first of these stories accompanies in frightening detail the thoughts and evasions of a *porteira* in Lisbon who, as a battered wife, prays (unsuccessfully) to protect her husband from the temptation of drink, thereby lessening the likelihood that he will return home inebriated and beat her. "Testemunha" and "A Instrumentalina," on the other hand, are based on each story's narrator's recollections of childhood, thereby entailing the juxtaposition of two times (adulthood and childhood) and two places (rural Portugal and North America). Finally, Jorge's story entitled "António," which treats the often harrowing experience of being beholden to one's (despotic) hairdresser, seems to belong in Pratt's third category, that of the "short story as a sample," whose point "is not just the events themselves, but their supposed typicality" (185).

Moving our discussion of the short story's contents and organization to the question of its interpretation, I should also note that, given the "incomplete" nature of this genre, the short story often requires the active participation on the part of the reader, whose job is to supply what the author has left out. By saying less than what is "expected" of it, the short story begs for the reader to use his or her subjectivity to fill in its blanks. This meaning-supplying gesture can often gain impetus from the larger whole in which the text in question is to be found. Therefore, when we examine the short story's status as a published text, we must remember that it usually depends upon its relation to this larger whole. As Pratt notes in her fourth proposition, "The novel is the whole text, the short story is not" (186). By its common inclusion in a larger reading experience, be it a collection of short stories, an anthology, or a magazine, the short story's already fragmentary nature is greatly reinforced. Rarely does a short story constitute a complete book, and its "meaning" is often derived from or enriched by the texts that surround it.

In order to illustrate better the manner in which a short story's relation to other texts helps to condition its interpretation, I turn now to the specific example of "Marido," the story that opens Jorge's volume and lends the collection its title. A table that appears at the end of the volume identifies this story as originally having appeared in the review *Vértice* in April, 1989. We are also informed that it was subsequently republished in a supplement to the women's magazine *Elle* in August, 1994. Now, it is true that these two publications enjoy at least one reader in common (myself); it is also true, however, that the contents of each publication presuppose a different type of reading experience. *Vértice* is what we may consider a "serious" publication comprised of articles that belong to the academic fields of history, sociology, literary criticism, and so on. *Elle*, on the other hand, is directed toward a middle-class female audience who may be as interested in reading about fashion, the home, and their jobs, as they are in reading "serious" fiction.[2]

It goes without saying that the experience of reading "Marido" will vary according to these two divergent contexts. This is a simple, yet moving, story of a working-class woman who, while systematically battered by her husband, cannot conceive of life without him. I contend, nonetheless, that its perspective and, ultimately, our interpretation of the protagonist's fate hinges on the other discourses that surround it. As this story enters into a dialogue with these framing texts, certain elements come to the fore while others recede into the background. In the first case, the readers of *Vértice* might identify more readily with the perspective of the *porteira*'s well-intentioned neighbors (the lawyer, the doctor, and the social worker) who urge her to leave her spouse. In the second context, it is quite possible that some female readers might have an easier time recognizing the protagonist's inability to imagine a life without her husband, sympathizing, initially at least, with her position that:

> para além do sacramento, seria triste a vida de porteira sem um marido que viesse da oficina-auto com o seu fato-macaco por tratar. Com quem ralharia, por quem iria ao talho, de quem falaria quando fosse às compras, para quem pederia protecção quando cantasse à janela por Salve Regina, a quem pertenceria quando os domingos viessem, e cada mulher saisse com seu homem, se ela nem mais teria o seu. (17-18)

In this latter case, for the readers of Elle, the story's shocking ending (in which the husband sets his spouse on fire with a lighted candle) would take on the proportions of a cautionary tale whose principal meaning is derived, perhaps, from their failure to appreciate the gravity of the situation.

It is quite possible to identify the original context of the other stories found in *Marido e Outros Contos* and, similarly, to try to imagine the readers' responses to the texts in question.[3] Once they were bound together in the volume, however, this original context was lost and, simultaneously, a new, different context, that of a short story sequence, was provided.[4] It is within this new context that "Marido" acts, first and foremost, as the introduction to the volume as a whole. In effect, the violent *dénouement* of the *porteira*'s story introduces the intertwined themes of contingency and loss that Maria Alzira Seixo has identified as constituting a unifying thread for the stories contained in *Marido e Outros Contos*. Seixo observes that these stories, while evoking "toda a literatura do desejo e da união," actually tend to register "a separação do par (…) e a emergência do desejo insistente e sensível" (25). This desire, moreover, is specifically identified as female desire. As we have seen in the case of the story that opens the volume, the protagonist's strong feelings of loyalty and her desire to maintain her union with her husband at all costs actually provoke the accident that occurs at the story's end. In choosing to open the collection with this particular story, Jorge prepares the reader for the repetition and development of its themes, which Seixo has identified as entailing "a articulação do feminino com a contingência e com a perda." In the loosely-knit sequence of intertwined narratives that follows, we will find the recurring portrayal of the female characters' desire for unity, union, or freedom, which is then either satisfied by chance or eliminated through sudden violence.

While the most salient qualities of a short story sequence are not in evidence in *Marido e Outros Contos*,[5] a quick look at the table that identifies the stories' original place of publication reveals, nonetheless, that these stories have been judiciously arranged in a progression that differs from that of a mere chronological ordering according to their dates of publication. In fact, the story that is ascribed the earliest date ("António," *Jornal de Letras*, August 1988) is actually the third text to appear, and "Marido" is identified as having first appeared one year later. The remaining five stories were all published between 1992 and 1996, but they, too, are not presented in any discernible chronological order. This sequencing leads me to believe that it is legitimate to attempt to discern an underlying pattern resulting from their juxtaposition and to assume, furthermore, that the author herself was responsible for this ordering.[6]

As is the case in any sequence of intertwined narratives, one may discern various relationships that link the stories in question, thus opting to trace several different geometries within the text (Luscher 154). One of the first patterns to emerge is the counterpoint that arises from the variation between the use of first-person narrators and a recurring omniscient narrative perspective. "António," "A Instrumentalina," and "Testemunha" (which are found respectively, in third, fifth, and sixth place in the volume's sequence) are all told from the point of view of women who make no effort to mask or to hide their identity as the texts' narrators. The first of these stories is narrated by a voice of a mature, urban woman whose perspective could easily be equated with that of the author herself. As she subjects herself to her hairdresser's "test," wondering whether she will be accepted by him, this narrator remarks, "Dentro de momentos, vou saber por mim mesma. Sei, porque me contaram por acaso. Contou-me uma joalheira que na idade se localiza entre mim e a minha mãe" (46). Upon being rejected by António, the narrator exits his salon and passes through the shopping center, noting that all of nature is on display in the shops' windows. In a fitting close to the story, the narrator's desire is then capped by an observation in which António, the hairdresser's name, is substituted with that of the Greek Antinous, symbol of a tyranny exerted by extreme physical beauty: "Eles não sabem, porém, como esse todo está representado até na secção de beleza. Elas não sabem o que se passa no salão de António. Ignoram, desconhecem. Até sempre António. Para sempre, Antínoo" (49).

In contrast to this personal/autobiographical focus that uses a banal trip to the hairdresser's shop to present an exemplary narrative on the nature and role of female beauty, the narrators' status in the latter two stories more closely resembles that of imagined, fictional characters. As these narrators encounter figures from their childhood and adolescence, they are reminded of a past which in both cases involves a return to a rural setting during the second half of the 1950s. Upon meeting with her long-lost uncle in a Canadian hotel, the narrator of "A Instrumentalina" is returned to the "nesga de campina ao sul do meu país" (80), where she first experienced affection, betrayal, and loss. "Testemunha," as its title indicates, does not recount the narrator's own past, but rather summarizes the experiences of a female acquaintance, parts of which have been witnessed by the narrator, and parts of which are told to her. In recalling her friend's family's difficulties, one particularly painful and humiliating childhood episode comes to the fore:

> Então uma das meninas disse, apontando para Zuzete. Aquela, aquela não tem calças. Laurentino deu um estalo com a língua como os ladrões de alpergata a chamar a chusma. E todas à uma. Distribuíram-se pelos pulsos e pelos braços, pelos artelhos de Zuzete, baloiçaram Zuzete como se fosse saca, atiraram--na dentro do trigo, e porque afinal Zuzete usava uma roupa interior amordaçada de elástico, a luta foi demorada e entrecortada de grandes brados, até que Laurentino atirou a cueca ao ar, por cima da cabeça de todos. Zuzete de coxa aberta no meio do trigo, Zuzete sem bolsa, Zuzete sem laços, Zuzete de choro alto, magoado, palhetas de aço a meterem-se pelos ouvidos dos colmos. (113)

However traumatic, this event belongs to the past, and it is the narrator who recalls this episode. At the time of narration, the vicissitudes of Zuzete's childhood have apparently been overcome while the memory of them, embodied in a concern for the aunts that she left behind, persists. The story ends, nonetheless, with a rather ironic, yet optimistic, observation regarding the distancing effects of time and space: "para lá voltar é necessário atravessar meio século de vidas, na asa de uma avião americano" (115).

While "Testemunha" counts on the presence of a clearly identified narrating subject, the story that is told belongs to another character. The narrator thus assumes a dual role, capturing and recording the voice of Zuzete speaking of her present situation while also allowing us to witness her past. This temporal alternation enables her to focus on the forces that contributed to the social formation of the character while at the same time registering Zuzete's conscious and unconscious reactions to these forces. In addition to providing an excellent example of Jorge's skill in vividly rendering the workings of her characters' consciousness, this alternating point of view between self and other enables us to link this story to the volume's other four narratives.

In these remaining narratives, multiple points of view are captured by an unidentified, third-person narrator. The style that is employed in the first, second, fourth, and seventh stories of the volume has been aptly described as emerging from "uma omnisciência formal, (...) que se esbate e se desdobra em múltiplas formas de cumplicidade, pelas pausas, pelos silêncios, pela indeterminação do olhar ou pela súbita aceleração do ritmo" (Silveira). While the sex of the narrator of these stories is not identified as specifically female, I believe that one can make a case, borrowing from Isabel Allegro de Magalhães, in favor of an approach that posits the "sex of the texts" as clearly feminine. In her gloss of Julia Kristeva's description of the "semiotic elements" employed by writers to challenge the prevailing (male) symbolic order, Magalhães explains that these are elements that "não estando embora expressos no discurso logocêntrico são visíveis por exemplo através do ritmo, da estrutura, do tom, dos silêncios ou de outros elementos" (23).

This narrative strategy based upon silences, incomplete utterances, and shifting points of view has the effect, of course, of challenging, destabilizing, or subverting the patriarchal order which, as Kristeva reminds us, is present in the very enunciation of sentences (noun + verb; topic-comment; beginning-ending). Female subjectivity, as it rejects this notion of linear time and gives itself up to intuition, rests on "anterior temporal modalities: cyclical or monumental" which, according to Kristeva, are revealed in "a problematic of a time indissociable from space, of a space-time in infinite expansion, or rhythmed by accidents or catastrophes" (192). It is this female subjectivity, I believe, that Jorge sets out to capture in her stories. However, as Toril Moi reminds us, Kristeva's "emphasis on the semiotic as an unconscious force precludes any analysis of the conscious decision-making processes that must be part of any *collective* revolutionary project" (170). While I do not pretend to posit *Marido e Outros Contos* as a socially revolutionary text per se, I do believe that this collection does make an attempt to identify and investigate various contradictory positions occupied by female subjects vis-à-vis society as a whole.

Moving now from a theoretical discussion of the disruptive language employed by Jorge's narrators to the analysis of the thematic preoccupations evident in her narratives, it is interesting to note that three of Jorge's stories quite literally focus on accidents or catastrophes. While only the first ("Marido") entails the main character's death, the death that is witnessed in the second ("Espuma da Tarde") and the death that nearly occurs in the third ("O conto do nadador") reflect a dynamic of female desire that is initially expressed in the wish to protect, to please, or to seduce. This desire is ultimately resolved, however, "numa epifania da consagração ritualizada na morte por acidente" (Seixo 25).

As we have seen in the case of "Marido," the *porteira*'s desire to protect her husband and to remain loyal to him ultimately costs her life. "Espuma da Tarde," the fourth story in the volume, recounts a young man's shooting by the police which is witnessed by his two friends and their waitress at a beachfront snack bar. While the story's opening focus is on the three men who debate whether the monotony of their lives is due to a lack of space, of money, or of interest, surprise, and action, the narrative perspective soon slides over to that of the girl whose seductive powers seem to have the effect of subtly challenging the most aggressive of the three men to action. By the story's end, after the *primeiro rapaz* is shot, the narrative focuses exclusively on the girl and on her reactions to the death that she has witnessed.

If at first she is incredulous ("Não, ela não tinha pensado que fosse assim, que não houvesse prolongamento, intervalo, continuação e um fim, renascidos doutro modo. Era aquilo que ela havia desejado ver? Só aquilo?" 73), she begins to feel a certain order fall over the afternoon and to turn herself over the silence let loose by the waves. The girl then realizes that "para que essa ordem fosse completa, para que aquilo que pudesse restar de incompreensível ou injusto fosse apagado da face da areia, ela apenas tinha de cumprir um pequeno rito que ainda não sabia qual iria ser," and we are told: "Apetecia-lhe desprender-se das meias, desprender-se da sedução. Pelo menos, para já, durante alguns dias ia ficar assim, pois nunca se sabia se aquele não ia ser o único gesto heróico que teria ocasião de presenciar durante toda a vida" (73-74).

If the epiphanic nature of this story's ending brings to mind certain aspects of Brazilian writer Clarice Lispector's collection *Laços de Família*, Lídia Jorge's own description of the dynamics that shape Lispector's stories also seems equally applicable to "Espuma da Tarde":

> Tem personagens, tem aventura, acidentes e desfechos. Só que (...) os personagens começando por ser comuns, logo se revelam incomuns, avançando como se não tivessem olhos para ver, e quando quisessem ouvir, não tivessem ouvidos. Ou inversamente, se têm ouvidos não têm sons, e se têm olhos não há paisagem que se veja. (n. p.)

In Jorge's story, the surviving rapazes remain as blind to what they have witnessed as they were at the story's opening:

> —'Pois bem. O que é que falta aqui? Em concreto, ninguém sabe, mas eu sei. O que falta aqui é um bocado de terra...' Estava-se diante do mar. Da orla da praia o Oceano partia na direcção duma lonjura sem limite e por isso não deixava de ser insólito que um tipo se pusesse a dizer que faltava um pedaço de terra diante de tanta água. (54)

At the end, the narrator observes, no less ironically, that they can explain "em profundidade" all that happened, while the girl, on the other hand, becomes aware of the precariousness and fragility of both knowledge and desire. As a result, she opts, momentarily at least, to remove herself from the game that had reserved for her a role based solely on the powers of seduction.[7]

In "O conto do nadador," the final story of *Marido e Outros Contos*, the desire to seduce also plays a central role in the events that unfold. This story narrates a young girl's near brush with death by drowning that takes place as she attempts to distinguish herself from her girlfriends before the gaze of a male onlooker. As they grow accustomed to "o calor do olhar" (124), the girls become more and more daring, venturing to a distant, almost deserted beach where they shed their clothes and play in the sea. Attempting to attract the attention the anonymous "voyeur" who watches them, Delfina, the most courageous and the only girl who almost knows how to swim, braves the ocean on the day following a storm. When she begins to drown, the other girls, tragically, are unable to assess the "reality" of the situation, and as the onlooker saves her life and administers resuscitation, they believe that they are witnessing a movie-like scene of conquest and the consummation of love:

> E aí o voyeur entrou na água, mergulhou, segurou ao peito a rapariga corajosa, abraçou a rapariga, ergeu no ar a rapariga, nadou com a rapariga para fora, atravessou as ondas estupidamente em rebentação, correu para o cascalho, depositou a rapariga de bruços na areia. Afagou-lhe as costas com as suas grandes mãos, virou-lhe o corpo, retirou-lhe o cabelo da cara, descobriu-lhe a boca, colocou a boca sobre a sua boca, voltou a massajar-lhe as costas e a comprimir-lhe o peito. E depois voltou a beijá-la. Beijou-a. Beijou-a como nos filmes que então se viam, sem se ver a língua nem os dentes. O amante respirava alto, soprava durante o beijo. Durante um instante, todo o seu corpo cobriu o dela. Tal e qual como todas e cada uma havia sonhado vir a acontecer consigo, em imaginação. (137)

The girls' dependence on references borrowed from popular culture as they seek to understand the real-life situations and emotions that they are experiencing brings to mind, of course, Jorge's highly acclaimed second novel, *O Cais das Merendas* (1982). There, the reader is frequently told of the characters' use of cinematographic images as a means of helping them to make sense of their actions.[8] Likewise, the physical setting of "O Conto do Nadador" (the events I have been discussing take place in the Algarve in 1955 and are recalled in a contemporary present by João Desidério, proprietor of the Hotel Paraíso) also bring to mind several thematic elements of *O Cais das Merendas*.

This reference to Jorge's earlier novelistic production brings me back, of course, to the discussion of the short story and its dependence on the novel with which I opened my reading of *Marido e Outros Contos*. Like both the critics whom I quoted in my introduction, I believe that a great number of useful comparisons can indeed be made between these stories and Jorge's novels. In addition to clear affinities in both plot and setting with *O Cais das Merendas*, parallels may be drawn between several of these stories and the experience of isolated, rural life that is evoked in *O Dia dos Prodígios* (1980), and with the emotionally charged, allegorical space that serves as the background of *A Última Don*a (1992). The author's use of language, moreover, is strikingly similar to that which we find throughout her work. Finally, I should note that, if we are to assume that these stories represent the sum total of the author's efforts within the short story genre, we must conclude that Lídia Jorge continues to work and publish first and foremost as novelist. The seven stories that I have been discussing appeared in print between 1988 and 1996; during that same period, Jorge also published three novels and, in the summer of 1998, immediately following *Marido e Outros Contos*, she published her eighth novel, entitled *O Vale da Paixão*.

That is not to say, however, that the stories of *Marido e Outros Contos* can or should be read as examples of a "minor" genre which only serves as a reflection of Lídia Jorge's "major" works, or as rehearsals for forthcoming novels. On the contrary, I believe that it has been both fruitful and illuminating to approach the collection as an integrated whole. I am reminded, in fact, of Robert M. Luscher's observation that, "As in a musical sequence, the short story sequence repeats and progressively develops themes and motifs over the course of the work; its unity derives from a perception of both the successive ordering and recurrent patterns, which provide the unity of the reading experience" (149). The stories contained in *Marido e Outros Contos* were not initially conceived as belonging to a short story sequence, but our experience of reading them has undoubtedly been enriched by examining then in the context of a collected volume.

As I have shown, the narratives positioned at the volume's opening, middle, and end highlight the collection's focus on multiple manifestations of female desire and draw explicit attention to this desire as both controlled and conditioned by the prevailing male hegemony. Traces of the same thematic may also be found in the other narratives contained in *Marido e Outros Contos*.[9] In fact, the other male figures who appear throughout (the hairdresser "António," both the uncle and the grandfather in "A Instrumentalina," and Laurentino, Zuzete's tormentor) similarly participate in an almost ritualistic determination of female identity as determined by the forces of violence and chance. We can read these stories individually, of course, as textual fragments that record fragments of a series of lives torn away from routine by the intrusion of contingency and loss. When taken together, however, they provide us with a much more complex view of female experience—that of the female subject's precarious positioning within a symbolic and social order that is beyond her control and that often places her in a direct collision course with the forces of that order.

Notes

[1] In addition to presenting a series of propositions regarding both the form and the contents of the modern short story, I find Pratt's article very useful due to the complete historical treatment that she accords to short story theory. As she sums up previous critical approaches to the short story, Pratt's article will serve, in the present analysis, as my principal source for a general theory of the genre.

[2] So as not to hinder the flow of my analysis, I will leave any discussion regarding *Vértice*'s readers' relationship with "serious" fiction for another occasion.

[3] Two of the stories contained in *Marido e Outros Contos*—"A Instrumentalina" and "O Conto do Nadador"—were originally published as separate books. The former is listed by Jorge's editor (Dom Quixote) as volume six of her *Obras Completas*. The latter was published in 1994 by Contexto and in its original version was accompanied by Alain Corbel's illustrations.

[4] Following Robert M. Luscher's lead, I have opted for the term "sequence" rather than "cycle." As Luscher defines it, a short story sequence is "a volume of stories, collected and organized by their author, in which the reader successively realizes underlying patterns of coherence by continual modifications of his perceptions of pattern and theme" (148).

[5] The book contains no preface, prologue, or epilogue, for example. Likewise, the title of the volume does not differ from that of the stories, nor are we presented with related characters or narrators (Luscher 150).

[6] As there is no evidence to the contrary, I believe that it is safe to assume that Lídia Jorge was responsible for the ordering of the volume's contents.

[7] The nature of the girl's "epiphany" sets her apart, I believe, from the protagonists of Lispector's short stories. In her introduction to *Laços de Família*, Jorge observes that "toda a obra vive do influxo do seu tempo histórico e a prosa de Clarice não se mantém asséptica em relação ao mundo mental em que viveu." This leads Jorge to identify points of contact between Lispector's writing and that of other well known Modernist writers—Kafka, Joyce, and Woolf. The characters and events narrated in Jorge's story, on the other hand, seem much more at home in a contemporary, post-Modern world, where emotions seem to have been exhausted and epiphanies, when they occur at all, are registered in a minor key, as indeterminate and of a decidedly immanent nature.

[8] Two of the most cited passages of this novel that deal with this epistemological dependence on the movies read: "Já alguma de vocês teve notícia de um party terminar assim? As amigas olharam umas para as outras e realmente ninguém tinha ideia, por mais que puxasse pela memória dos filmes, os olhos perdidos no fim do mar" (41), and "estávamos todos desmemoriados, sem sabermos, por exemplo, se as segas se faziam na primavera se no outono. Eu tenho uma ideia de ver num filme colorido mulheres a ceifarem com uma luz alaranjada própria da queda da folha entre nós" (244).

[9] A possible exception to this emphasis on female desire can be found in "A prova dos pássaros," which I have opted to exclude from my analysis. In this story, it is the male protagonist who desires to find proof of God's existence. His needs are met, however, as the result of his interaction with a young woman and her baby, thereby leading me to interpret his quest as fulfilled by means of his symbolic encounter with the maternal.

Works Cited

Jorge, Lídia. *O Cais das Merendas*. Lisbon: Publicações Europa-América, 1982.

———. *Marido e Outros Contos*. Lisbon: Dom Quixote, 1997.

———. Preface. *Laços de Família*. By Clarice Lispector. Lisbon: Afrontamento, 1990. n.p.

Kristeva, Julia. "Women's Time." *A Kristeva Reader*. Ed. Toril Moi. New York: Columbia UP, 1986. 187-213.

Luscher, Robert M. "The Short Story Sequence: An Open Book." *Short Story Theory at a Crossroads*. Eds. Susan Lohafer and Jo Ellyn Clarey. Baton Rouge: LSU Press, 1989. 148-67.

Magalhães, Isabel Allegro de. "O Sexo dos Textos: Traços da Ficção Narrativa de Autoria Feminina." *O Sexo dos Textos*. Lisbon: Caminho, 1995. 15-53.

Moi, Toril. *Sexual/Textual Politics*. London and New York: Routledge, 1985.

Pratt, Mary Louise. "The Short Story: The Long and the Short of It." *Poetics* 10 (1981): 175-94.

Seixo, Maria Alzira. "In-Citações: Contos de Lídia Jorge." *Jornal de Letras, Artes e Ideias* (28 January, 1998): 24-25.

Silveira, José Nobre da. "Os Gestos do Sonho: Sob a Forma do Conto, a Ficção como Aventura da Linguagem." *Expresso* (14 March, 1998): 24.

Picturing Time: Some Photographs of Lídia Jorge

Memory Holloway

On the cover of this issue of *Portuguese Literary & Cultural Studies* is a photograph of Lídia Jorge taken by Luís Ramos in 1991. This photograph and others of her by the same photographer were first published in *A Imagem das Palavras*,[1] a book which featured photographs of contemporary Portuguese writers according to a set of conventions which included a portrait of the writer, the writer's study or place of work, and the region or immediate environment of the writer.

In his portrait picture, Ramos presents Lídia Jorge not once, but twice in the same photograph, both as an adult and as a child of eighteen months. This simultaneous, repetitive, and double representation of the writer was achieved with her collusion in an event staged for the occasion, much as a director might locate an actor. She holds the photograph of herself up for the viewer to inspect, pressing it towards the camera eye. More correctly, she *frames* the photograph with her hands, cupping its left edge in one hand and securing its right edge with the other. The photograph of the child is in sharp focus; the adult writer, fixed in planar recession, is blurred, and she gazes back at the spectator, her eye just grazing the top deckled edge of the photo. Underneath are the words of the title of this issue: *Lídia Jorge in Other Words/por Outras Palavras*. Image and text work here to reinforce one another in the way that the title lays claim to the photograph by giving a name to what is represented, the two Lídias. Even more, the photograph, and the discourse that circulates around it, is presented as another language, "in other words," a visual language.

There are several conventions with which the photograph plays. The most immediately striking is the commemorative photograph where a political adherent or family member carries a large photograph in a public setting either to eulogize the heroic virtues of the leader or to immortalize and mourn the dead. We think of the mothers whose children disappeared for their acts of political resistance, marching year after year around the central plaza in Buenos Aires. Or funeral processions in India, where the deceased is honored with a photograph taken in the prime of life. Or the photographs of those killed by drunk drivers held up for all to see. Or figures who by their heroic acts, have been elevated to the status of martyrs in the service of the State. Presenting the photograph to the viewer, pressing it forward to the very front of the picture space is a visual command that requires the spectator's acknowledgment. Yet this photograph of the writer re-presenting herself as a child is commemorative only in the sense that it registers a passing of time. The child is still alive in the adult, and the location of the photograph in public space only becomes so with its publication. There is nothing here of public mourning, of parades or processions or protest, but rather a quiet sense of shuffling through the family archive and the passage of years. Picturing time is measured as a physical trace in the residue of what is left over: only a photographic record of what once was.

Childhood, it could be argued, is a physical reality located in the past. But according to a psychoanalytic model, there is no "past reality," only continuity. As Freud pointed out, there is no time in the unconscious. There is only the present, constructed all at once by past events, actual or imagined, and their effects in the present. The intervening space between Lídia Jorge as adult and Lídia Jorge as child is collapsed into the present. Lídia as a child is Lídia at eighteen months, the end of that crucial period which begins at six months when the child completes an image of the unity it will achieve and what it will become. Catherine Clement describes it as that "moment when one becomes oneself because one is no longer the same as one's mother."[2] Lacan, who formulated this notion, called this the "mirror phase," a concept well known in discussion of the formation of the subject. It begins somewhere between six and eighteen months and ends with self-recognition and the acquisition of language. This recognition of Freud's "body ego" emerges from the idea of a disorganized state of the body in pieces, that is to say, from a pile of fragmented parts into a bounded identity. And it is exactly this moment that the photograph records, the moment when the child will begin to speak.

When Lídia Jorge was asked in an interview whether as a woman she was conscious of writing in a manner that distinguished her from other Portuguese writers, she replied that within the peculiarity, or even a certain style which is her own, she recognizes herself in the memory of the girl she once was, of the books she read which touched her the most, and of the music and words that she was storing away. "Having been a girl must have marked my mode of expression," she told the interviewer.[3] Her women are, as she describes them, powerful, invisible, subversive, and as a writer she records ("echoes" is her word) the violent changes that have taken place since she has begun to write. She does not claim her writing as that of a traditional feminist, and she does not claim to write feminist texts. Elizabeth Grosz, writing on "Feminism After the Death of the Author,"[4] has recently reevaluated the criteria by which a feminist text is determined. The gender of the author, she claims, does not guarantee the text's position as feminist or not, and the reader can't know the author's intentions, emotions, psyche, or interiority. None of these can fix or control the meaning and inherent ambiguity of a text. Nor does the content of the text insure its status either. There can be no assumption that women are a homogeneous group, or even that they share common experience given the cultural, geographic, political, and historically diverse backgrounds from which they come. There is no particular topic, content, or issue that belongs only to women's writing. Neither the gender of the reader nor the style of the text can be claimed *a priori* as a schema or mode of classification. "Indeed," she writes, "it seems that there is no one characteristic which could ensure a text's feminist status." Instead, for a text to be regarded as feminist, it needs to make visible the patriarchal or phallocentric presumptions that govern its contexts, and it needs to shake up and unsettle the phallocentric equation of masculinity and humanity. New styles, new modes of analysis, and new arguments need to be generated. "Being a woman and being called Lídia," says Lídia Jorge, mark her as female and her writing as produced by a woman, but they do not mark her work as feminist texts.

A photograph can, however, say something about the writer in the same way that other photographs of other writers say something about their working habits, the rooms in which they write, the houses in which they live and so on. Photographs of writers writing or artists painting constitute an entire genre as familiar in painting as in literature. But they don't tell us much. Certainly they don't reveal the secrets of artistic production. A photograph of an artist at work or on holiday, as Barthes confirmed, operates on the level of myth.[5] The writer who joins leisure with the prestige of a vocation is part of our time, a worker like the rest of us, yet also singular and different. Although he fraternizes with other workers on holiday, unlike them he doesn't cease to work. Writing is his "natural" activity; the writer is always writing, like an involuntary secretion. No matter where the writer is (on the beach, in the country, going down the Congo, in the Algarve) the writer is still a writer. So, Barthes concludes, the photograph of a writer participating in a prosaic spectacle operates as an effort to demystify, but works in exactly the opposite direction. If she's part of everyday life, her art is even more divine. If Lídia Jorge's simple, polished *escritório* appears to be stripped any attributes of a writer, it enables us to believe even more in the internal noise that goes into the writing. We want to elevate our artists, and we resist de-sanctifying them in the most mundane of terms, in their dress, their eating habits, or the places in which they work. What we want from photographs of writers is evidence: evidence of difference and evidence of likeness.

The other photographs in this issue taken by Luís Ramos of Lídia Jorge draw on this genre which represents artists and daily life. But these are photographs, as I have said, that play with the very conventions in which they participate. The *escritório* is empty, with hardly enough light in its cool interior to illuminate a page. The writer walks along a stone wall that forms a backdrop. The writer digs into a coat to resist the wind. These images tell us nothing about how her texts are achieved or what is contained in them, nor should we ask them to. If there is an "effect of the real," photography's effective claim according to Barthes, it issues from the look of "non-art" and the studied spontaneity that aligns the first two of these to documentary photographs, and the third photograph to the genre of the portrait. Yet, like the others, this portrait of the writer works against the traditional sense of the genre, in this instance the sitter posed in the studio. Nor is the writer pictured with anyone else (other than herself). The social network is effaced, and the way opened for the operations of myth: the writer producing in isolation, when in fact the stories and novels of Lídia Jorge point to a way of working that is with and through the voices of others. In *O Dia dos Prodígios* the voices of the women are woven into a relentless litany of opinion and comment: "E Macário disse… E Matilde disse… E Manuel Gertrudes disse… disse Carminha Rosa… E Jesuína Palha disse."[6]

It was precisely this location of the human subject in a network of social relations that Walter Benjamin thought was photography's smartest achievement, a point he argued in his early essay of 1931 on "A Small History of Photography."[7] Portraits, in their early historical incarnation, could and did place the individual in the social formation according to the professions they chose or the class to which they belonged, visually legible by the dividing lines of dress or professional attributes as in the hat the sitter wore, such as the cloth cap of the working class or the bowler favored by middle class professionals. "Stamped on the photographic portraits made during the first decade of the medium's existence," writes Rosalind Krauss, "was the aura of both a human nature settling into its own specificity…and a social nexus exposed in terms of the intimacy of its relationships" by these amateur practitioners (Hill, Cameron, Hugo) who were making portrait pictures for their friends.[8] These intimate relationships are the stuff of Lídia Jorge's writing, the links, the voices both modern and mythical, the sense of social space that marks her work.

How we interpret the photographic portrait depends to a large extent on the photographed subject's gaze. How and where the look is directed has a bearing on what message is sent. A direct gaze into the camera eye can be considered in several opposing ways. In doing so, the subject acknowledges the presence of the photographer and the camera, but what are we to make of this? (It must be said, however, that the photographer and the camera eye aren't always synonymous. In Wim Wenders' *Lisbon Story*, the filmmaker hangs his camera on his back from which vantage point it records everything that he *doesn't* see.) Film theorists take differing positions on the meaning of this gaze, with the question of voyeurism as the central issue. If the subject meets our gaze, so the argument goes, voyeuristic peeping is diminished. Or, as Christian Metz argues in relation to cinema, the return gaze can be considered as the subject's permission to be watched.[9] Lídia Jorge not only gives us permission to look, but in her returned gaze and the offer of the photograph, she actively invites the spectator to do so.

That offer is literally framed by the writer's hands, which surround the photograph of the child. This frame, all frames, call attention to the picture, while at the same time separating it from the world that it reproduces. The hands section off the past from the present, childhood from adulthood, and hollow out a deep space between the face of the adult and the body of the child, as though to emphasize temporal distance. In the physical gap between the two resides human memory, the sense of what was and what is, what one has become. C.S. Sherrington, writing in the nineteenth century, referred to a sixth sense to which he gave the name "proprioception," described as the individual's consciousness of the body that confirms physical identity.[10] The adult memory of this child (Lídia Jorge remembering Lídia Jorge) is a physical, corporeal memory, as well as that imagined and handed down by others. Memory might be thought of as a seventh sense, as a record of antecedent existence upon which our intellectual identity depends.[11]

So, movement circulates between the active subject, the writer who offers the image of herself, the writer who produces meaning by writing, and the passive object of the photograph which receives the meanings constructed by the spectator in looking. Many acts inform the ways in which we see and the ways in which we remember our photographed past: projecting our own meanings onto photographs, voyeuristic looking, fantasy, and desire. In this instance, the camera doesn't present us with visual facts of the writer's life that are "simply there." Neither the photographer nor the spectator is disinterested. Each works with frames already in place to construct some particular picture according to a stock of available signs. That is why the figure of the writer framing herself adds yet another layer to available meanings.

Painters, of course, have long known the value of frames, both in the economic terms of their potential material richness and as a means of regulating the gaze. "Frame the work," Poussin commanded, so that "the gaze is contained and not scattered outside receiving other neighboring images pell-mell and confusing them with what is in the painting."[12] So as not to call attention to the frame itself, Poussin insisted that it be simple and not overly ornate. Matisse claimed that the frame was an important part of the picture in that it signaled the edge of the work, and that beyond the frame the continued movement of the picture could be implied. And Picasso, always alert to the ways in which common objects could be drafted into the service of art, looped a thick piece of rope into a frame surrounding the oval of his 1912 *Still Life and Chair Caning*, a gesture that revised the notion of the frame by using common materials that suggested the local vernacular of everyday speech. Framing is another way of controlling what is framed.

Finally, we might want to think of the role the family archive of pictures has in constituting individual memory, and how one is framed by that archive. Here is Roland Barthes, as he searches for a photograph of his mother after she died.[13] He is searching through the archive, and he begins in this way by working "back through a life, not my own, but the life of someone I love. Starting from the last image taken of his mother before her death, he arrived, traversing three-quarters of a century, at the image of a child. He stares at what he calls "the Sovereign Good of childhood." And what he finds in her first photograph, the photograph of the child, is also the last one that he finds. Perhaps this can tell us something about our photograph of "Lídia Jorge and Lídia Jorge," about the "Sovereign Good of childhood" and its survival in the adult.

Notes

I would like to thank Lídia Jorge and Luís Ramos for their generous permission to publish the photographs in this issue of *Portuguese Literary & Cultural Studies*.

[1] Comissariado Português Para a Europalia 91, *A Imagem das Palavras* (Lisbon: Contexto, 1991).

[2] Catherine Clement, *The Lives and Legends of Jacques Lacan* (New York: Columbia University Press, 1983) 76.

[3] Stephanie d'Orey, Interview with Lídia Jorge. In this issue of *Portuguese Literary & Cultural Studies.*

[4] Elizabeth Grosz, "Feminism after the Death of the Author," *Space, Time and Perversion: Essays on the Politics of Bodies* (New York: Routledge, 1995) 10-24.

[5] Roland Barthes," L'Ecrivain en vacances," *Mythologies* (Paris: Éditions du Seuil, 1957) 29-32.

[6] Lídia Jorge, *O Dia dos Prodígios* (Lisbon: Publ. Dom Quixote, 1995) 96-97.

[7] Walter Benjamin, "A Small History of Photography," *One Way Street and Other Writings*, trans. Edmund Jephcott and Kingsley Shorter (London: NLB, 1979).

[8] Rosalind Krauss, "Reinventing the Medium," *Critical Inquiry* 25 (Winter 1999): 291.

[9] Christian Metz, "From the Imaginary Signifier," in *Film Theory and Criticism: Introductory Readings*, eds. Gerald Mast and Marshall Cohen (New York: Oxford University Press, 1985) 782-802. A full discussion of the meaning of the subject's gaze and its role in photographs of non-Western subjects can be found in Catherine Lutz and Jane Collins, "The Photograph as an Intersection of Gazes: The Example of National Geographic," in *Visualizing Theory: Selected Essays From V.A. R. 1990-1994*, ed. Lucien Taylor, (New York: Routledge, 1994) 363-84.

[10] Oliver Sachs, "The Disembodied Lady," *The Man Who Mistook His Wife for a Hat* (London: Picador, 1985) 42-43.

[11] David MacDougall discusses the ways in which memory is translated in film dealing with historical periods in "Films of Memory," *Visualizing Theory: Selected Essays From V.A.R. 1990-1994*, ed. Lucien Taylor (New York: Routledge, 1994) 260-70.

[12] Nicholas Poussin, Letter to Chantelou, 28 April 1639, in *Correspondance de Nicolas Poussin*, ed. C. Jovanny (Paris: F. de Nobele, 1968) 20-21. On a discussion of the frame, see Louis Marin, "Du Cadre au décor ou la question de l'ornement dans la peinture," *Rivista di Estetica* (1982): 18-20.

[13] Roland Barthes, *Camera Lucida*, trans. Richard Howard (New York: Hill and Wang, 1981) 71.

Luís Ramos, "Lídia Jorge," 1990.
A Imagem das Palavras.
Comissariado Português Para a Europalia 91.
Lisbon: Contexto, 1991.

Luís Ramos, "The Writing Room in the Algarve," 1990
A Imagem das Palavras.
Comissariado Português Para a Europalia 91.
Lisbon: Contexto, 1991.

Luís Ramos, "Lídia Jorge in the Algarve,"
A Imagem das Palavras
Comissariado Português Para a Europalia 91.
Lisbon: Contexto, 1991.

O Romance e o Tempo Que Passa ou A Convenção do Mundo Imaginado

Lídia Jorge

Senhor Embaixador de Portugal em Londres
Amigos

1. Sempre hei-de recordar com inquietação, mas também com alguma malícia, certa carta anónima que recebi em 1980, ano da publicação d'*O Dia dos Prodígios*. Como estarão recordados, por essa altura, em Portugal, surgiram títulos e nomes que depois viriam a marcar a década de 80, e entre eles, esse meu primeiro livro não deixou de criar o seu rumor. Naturalmente que nem sempre concordante, e a carta a que me refiro ombreava com a opinião daqueles que nada de especial viam nessa narrativa e se insurgiram contra o bom acolhimento de que era alvo. Suspeito que ainda mantenha essa folha dobrada, metida no seu envelope, misturada com os papéis que sedimentam dentro das gavetas, transformada no pó arqueológico para onde se vai arrumando parte da desordem interna, e tê-la, desse modo, é o mesmo que não a ter, embora na memória se mantenha intacta.

Era uma carta de letra desenhada, inclinada para trás, riscos bicudos e retorcidos, em que o autor se apresentava sob o disfarce de UM INCONFORMADO. O inconformado começava por fazer uma listagem das imperfeições tipográficas da primeira edição desse texto, seguida duma crítica à inverosimilhança da história narrada n' *O Dia dos Prodígios*, para o que invocava por contraste, Alves Redol e Carlos de Oliveira, e terminava—nisso residia o mais interessante da carta anónima—com uma balada à morte do romance como género, ao que juntava alguns títulos preciosos de obras indispensáveis para que eu compreendesse como esse tipo de narrativa, a que eu andava a dizer pelos jornais ser o meu espaço de eleição, se encontrava à beira de desaparecer. Se acaso *O Dia dos Prodígios*, em si mesmo, não era já o sinal perfeito de que esse género se encontrava liquidado. Entre os livros indicados, como obra máxima recomendada para minha instrução, a dita carta sugeria *Le Livre à venir*, de Maurice Blanchot, já datado de 1959, e punha em relevo um dos capítulos sobre esse livro futuro, com o título de ECCE LIBER.—"Ecce liber," repetia várias vezes o cavalheiro anónimo da carta.

Ora "Ecce Liber" corresponde precisamente à primeira parte do quinto capítulo d'*O Livro por vir* publicado em Portugal só em 1984, mas está longe de constituir o anúncio do fim inefável do romance, da Literatura ou do quer que seja. Anuncia, sim, uma mudança, mas de outra natureza e alcance, um convite ao silêncio que escuta o sentido íntimo do livro em si, o que de modo nenhum era entendido, em 1980, pelo meu anónimo correspondente. Seja como for, essa carta que guardo na memória, e na altura me inquietou, não deixou de condensar à sua maneira, no diálogo que estabelecia com uma principiante desconhecida, a desconfiança que desde há muito se tem vindo a estabelecer em torno do destino da Literatura, muito em particular em torno do seu género mais acessível que é o romance. Por isso mesmo, mergulhado em áspero desencanto, o anónimo correspondente aconselhava-me a escrever pequenas histórias, breves contos incisivos, secos, que fossem direito ao proveito e exemplo e pudessem ser lidos enquanto se esperava pelo autocarro ou na fila do correio. Acaso eu não via que o tempo de leitura não se compaginava mais com o mundo actual? Acaso pertenceria eu, jovem autora, ao grupo daqueles que teimavam em não querer ser contemporâneos?—Perguntava, mais ou menos por estas palavras, o interlocutor anónimo. E era inquietante, claro. Na altura, ao contrário do que o encapotado aconselhava, estava eu a meio de *O Cais das Merendas*, um livro em tudo oposto ao que a carta predizia—era longo, descritivo, não ia direito ao exemplo, nem estava a ser construído para ser lido enquanto um autocarro chegava e outro partia. Pelo contrário, precisaria duma sólida mesa-de-cabeceira que o pudesse acolher e dum bom marcador para ser lido devagar, noite após noite, no sossego da casa. Fosse para que fosse, eu escrevia.

2. Escrevia porque na verdade nada se encontra predestinado, nem os géneros literários para cuja integridade, enquanto "géneros naturais," há todo um edifício feito que parece indestrutível. Só que os géneros e seus subgéneros são aniquilados ou desenvolvidos ao sabor do segmento da vontade individual de cada um, o que, no seu conjunto, herda e constrói a alma colectiva onde mergulhamos e donde emergimos, tão enredados e tão livres nesse fluxo

quanto o somos pelo impulso inevitável da História. Quer queiramos quer não, esbracejamos no tempo que já passou como náufragos, ainda que alegres naúfragos. Esbracejamos no presente, por instinto, como cegos, ainda que alegres cegos, e por isso é difícil qualquer um predizer ou adivinhar o que está predestinado. E em princípio, quem escreve é comandado por uma ordem interior, indiferente à curva da oportunidade. Pois tão útil é a pessoa que participa num tempo que declina, quanto aquele que participa naquele que ascende, desde que o seu projecto seja uma seta disparada a partir de dentro. Por isso, em relação ao romance, sua oportunidade e função, hoje em dia, encontro-me—já me encontrava—nos antípodas do anónimo inconformado da carta. Creio que o romance continua a desempenhar uma função que nenhum outro género desempenha, até porque o romance, género de narrativa recente, é o rosto visível do mundo contemporâneo, e mãe duma antropologia nova que ainda só há dois séculos fundámos, e que não pode estar prestes a terminar. Sou daqueles que se inquietam mas que crêem que a maquineta de Guttemberg não acabou, nem a Literatura nem sequer o romance, a forma literária mais versátil, dir-se-ia mesmo até a mais promíscua, no sentido positivo da plasticidade que "promiscuidade" pode assumir. A forma mais híbrida e adaptável da criação poética, não pode declinar a sua função deixando vazio o lugar que lhe pertence e nenhuma outra realidade até agora substitui.

3. No passado, sobretudo durante os anos 20 e 30, também se julgou que o cinema acabava de aniquilar o romance, incorporando a sua narrativa e ultrapassando-a pela visibilidade. O romance, que havia alcançado o ponto máximo com as coloridas e detalhadas páginas do romance realista e naturalista, parecia declinar, principalmente à medida que os filmes de Chaplin e Murnau davam lugar ao cinema falado. A palavra escrita, o resto da narrativa escrita, que era a legenda, desaparecia e mergulhava no fluxo oral da fala dos personagens, passando a palavra a ser tão evanescente e volátil como a música. No entanto, o cinema, como se sabe, não matou o romance, apenas o obrigou a transformar-se, a deslocar o seu ponto de vista para o interior dos seres. Como bem o provou Viginia Woolf, a partir de então já não se poderia mais descrever um gesto mas, sim, invocar o impulso que o impele. Nem a forma e a cor dum vestido, antes a intenção e o sentimento que explicava o seu uso ou exibição. Como se sabe, o romance saltou para dentro dos seres e acompanhou as trajectórias invisíveis e impalpáveis, a sudação interior dos rostos. Sobreviveu, precisamente, ao excesso de

visibilidade do cinema, ampliando a parte da sua câmara escura até às zonas abruptas do ser, aproximando-se mais e mais do incógnito coração do homem.

Mas os anos 40 e 50 desencadearam outro tipo de pessimismo. Tendo nascido no regaço da burguesia, acaso o romance não estava trespassado dos sentimentos de contradição que o mundo de contrastes sociais arrastava consigo? Não era o romance o género próprio da desavença inglória das paixões tristes, dos sentimentos frustrados por incapacidade, sentimentos de miséria narcísica que o romance explorava de forma gostosa? Era. Pois um dia, quando as sociedades fossem justas e viris—e isso iria acontecer amanhã—o romance iria ser expulso desse lugar pernicioso onde engendrara a sua fórmula condenada. Morreria de morte natural, à medida que a igualdade de oportunidades fizesse de cada cidadão um homem feliz, integrado, teleologicamente, num todo salvador da terrena Humanidade. Isso era o que os jovens universitários dos anos 60 pensavam, encarando a teia de *La Jalousie,* de Alain Robbe-Grillet, como uma obsessão infértil e reaccionária, ainda que muitos de nós nunca tivessem lido teóricos como George Lukács. Mas como ele pensávamos que, por certo, o romance viria a desaparecer sucumbido sob as luzes da Liberdade, da Igualdade e da Fraternidade. O que, infelizmente, como se sabe, não aconteceu. Desse ponto de vista, pelo contrário, o Mundo tornou-se cada vez mais ficcional. A previsão de Lukács funcionou na direcção oposta. E depois? Depois, juntou-se o argumento da velocidade, da fuga do tempo, da comunicação simultânea, do circo mirabolante da rapidez, acção, acção, ser como acção, rapidez como fibra do ser, modo a que já se associava, de forma tortuosa, o interlocutor da carta anónima.

Ainda nos anos 70, a ideia de que os grandes paquetes tinham sido afundados ou enferrujavam nos cais e que os comboios iriam ser ultrapassados para sempre por uma outra qualquer máquina deveria ter criado nessas nossas cabeças românticas o pressuposto de que já não haveria mais aquele cavalheiro de bengala e fato de linho com um romance aberto sobre os joelhos tranquilos. Porém, o avião, os aeroportos, ironicamente, iriam ser contemporâneos duma difusão de livros e dos romances, com uma nova lógica, talvez surpreendente lógica, mas que de modo nenhum pode estar ligada a qualquer ideia de morte do romance. Nunca se saberá avaliar, evidentemente, quanto Milan Kundera ou Umberto Eco devem à difusão livreira dos aeroportos. Passando adiante, hoje, o argumento é outro.

Talvez mais sério, talvez mais radical. O que hoje se diz é que o romance, na era da informação e da criação da realidade virtual, não só já não conta nem informa, como não pode competir com a força da "vida vivida" directamente oferecida pelo ciber-espaço, em contraste com a "vida pensada" que o romance oferece. Isto é, vivendo o romance da pantalha imaginada pelo leitor e da captação individual do sentido, estaremos perante a explosão total da informação, assistindo à implosão do significado, segundo diz Baudrillard, pois estaremos à beira da dispensa do tempo do intervalo. O intervalo, o tempo de repouso que medeia entre abrir um livro e reconstituir uma cena ou apenas ler uma frase e imaginar a cena ou movermo-nos por dentro dos sentidos múltiplos da frase. À beira de perder o intervalo da participação pessoal. E assim, o verdadeiro pós-modernismo estaria aí estipulando e estrangulando não só o romance mas também a própria escrita. E todos estes argumentos seriam não só fortes como decisivos, não fora o facto de que, cada dia que passa, novos leitores aparecem, novas linguagens surgem cruzadas e novos cultores do romance surgem, novas formas se engedram dentro dele, imperturbáveis na sua permanente metamorfose, parecendo ser melhores aqueles que reivindicam para dentro do corpo ficcional o que continua a ser-lhe específico—o jogo activo das personagens no seu espelho de criação de alteridades, e a poética do discurso construído na ideia de que, ao mundo e seu ruído, é preciso juntar palavras rodeadas de silêncio. Hoje em dia percebe-se, como se houvesse um decreto implícito, que à vida humana e sua fábula é indispensável acrescentar fábulas.

4. E no caso português?

No território cultural português, onde os rumores de fim são sempre acolhidos com particular agrado, a estas oscilações de crença e descrença no género tem acrescido a convicção particular de que não somos dotados para a narrativa, apresentando-se o lirismo como a base propulsora do nosso espírito criador. Qualquer balanço cultural, alargado ou conciso, apresenta como ponto assente que os portugueses são visceralmente inclinados à Poesia, com destaque para Camões no século XVI e, mais recentemente, Pessoa. Na narrativa, entre um ou outro nome desgarrado, apenas brilha Eça de Queirós, no século XIX. Quando se procuram duas linhas para condensar os países, não há pois muito que sofrer connosco. A síntese já aparece feita.

Aliás, por vezes, torna-se mesmo interessante ver como aqueles que mais acreditam na ficção portuguesa, esses mesmos, precisam de buscar na raiz poética o esteio que dê unidade à produção romanesca. O próprio Eduardo

Lourenço, entre nós, de longe o ensaísta mais destacado, para proceder ao balanço do romance português não raro se socorre das balizas da Poesia. Célebre se tornou um dos seus ensaios datado de 1966, publicado então na revista *O Tempo e o Modo*, para o qual encontrava como epígrafe a certa frase de Léon Chestov: "Obedece-se, na vida literária, ao costume dos naturais da Terra do Fogo: os jovens matam e comem os mais velhos." Mas avaliado um conjunto diverso de escritores de romance tão diferentes entre si quanto o então recém--aparecido Almeida Faria e Agustina Bessa-Luís, Cardoso Pires, Abelaira, Ruben A., Maria Judite de Carvalho ou Vergílio Ferreira, Eduardo Lourenço deduziria, em sentido contrário ao de León Chestov, que "há jovens tardios e velhos precoces, no sentido próprio e figurado," e utilizava como denominador comum para esse grupo heterogéneo de ficcionistas, como título, uma imagem retirada de uma das sombras mais vitais de Pessoa—"Uma Literatura Desenvolta ou os Filhos de Álvaro de Campos." Aliás, em determinado momento, escrevia mesmo: "A nova prosa deita-se na antiga cama da Literatura portuguesa com o à-vontade supremo do gato de Pessoa."

Passados quase trinta anos, ainda é nessa perspectiva, a da raiz poética, que se continuam a fazer muitos dos balanços sobre a fortuna do romance escrito em Portugal. É comum fazer confrontar os escritores de romance actual não só com a aporia de que a prosa actual parece filha da "narrativa" de Álvaro de Campos, na sequência daquela síntese de Eduardo Lourenço, como, mais proximamente, é costume apresentar a publicação do *Livro do Desassossego*, no final da década de 80, como o grande acontecimento, em torno do qual as narrativas ficcionais facilmente se arrumam em forma de constelação. Isto é, os que lhe são parentes e os afastados—ou aqueles romances que desestruturam por dentro o pensamento, des-narrando, como Pessoa na máscara de Bernardo Soares, e os que se envolvem com uma narrativa unida com a História comum, ou pelo menos mais próximo da convenção do calendário social reconhecível. Mas felizmente, tanto quanto me lembro, na carta do meu correspondente anónimo, não surgia este argumento—o argumento lusitano de que o génio português é lírico, e que, por isso, acrescidamente, não seria oportuno enveredar pelo caminho do romance.

5. Aliás, regressando à carta anónima e ao momento em que foi escrita, 1980, será uma falta imperdoável não reconhecer que, a partir desse período, se começou a falar em termos respeitosos do romance português, em questão de quantidade, diversidade, bem como em originalidade. No início dessa

década, assistiu-se a um encontro interessante de duas gerações que coexistiram e que, à parte os desentendimentos típicos, dialogaram, naquilo que se entende por diálogo na criação—a uns livros sucederam outros, com propostas estéticas diversificadas, empurrados que nos encontrávamos pelo momento de inquietação que a mudança social e política proporcionava. Só assim se entende que escritores de obra já então produzida, como José Cardoso Pires, Vergílio Ferreira, Urbano Tavares Rodrigues, Fernando Namora, Maria Isabel Barreno, ou Maria Velho da Costa, tenham revigorado as suas obras, publicando alguns dos melhores livros durante esses anos, e que ao mesmo tempo um número tão significativo de novos autores tenha surgido—era o momento em que João de Melo, Mário de Carvalho, Mário Cláudio, Lobo Antunes, Teolinda Gersão, Hélia Correia e muitos outros publicavam o primeiro livro, alguns deles, o segundo. Mas de entre todos, o caso mais particular viria a ser o de José Saramago, que, pela idade, se colocava entre os mais velhos, mas pela forma alinhava entre os mais novos, colocando-se-lhes à frente, na experimentação, no virtuosismo e também no volume de produção. Naturalmente que nunca existem causas suficientes para explicar um momento. Talvez este nunca se explique.

A menos que se possa associar o que foi a feliz coincidência de ter havido em Portugal uma Revolução muito própria, já que se tratava dum movimento que punha termo não a uma ditadura qualquer mas a uma ditadura de 48 anos que albergava dentro de si não só um colossal atraso mas também a última guerra colonial em África, movida pelo último país europeu obstinado na determinação de ser multicontinental, segundo o modelo imperial do século XVI, com o facto de ter sido contemporânea, essa revolução, da vitalidade e crença na narrativa ficcional, que o romance sul-americano estava desencadeando nos anos 70, fazendo reagir, a vários níveis, a ficção europeia. Continuo a suspeitar que foi da acção desses dois factores—a História portuguesa que eclodia na nossa sociedade e o tipo de vitalidade que as obras amplamente difundidas de Juan Ruflo, Vargas Llosa, Cortázar, Lezama Lima e Gabriel Garcia Márquez demonstravam face aos modelos anémicos e desconstrutivistas, sobretudo o dessorado romance francês de então, bem como o já repetido romance de matriz pascaliana e existencialista e, em particlar, o *nouveau-roman*—que se impôs a certeza de que a aposta nos modos tradicionais de dizer, na exuberância barroca da forma, no feixe de elementos constitutivos da identidade dos países, na sua história particular, no seu fabulário e fantasia, nessa espécie de capacidade de universalizar o regional, foi tudo isso em conjunto que permitiu que a crença no romance como género se afirmasse de novo. Voltando à História, a portuguesa, acontece uma vez no século, na vida de cada país, tanta mudança operar-se em conjunto.

Na verdade, o que sucedia a Portugal em 1974 era alguma coisa mais do que passar dum estado de ditadura para uma democracia. Em 25 de Abril de 74 assistia-se ao encerramento dum ciclo imperial iniciado no século XV, e que vinha a prolongar-se em agonia com a ditadura. Isto é, o país de dois milhões de habitantes que havia liderado os Descobrimentos marítimos ibéricos e europeus, e que havia dilatado a sua geografia pelo Mundo, era obrigado, naquela madrugada de 74, a confrontar-se com o apoucamento do seu corpo imperial fantasmático até à dimensão do núcleo original—umas centenas de milhares de quilómetros de costa atlântica, no extremo oeste do continente europeu. O que significava que iria ser forçoso escolher outro apoio e outro compadrio geográfico, e que a nossa hiperidentidade iria ser posta à prova face à Europa que nos viria a acolher. O que significou também que o nosso projecto de futuro, do novo futuro, ficaria em causa e em discussão. E que o passado precisaria de ser revisto e de novo narrado. A Guerra Colonial sonegada, o exílio, o isolamento da juventude portuguesa, bem como a ocultação, todas as ocultações, passando pelo número dos mortos e estropiados, até outras mais subtis, como era a ocultação dos sentimentos da memória e a ocultação do corpo, de súbito, tudo isso poderia ser revelado. Ficcionalmente, esse momento permitia um ajuste de contas com a realidade, desmedido de amplo e novo que era. Todas as Artes estavam implicadas nessa provocação. Creio que os ficcionistas portugueses cumpriram-no em toda a dimensão, incluindo a parte do ajuste, que é sempre o objectivo mais mesquinho, na globalidade dum acto criador, e contudo não menos vivaz.

No seu conjunto, os escritores portugueses, na década de 80, foram capazes de construir a partir do território do país, o romance a que Carlos Fuentes tipificou como "Segunda História," isto é, o romance como escrita da história, engendrada contra o realismo de a contar. A propósito do romance como género, escreveu esse escritor em *Geografía de la novela*: "Trata-se da criação da outra história, de uma segunda história, que cega e diminui os historiadores de arquivo. E a segunda história manifesta-se através da escrita individual, porém, propõe-se como a memória e projecto (quer dizer, como realidade verdadeira) de uma colectividade, por definição, danada. E à luz da redenção, no dizer de Adorno, o mundo aparece, inevitavelmente, deformado."

Penso que foi isso exactamente o que os escritores portugueses da década de 80 foram capazes de fazer, ordenando-se, naturalmente, pelas suas diferentes sensibilidades em torno do que se poderia chamar ora de uma poética angélica, que engloba escritores como Hélia Correia, João de Melo e mais claramente José Saramago ou José Cardoso Pires de *Alexandra Alpha*, ora duma poética de expressionismo psicológico própria de Lobo Antunes e Almeida Faria, ora uma poética de reconstituição como é a de Fernando Campos, João Aguiar, por vezes Mário de Carvalho e principalmente Mário Cláudio. A estes aspectos de crónica do tempo e da história me parece dever acrescentar-se o facto de, no plano da linguagem, o romance português desta década ter apostado particularmente na vertente metafórica da língua, não enjeitando nem os aspectos da ruralidade arcaica, nem da assimilação dos estrangeirismos como modo poético, sem jamais ceder aos modos apaziguadores da narrativa ligeira, aquela em que a acção parece delineada de propósito para se converter em *script* para cinema ou televisão.

Pelo contrário, o que fez a estranheza do romance escrito em Portugal, nesta época, e que lhe dá identificação e singularidade, é a aposta no plano contrário—a aposta nos recursos poéticos da língua e na forma entornada, quando não labiríntica, de narrar. A aposta em estruturas paralelas que por vezes lhe retiram unidade mas as transformam em peças barrocas muito próprias. A que se deve acrescentar outro aspecto—o facto de o romance, saído das mãos das mulheres, ter surgido assumidamente com a marca feminina, incorporando a desenvoltura legada pela escrita de mulheres que as precederam. A incorporação do ponto de vista próprio da mulher, em geral atravessado, no plano simbólico e metafórico, por um corpo poético de resolução circular, ajudou a enriquecer o romance da década de 80, cujos traços se prolongam pela década actual. Por isso partilho da opinião de Georges Frassard quando afirma a propósito da actual ficção portuguesa: "Os portugueses, a meio caminho entre a Europa, a África e a América Latina, e revitalizados na sua consciência por uma forte experiência traumática em África, terão criado, durante os anos que se seguiram à Revolução, uma das mais genuínas e singulares poéticas do velho continente, cujo pequeno país a que pertencem não tem meios de promover à altura."

6. Mas todo o momento, por unido que seja, não passa de um intervalo, e olhando para anos mais recentes, pode-se dizer que actualmente se assiste, em conjunto, a uma trajectória que se inclina rapidamente para outras direcções. Sem querer fazer depender a criação literária da conjunção

histórica —que só em parte e misteriosamente a determina—, diria que o ciclo do país que se iniciou, o novo ciclo que a Europa está a atravessar, e o próprio momento do Mundo na sua alteração de valores e definição de metas, bem como a perplexidade que a presente mutação está erguendo, parece determinar novos caminhos e abrir a narrativa a novos modos e inquietações, de onde sobressai uma relação alargada com o devir global. A maior parte dos romances publicados durante o ano de 1995 é atravessada por um acentuado cunho escatológico, e entre eles, *Ensaio sobre a Cegueira* constitui uma das parábolas mais terríveis de aviso sobre a lógica do mundo ocidental. Mário Cláudio, na senda de Eça de Queirós, de um outro fim de século, publicou *A Batalha do Caia*, narrativa sobre um imaginado aniquilamento cultural do país face à invasão exterior. O livro de Mário de Carvalho sobre o fim do Comunismo, escrito de forma irónica, tem o título displicente de *Era Bom que Trocássemos Umas Ideias sobre o Assunto* e solta um riso lacónico sobre a desorientação das ideologias. Em *A Casa da Cabeça de Cavalo*, Teolinda Gersão mistura os tempos criando uma dramaturgia de abraço entre mortos e vivos. Baptista Bastos publicou *O Cavalo a Tinta da China*, reconstituição dos tempos do ditador, visto agora à distância e devolvido para o futuro com o desprendimento que o correr do tempo dá. Manuel Alegre também aí regressa, ainda que por outra via—*Com Alma*, um livro de extraordinária frescura. É o mundo dos anos 40 e 50 que regressa, atravessado da lembrança reveladora duma infância que explica a própria poesia do autor enquanto poeta. Eu mesma publiquei *O Jardim sem Limites*. E muitos outros que seria oportuno enumerar, mas fastidioso e inútil nestas circunstâncias. Para não esquecer nomes mais recentes como são os de Pedro Paixão ou José Riço Direitinho, com um outro acento, mais descontraído e mais ligeiro. Não interessa. No conjunto, de novo regressa a vitalidade, e o sentido da contemporaneidade, aos romances portugueses.

7. No entanto, nem todos estarão de acordo com estas palavras. Sei que nem sequer os meus colegas directamente implicados costumam fazer um balanço tão positivo como este. Não desconheço que muitos até entendem que além de si mesmos, o resto é paisagem de pasto curto. Não duvido que por vezes entre os balanços que fazemos—e não são fáceis—sucedem disparidades de avaliação, principalmente quando têm a palavra os mais conhecidos. Faz parte do reforço do ego dos criadores, e do jogo fratricida que funciona, por vezes, como estímulo pelo menos para os próprios. Mas nada disso importa.

Aliás, talvez a dificuldade que por vezes se encontra ao falar da Literatura mais recente esteja no facto de cada um de nós ter investido em caminhos muito pessoais e ter buscado trilhos que não raramente se encontram mais frequentados por escritores longínquos do que por escritores da mesma nacionalidade. E eu mesma me pergunto se a língua comum, as línguas nacionais, continuarão a condicionar de forma determinante como até aqui. É que de súbito, para o bem e para o mal, o mundo ficou mais próximo, e todos nós ficámos nómadas. As minhas inquietações têm fronteiras cujos limites não sei determinar, e os meus gostos coincidem pontualmente com os de escritores de países distantes como se estivessem perto. Escrevi *O Dia dos Prodígios* e *A Costa dos Murmúrios*, mas dou por mim a desejar ter escrito um livro como *Porto-Sudão* de Olivier Rolin. Desejaria ter sido eu a escrever aquelas linhas sobre a Geração de 60 partida ao meio, metade cínica, materialista e tiunfante, e metade vencida, cabisbaixa, agarrada a uma flor de utopia destroçada, tal como ele escreveu a propósito de África. *Porto-Sudão* é, na minha cabeça, a continuação d'*A Costa dos Murmúrios* que outro escreveu por mim, em meu nome. Ou Cees Noteboom. *A História Seguinte* é uma narrativa que eu quereria ter escrito. Quereria ter escrito não só porque se trata da divagação dum homem que se deita em Amesterdão e acorda "morto" num hotel de Lisboa, e por Lisboa divaga, mas sobretudo porque passa em revista a poética ocidental sobre as estrelas do firmamento. Quereria ter sido eu a escrever as breves páginas desse livro quase sem espessura material e tamanha espessura de sentidos. Queria ter inventado aquele barco que se desloca com um professor de Filosofia a invocar a História mitológica das constelações. Não escrevi nenhum deles, escrevi *O Jardim sem Limites*, um livro sobre a história dum homem parado numa praça, resistindo e superando-se na sua imobilidade até à morte. Talvez Cees Noteboom e Olivier Rolin nunca cheguem a ler as minhas páginas. Se as lerem talvez nem desejem tê-las escrito por seu punho, como eu desejei ter feito com os seus próprios livros. Talvez. Mas aí entra o sentido exacto do capítulo de Maurice Blanchot, "Ecce Liber," baseado, sobretudo, na poética de Mallarmé e que remete para um livro único que está escrito, do qual cada um de nós atinge uma página, talvez uma linha ou uma palavra, ou outros a acham por nós, e não importa o nome de quem a acha, porque o escrito poderia ser anómimo, e mesmo assim, cada um continuaria a narrar mesmo que não assinasse. Escreveu Mallarmé, poeta entre os poetas: "Julgo tudo isto escrito na natureza de maneira a só deixar fechados os olhos aos interessados em não ver nada. Esta obra existe, toda a gente a tentou sem saber; não há génio ou farsante que não tenha encontrado um traço dela no seu rosto."

8. Assim é.

Compreenderão agora por que razão decorei a carta do anónimo insatisfeito que me escreveu a propósito de *O Dia dos Prodígios*. Maliciosamente, à distância, acho que ainda bem que a escreveu, para lhe poder dizer que se enganou redondamente, em tudo e em toda a linha. O tempo passa, os livros visíveis acontecem, o Inconformado não tinha razão.

Interview with Lídia Jorge

Stephanie d'Orey
Translated by Stephanie d'Orey
Assisted by John Brookesmith

When did you decide to become a writer, and what were the influences that helped you?

There is a considerable difference between writing as a way of being, which implies having an inventive attitude of mind to life itself and to being a writer, with all its professional and ontological implications. I know that I decided to write very early—at fifteen I was already publishing short pieces. I understood what it meant to be a writer only when I published my first novel. The idea of writing and being a writer had been taking shape in my head for a long time, without my being able to state it—it was possible only when my first novel had appeared.

Is your first book O Dia dos Prodígios, *to some to some extent autobiographical? If so, which are the elements of it that relate to your childhood experiences?*

The autobiographical elements of *O Dia dos Prodígios* are contained in the atmosphere, the imaginative experience of the rural world where I spent my childhood, the kind of relationships I consciously observed, particularly between individuals and the community in a world closed in on itself, but susceptible to dreams and fantasy. The physical space, the prophetic voices of the characters, the interpretation of life through metaphor, the slow pace of life, people's capacity for an almost enigmatic patience—these are all things I myself lived through and can be said to be autobiographical. Just as I endured a fear of snakes, strongly associated with the fascination unleashed by them. Aspects of some characters, such as Manuel Gertrudes or Jesuína Palha were drawn from real people. None of the rest were. But as for the rest of them, that is open to question.

Some passages in O Dia dos Prodígios *describe the condition of women in minute detail; for example, Carminha washing a window. What are you wanting to say about the female characters in the book?*

The women in *O Dia dos Prodígios* are still prisoners of "tent and clan," that is to say, of home and family. Few ever leave that place except in their dreams and in their connection to an ideal of an outside world. Curiously, more or less the same thing happens to the men in Vilamaninhos. However, this should not be interpreted as an accusation. It is simply the case. Nobody knows why fine and good characteristics are not always balanced. The three female figures, Carminha, Carma, and Branca, who express the most their sense of imprisonment, are also the ones who make use of the rituals of magic. Carminha washes windows as if waving goodbye, and there she remains, still cleaning them. It is a gesture I associate with women, in all places and ages, an unspoken expression of feeling. It is an appeal and at the same time an affirmation.

As a woman writer, what do your novels say about the condition of women in Portugal?

I think my novels take stock of a Mediterranean image of woman. Their strength is powerful and subversive, more invisible than socially apparent. Politics may still pass them by. The family still seems as if a given by nature rather than by the culture. In my novels the women complain about their lot. As I am not a feminist writer, in the traditional sense, I don't portray them as victims; neither do I give them good characters to contrast the evil ones. I'm not constructing a simplistic dichotomy. Humankind has two faces—the angelic and the savage. My women have too. The lament I make about the human condition is staged mainly around the women because I am more familiar with them. And also Portuguese women have been the interpreters of the most violent change. I cannot help but echo such difficult times.

What kind of roles do the women play in your novels?

In general the men they love neither understand nor listen to them. The incompatibility of language between men and women is one of my themes, just as another theme is the lack of communication between citizens and institutions. When it comes to women, they are often in the company of their children, whose language also escapes them. I don't know if what I am saying is really true, but I suspect that the women in my books, in general, confuse their love of men and their loyalty to God or country. They are not virile heroines. They are figures of protest.

Are you conscious of writing in a different way to other Portuguese writers because you are a woman?

We can't take ourselves to pieces. I am a woman of professional standing, and I have to say that some of my writings must be a record of the passing of time and others about life as I imagine it. How could I write at all without such a distinction—being a woman and being called Lídia? Certainly my books talk of a world of which another person couldn't speak at all. From my themes to the very structure of the text, everything has to be impregnated with my own style. Without wanting to judge myself, I recognize in myself a peculiarity, or even a certain style. Within that there is the memory of the girl I once was, of the books I read which touched me the most, of the music of the words that I was storing away in my head. Having been a girl must have marked my mode of expression.

O Dia dos Prodígios *was first published in 1980. When did you start writing it, or thinking about it?*

I started thinking about *O Dia dos Prodígios* after the Revolution[1] and it was written between 1976 and 1978. It was a book about a community which nonetheless originated in reality: my own grandfather, José Jorge Júnior, lying in his sick bed, confusing the dead with the living, my face with those of his wives and his lost daughters. In one hour the sky fell to earth. I believe this happened in 1975.

When was it finished? Would it have been possible to have published this earlier if you had wanted to? (that is, before 1974?)

I finished writing it in the summer of 1978. No, it would not have been possible to have published it earlier. In the first place because I myself would not have been able to have written it, and secondly because the book is rooted in a metaphor of liberation that wouldn't have been compatible with the previous régime.

How did this book relate to other writing being published at the time?

Around 1980 books started to be written by my generation about the themes of oppression and freedom, politics and ontology, if you can call it that, that assumed a great importance. Older writers were also sensitive to the change. The public itself was receptive to this totally new way of seeing things as they are. The theme of liberation from oppression inspired us enormously.

Do you see yourself as belonging to a particular school of writing? (or group of writers) If so, how would you describe it and which other writers belong to it?

As I said earlier, I can't isolate myself from an experience at the very heart of the particular recent history of this country. I am part of a generation which has witnessed change very much its own, and includes writers Maria Velho da Costa, Almeida Faria, Mário de Carvalho, Teolinda Gersão, Lobo Antunes, João de Melo or Hélia Correia, to name but a few. But in relation to writing, each one of us has a personal way of spelling out what has to be told. From this point of view I feel much closer to some writers of other generations and other literatures. This has to do with my temperament and with my reading at the time my taste and literary personality were being formed.

What are your own views on European social and ethical questions? Are these reflected in your work?

I feel happy in large spaces. I like flags but not frontiers. The idea that Portugal could become included in a space far larger than the Peninsula always seemed desirable to me, especially because I observed firsthand what would be going to happen with Africa, which has become not unnaturally our second territory. The option of Portugal to link itself with other European countries, at a time when the Community was expanding, seemed to me not only to be a good idea but inevitable. Today, I fear what everyone fears: that the rich diversity is succumbing to changes in social organization which are now taking place, [and] also that Portuguese culture, although resisting, will survive only in a vestigial form. But this issue is being hotly debated. In other sectors of activity, some people may feel depressed. Those who are writers know that on this topic there always remains something to be said. Words exist to be spoken. Somebody is going to say what they mean. In my books, it is true, some of my characters are destined to be afraid of being themselves; they wish to be like everyone else, bowing down to the rest of the world and barely raise their own flag. It seems that is what I've said, but not on purpose. My second book *O Cais das Merendas* has this idea as its central motive.

How did the experience of living in Africa influence your work?

Living in Africa was a decisive experience. Africa spread before my very eyes the theatre of life. I'm referring to the end of the sixties and the first half of the seventies. From the position in which I found myself, I understood what it was to oppress and to be oppressed, what is was to have a comfortable life as well as to be alienated, what it was to be a guerrilla and a soldier. But, as time went on, life as lived in the Portuguese colonies also taught me that what exists on one side is found also on the other. Each is a mirror image of the other. Death and amputation, too often present, made this duplicity clear. These conditions proved in the main that insofar as one Utopia is being built up, another will be about to fail. Liberation would be followed by another war and another betrayal. The wheel of civilization and history was plain to see. It was impossible for me to disengage myself from Africa's future. My writing was almost writing itself, with the destiny of that land as its horizon. *A Costa dos Murmúrios* is a novel about the memory of war in Mozambique at the end of the sixties. It is a record of a lull in the drama of a confrontation between cultures, and it was written to assist in preserving the memory of that time.

Your last book, O Jardim sem Limites *has been immensely popular. What is it saying about living in Portugal today?*

This is an unusual book, but not too far removed from earlier ones. Its youthful characters marginalize themselves in Lisbon as it becomes an international city. They want to belong to this cosmopolitan world, which they perceive as a garden. But in contrast with those who were indeed born in Eden, born between the fantastic rivers which surrounded it, the characters of *O Jardim* have to make the circuit of the garden which they are exploring. The book tells of their bitter, violent, and fragmented journey, in a language of their own which portrays their lifestyle. They are heroic, tenacious, with enormous staying power. I am writing about people who make use of these capacities without knowing how. It is a book about the new indifference. This tribe of young people wanders the streets of Lisbon, blinkered from each other. They are not just a group of young people: they are also ourselves. The Rua Augusta, the street where the characters roam about, is superimposed upon a much larger canvas. That too is ours. If this were not the case, I wouldn't have written it.

Do your books sell well in Portugal?

Well, in Portugal there's no way you could sell as many as ten million copies of a novel—editions of 3,000 are customary. So, I can't complain—some of my books have run to ten impressions, and one sold over 50,000 copies in under a year. Not all sales have been as good as that, but I don't think things have been too bad.

Which titles are selling best?

The titles that have sold best are *O Dia dos Prodígios, Notícia da Cidade Silvestre, A Costa dos Murmúrios*, and *O Jardim sem Limites.*

What type of readers do you think read your books?

I don't really know how to estimate this. I think my public is very mixed. Although reader surveys indicate a mainly sophisticated or academic readership, I have been surprised by a scattered readership from very diverse backgrounds. In Portugal, the percentage of women readers is high, and this is an important factor. I suspect that many of my readers are women.

How are women writers regarded now in Portugal?

I think that today there is no discrimination at all—either positive or negative. There are fewer women writers than men, but they progress through the normal channels and gain a public that corresponds to their styles of writing. Any tensions that do exist are due more to personalities or the works themselves, rather than to gender.

Have attitudes towards women writers changed since your book was published?

When *O Dia dos Prodígios* was published, other women writers were also emerging. We were newcomers at the time, and it was said that there was feminist solidarity around our books. I really don't accept that. Other types of solidarity were created, both vis-à-vis male writers and in support of already known women writers. I think this continues to be the case—that qualities which make a work unpopular with one section of the public can make it appreciated by another. I'd like to believe that as far as published writing goes, Portuguese women's writing is as much respected or disrespected as writing by men.

What do you think was, at that time, the real significance of the New Portuguese Letters, *by "The Three Marias"? Did it influence your work?*

The *New Portuguese Letters* is about female desire. This was considered a crime in the seventies. Through the discourse itself, and the audacity of those amazing women writers, this book became a literary icon. It opened a way for us, which we have all more or less followed. Today, sensuality and eroticism are expressed in free and fluid language through fictional characters, helping to define their personalities. These are different times. Nowadays, assertion of our independence in matters of sexual behavior no longer has any great literary impact. This has now been achieved throughout western culture. Now the thematic contradiction, which we are struggling to resolve, focuses on the diffuse subject of love, which appears to be almost unattainable. This is a major theme of today.

Are there more women writers now than there were then, and do you think that women writers are still under-represented in contemporary Portuguese literature?

The number of women writers has been increasing, but yet comparatively little writing is being produced, due not to lack of talent, but to pressures upon their lives. I'm talking about professional and personal lives. The literary promise of woman writers, with some notable exceptions, continues to be less incisive and less productive.

Into how many languages has your work been translated?

Spanish, French, American English, German, Italian, and Dutch.

Which books have been most translated?

A Costa dos Murmúrios, *O Dia dos Prodígios*, and *Notícia da Cidade Silvestre.*

What do you think of your readership abroad? Is it different from that in Portugal?

I think there isn't much difference. My books aren't very popular. I think they are bought by the public interested in Portuguese literature; other readers are curious to read books originating in an Iberian culture, written by a woman. I don't know about the rest.

Have they been selling well?

Some have, especially those published in German by Suhrkampf. In Spain and France, luckily, sales seem reasonable.

Which books are being translated at the moment?

O Jardim sem Limites and various short stories are now being translated into German, French, and Spanish.

What do you know about other Portuguese writing in translation? Does it fall into any particular category?

Some Portuguese writers are having a lot of success in translation. Apart from Fernando Pessoa—the great discovery of this last decade!—and some young novelists and poets, there are older writers such as José Saramago,[2] Lobo Antunes, Agustina Bessa-Luís, João Cardoso Pires, and Vergílio Ferreira. I think there is a fascination with writers judged to be difficult, who can tackle poetic themes within structures that have a certain complexity, that deserve careful attention. I think that people who are acquainted with Portuguese fiction may also appreciate it as being from the outer limits of Europe, and as having unusual inventiveness and original patterns of development. This is without mentioning the not displeasing impression it gives of life in this country. As one knows, Portugal is a nation which, due to its history and geography, has acquired clearly defined relations with other cultures. I'm not saying that Portuguese literature has been overlooked, but a great deal would be lost if one were to do so.

An abridged version of this interview was published in October 1997 by the European Bookseller, *London, UK.*

Notes

[1] The Portuguese Revolution, 25th April 1974.

[2] Winner of the 1998 Nobel Prize for Literature.

Selected Bibliography

Cláudia Pazos Alonso

I. Primary Sources

Jorge, Lídia. *O Dia dos Prodígios*. 1980.

———. *O Cais das Merendas*. 1982.

———. *Notícia da Cidade Silvestre*. 1984.

———. *A Costa dos Murmúrios*. 1988.

———. *A Última Dona*. 1992.

———. *A Instrumentalina*. 1992. (conto)

———. *O Jardim sem Limites*. 1995.

———. *A Maçon*. 1996. (teatro)

———. *Marido e Outros Contos*. 1997.

———. *O Vale da Paixão*. 1998.

Translation into English

Jorge, Lídia. *The Murmuring Coast*. Trans. Natália Costa and Ronald W. Sousa. Minneapolis & London: University of Minnesota Press, 1995.

II. Secondary Sources

1. General on Portuguese Women's Writing since 1974

Ferreira, Ana Paula. "Reengendering History: Women's Fictions of the Portuguese Revolution." *After the Revolution: Twenty Years of Portuguese Literature*. Ed. Helena Kaufman and Anna Klobucka. London: Associated University Presses, 1997.

Magalhães, Isabel Allegro de. *O Sexo dos Textos*. Lisboa: Editorial Caminho, 1995.

———. "Portuguese Fiction Written by Women after April 1974: Some Innovative Features." *Portuguese Studies* 10 (1994). Revised version in *Gender, Ethnicity and Class in Modern Portuguese-Speaking Culture*. Ed. Hilary Owen. Lampeter: Edwin Mellen Press, 1996.

Owen, Hilary. "'Um Quarto Que Seja Seu': The Quest for Camões's Sister.'" *Portuguese Studies* 11 (1995): 179-91.

2. On Lídia Jorge

Berg, Eliana. "*O Dia dos Prodígios*, Escrita Prodigiosa." *Colóquio/Letras* 132-133 (1994): 148-56.

Bulger, Laura. "*O Cais das Merendas* de Lídia Jorge: Uma Identidade Cultural Perdida?" *Colóquio/Letras* 82 (1984): 51-57.

Cabral, Maria Manuela Lacerda. "*A Costa dos Murmúrios* de Lídia Jorge: Inquietação Pós-Moderna." *Revista da Faculdade de Letras do Porto* XIV (1997): 265-87

Engelmayer, Elfriede. "Fronteiras, ou, por Outras Palavras, o *Jardim sem Limites* de Lídia Jorge." *Actas do Quinto Congresso da Associação Internacional de Lusitanistas*. Oxford-Coimbra, 1998. 631-636.

Ferreira, Ana Paula. "Lídia Jorge's *A Costa dos Murmúrios*: History and the Postmodern She-Wolf." *Revista Hispánica Moderna* 45 (1992): 268-78.

———. "Lídia Jorge's Strategies of Navigation: Eating and Psychoanalysis in *O Cais das Merendas*." *Symposium* 1992: 176-94.

Gomes, Álvaro Cardoso. *A Voz Itinerante*. São Paulo: EDUSP, 1993. (Chapter on Lídia Jorge, and interview with the author.)

Heß, Renate. "Schreiben heißt: sich erinnern. Zum Werk von Lídia Jorge." *Portugiesische Literatur*. Ed. Henry Thorau. Bonn: VG Bild-Kunst, 1997. 501-20.

Jordão, Ana Paula. "Os Murmúrios da Identidade em Dois Romances de Lídia Jorge." *Actas do Quinto Congresso da Associação Internacional de Lusitanistas*. Oxford-Coimbra: Lidel, 1998. 857-63.

Kaufman, Helena Irena. "Ficção Histórica Portuguesa do Pós-Revolução." Diss. University of Wisconsin-Madison, 1991. (Chapter on *A Costa dos Murmúrios*.)

———. "Reclaiming the Margins of History in Lídia Jorge's *A Costa dos Murmúrios.*" *Luso-Brazilian Review* 29 (1992): 41-49.

Lepecki, Maria Lúcia. *Sobreimpressões.* Lisboa: Editorial Caminho, 1988. (Article on *O Cais das Merendas.*)

Magalhães, Isabel Allegro de. *O Tempo das Mulheres.* Lisboa: Imprensa Nacional-Casa da Moeda, 1987. (Chapter on *O Dia dos Prodígios.*)

Medina, Cremilda. "Lídia Jorge." *Viagem à Literatura Portuguesa Contemporânea.* Rio de Janeiro: Nórdica, 1983. 483-505.

Moutinho, Isabel. "A Collapsing Empire: Cultural Decay and Personal Transformation in the Recent Work of Portuguese Women Novelists." *Romance Languages Annual* 5 (1993): 484-90. (Comparative study of three novels by Joana Ruas, Wanda Ramos and Lídia Jorge's *A Costa dos Murmúrios.*)

Owen, Hilary. "[W]Rites of Passage." Diss. University of Nottingham, 1992. (Chapter on *Notícia da Cidade Silvestre.*)

Pazos Alonso, Cláudia. "A Voz do Poder e o Poder da Voz em *A Costa dos Murmúrios* de Lídia Jorge." *Actas do Quinto Congresso da Associação Internacional de Lusitanistas.* Oxford-Coimbra: Lidel, 1998. 1211-18.

Sadlier, Darlene. *The Question of How: Women Writers and the New Portuguese Literature.* New York & Greenport: Greenwood Press, 1989. (Chapter on *O Dia dos Prodígios.*)

Santos, Maria Irene Ramalho de Sousa. "Bondoso Caos: *A Costa dos Murmúrios* de Lídia Jorge." *Colóquio/Letras* 107 (1989): 64-67.

———. "Da História como Memória do Desejo: *O Cais das Merendas* de Lídia Jorge." *Colóquio/Letras* 109 (1989): 60-68.

Saraiva, Arnaldo. "Os Duplos do Real e os Duplos Romanescos." *Arquivos do Centro Cultural Português* 29 (1991): 39-48.

Sousa, Ronald W. "'I Was Evita' or *Ecce Femina.*"(forthcoming)

———. "The Critique of History in *A Costa dos Murmúrios* or Helen of Beira Meets Luís of Troy." *Cincinnati Romance Review* 16 (1997): 135-43.

Reviews / Recensões

Apresentação de *O Vale da Paixão*, de Lídia Jorge, a 8 de Julho de 1998, na Livraria Barata, Lisboa.

Elfriede Engelmayer

Dito assim pode parecer um absurdo que a matéria-prima de um romance seja a ausência. Mas o último (e belíssimo) romance de Lídia Jorge, *O Vale da Paixão*, mostra que esta matéria-prima pode ser tecida numa densa trama poética semeada de luminosas miniaturas.

Reparemos na jovem leitora (*Noia llegint*) da capa do livro, reprodução de um quadro de Montserrat Gudiol—na posição do corpo, que mostra como está fechada sobre si própria—e sobre o que lê, na contradição entre a mão direita, fechada, e a fragilidade que se revela no brilho sedoso do cabelo. Juntemos a essa imagem tocante o duplo sentido do título, *O Vale da Paixão*. Ainda não começámos a leitura, mas já estamos no centro da narrativa.

Também no romance se repetirá a alternância entre o claro e o escuro, o contraste que dá ao quadro de Montserrat Gudiol uma aura irreal e etérea. Na cena chave do romance é uma cortina de chuva que, à noite, esconde dos outros o encontro entre aquela rapariga de quinze anos, calada, e o seu pai, aquele pai que à luz do dia se torna em tio por força das convenções sociais e familiares. O pai que, naquela casa em que todos os passos se ouvem, tem de tirar os sapatos para subir a escada até ao quarto da filha. O pai cuja paternidade é selada nesse encontro único, mas que, por ter sido único, a filha vai buscar à memória uma, outra, outras vezes, como se se tratasse de rebobinar o mesmo filme; o filme de Walter Dias trota mundos, atravessa mares; o soldado Walter, para a família (pelo menos, para muitos membros da família) um mandrião. Ao verdadeiro significado da paternidade, a presença do pai, contrapõe a filha o ritual do filme que se projecta na sua cabeça; um fetiche comparável ao revólver Smith, a arma do soldado Walter sobre a qual dorme anos a fio e que a protege dos medos nocturnos melhor do que qualquer figura paterna.

O Vale da Paixão conta-nos as dores que se passam para encontrar a identidade, sobretudo quando um dos elementos constitutivos dessa identidade está ausente. Nunca somos só filhas e filhos, mas filhas e filhos de um pai e de uma mãe. No entanto, a sua ascendência tem para aquela filha o tamanho insuportável da culpa. "Ela sabia desde há muito, que para si mesma, em certas noites de chuva, a história do seu pai, por indigno que fosse pensá-lo, quanto mais dizê-lo, ainda que o fizesse em voz baixa" (209). Mas também a história da humanidade é uma cadeia de destinos individuais em que cada elo está ligado ao anterior e ao seguinte. Não é por acaso que, depois da partida do pai, a filha se refugia na sua leitura preferida—a *Ilíada*, de Homero, em que as genealogias não são apenas a topografia de cada um na sociedade, mas também o destino a que cada um não pode escapar, porque é essa a vontade dos deuses. E é aí também que a rapariga, intuitivamente, vai reconhecer um padrão imemorial: o dos homens que partem à demanda, o das mulheres e filhas que ficam cativas dos destinos deles.

No universo poético deste romance, na aldeia de São Sebastião de Valmares, algures entre Lagos e Faro, dá-se no ano de 1963 esse encontro singular entre pai e filha; num Portugal de estruturas patriarcais em que as mulheres se definem em função dos homens que as possuem (no duplo sentido, mais uma vez, da palavra). É nesse lugar que, cerca de dezasseis anos antes, a jovem Maria Ema, já grávida da rapariga, vai a casa do pai de Walter, o homem que a desgraçou. E volta a pé, no pó da estrada, atrás da charrete onde os pais a não aceitam. Não foi aí ainda que a paixão—o sofrimento—de Maria Ema atingiu o ponto culminante. Foi naquele ano de 1963, já casada com Custódio (irmão mais velho de Walter), e mãe de três filhos desse casamento, em que sucumbiu à paixão como se de uma doença se tratasse, quando Walter voltou à casa de Valmares.

O clímax deste romance, dividido em cem sequências de diferentes dimensões, encontra-se precisamente na quinquagésima. No Chevrolet preto de Walter a família vai de excursão até Sagres, uma viagem em perigosa euforia a que só se pode seguir a queda. É que Maria Ema está tão vulnerável que a visão do abismo elementar entre o promontório e o mar se transmuda no abismo existencial em que se quer precipitar. Mas Walter ainda a consegue agarrar, e ela virá a libertar-se daquele amor, ao contrário da filha.

Deixem-me que volte aos passos silenciosos de Walter Dias naquela noite de 1963, antes de ter partido para não mais voltar, depois daquela quase conseguida tentativa de suicídio de Maria Ema. Deixem-me que volte àquela cena que a filha faz passar constantemente na cabeça, numa espiral que dá ao romance a sua peculiar estrutura. A cena passa-se simultaneamente em dois planos temporais, o passado do ano de 1963 e o presente da narrativa, em que a voz feminina, na primeira pessoa, na presença da velha manta de soldado que herdou, invoca e convoca o pai ausente. A fragmentação temporal e formal (nos fragmentos narrativos que se referem ao passado ela é ora a filha, ora a sobrinha de Walter) espelha também a sua identidade fragmentada, já que, "(...) a vida não pertencia apenas a quem pertencia, mas também a quem a relatava" (54)—e, acrescentaria eu, a quem a nomeava. A quem, mesmo no singular testamento, chama sobrinha à que sua filha era. Ou à narradora, mulher adulta agora, que em trabalho de luto se despede do pai.

Só que a evocação de Walter Dias não conduz à catarse, nem no sentido aristotélico, nem no da psicanálise. O amor para com o pai não é sepultado, nem o coração é dele "purificado." A narradora, mulher sem nome, enterra a velha manta de soldado, mas um amor só se pode enterrar quando já está morto. Não é possível libertar-se de um amor que ainda está vivo.

Este pai, que numa noite inesquecível confessa nunca ter dado nada à filha, este pai que lhe escreve "Deixo à minha sobrinha, por única herança, esta manta de soldado"—este pai é uma ferida aberta. A sua ausência, tão forte que leva a que esteja constantemente presente na vida da filha, só depois da morte perde o sabor amargo. É que a morte é a ausência definitiva. Mas nessa altura já a filha percebeu que não é isso que interessa, e é por isso que pode enterrar a manta de soldado. Porque o que o pai foi, e o que o pai é, trá-lo ela no coração e na memória. Intocável.

The Politics of Postmodernity. Ed. James Good and Irving Velody. Cambridge: Cambridge University Press, 1998.
Hermínio Martins. _Classe, Status e Poder_. Lisbon: ICS, 1998.

Carlos Leone

From a continental standpoint, although not a French one, there are some unavoidable perplexities concerning the debate about postmodernity in the Anglo-American context. The gap between the concept and the social reality it aims to address on the one hand, and the debate itself on the other, stands out most prominently. Twenty years since the publication of Jean-François Lyotard's *Rapport sur le savoir*, the debate on the Continent (predominantly staged in France, Germany, and Italy) revisited the classical dispute between philosophers and sophists in the form of the confrontation between Habermas vs. Lyotard (with a sort of quasi-aristotelian stance in an essay by Karl-Otto Apel). However, in the English-speaking world, things became autonomous —as it usually happens—in a very particular way. On the Continent the discussion was primarily academic, centered in the social sciences, and only later on evolved to the press in a quite irrelevant way—maybe because the *gauchisme* of the continental press was a real opponent to the skepticism inherent in suspicions towards *grands récits*. Curiously, this strangeness to continental ideology proved to be totally absent in the reception of Lyotard's essay on the Anglo-American circuit, where the notion of "postmodern condition" soon became associated with, but unrelated to, a number of theories and concepts originating from French authors like Derrida (deconstruction) and Foucault (*episteme*). The problem is that postmodernity turns out to be a very pervasive notion, much more so than the others I mentioned and, consequently, its meaning became equivocal.

The key point is this: the postmodern condition is one of modernity, that is to say, a condition of knowledge (*savoir*) in modern western societies. Lyotard characterized it through a constant attention to the expanding information flow within western industrialized societies that would gradually predominate over the possession of capital. I'm cutting it short, but I trust that I am keeping in terms with Lyotard's viewpoint. This would inevitably put under serious stress the all-encompassing *grands récits* that legitimized the very societies where these changes occur. All of this must sound familiar in the days of the global economy, the internet, and other undisputed realities of the same modern societies based on an essentially liberal conception of politics and social organization—the only ones that allow these changes to take place effectively and peacefully. Unfortunately, this interpretation of modern societies was appropriated in the English-speaking world by the impenitent drive for theoretical support in French thinking consistently carried out through the years by feminists, cultural studies gurus, and so on. Just the same way Derrida's deconstruction became a method*ism* in the U.S., the postmodern condition became postmodernism, as if something called "modernity" had simply ended and something else showed up to take its place posthumously. At this point, I should recognize that this is a misinterpretation of the postmodern condition of knowledge also current on the Continent. In Europe, however, the discussion has been for a long time kinder, gentler, and almost imperceptible. Thus, the effects of this are far more visible in the Anglo-American world, as the Sokal affair so eloquently reiterates, with a resonance almost entirely limited to France and French-dependent cultures like, say, Portugal.

So, if this is a valid standpoint, we could describe the picture in terms of a continent where postmodernity has been a minor matter for a long time and an English-speaking world where it has become overstressed, has obtained a specific identity, and has been internalized in academic disputes (again, the Sokal affair is a perfect example). In this process, one might add, postmodernism reproduces some of the more well-established *clichés* concerning the differences between the Anglo-American tradition of philosophy (more analytical and empirical) and its continental counterpart (more literary and speculative). A good case for sustaining this perspective is *The Politics of Postmodernity*, edited by James Good and Irving Velody. Both in its structure and in its underlying assumptions, this book is pinned to the framework of an English-like postmodernity—and surely a very good one at that. It comes from a well-known topic, the reference to a crisis, ironically one of those dramatic events that one of the few thinkers of Anglo-American provenance with a good grasp of the Continent's activity (Richard Rorty) so frequently urges us to abandon. Thus, the editors tell us that "the crisis in the political is very much an aspect of crises of interpretation and representation in the social sciences. That is to say, the crisis in the political is but one dimension of a more general sense of disintegration in the human sciences." To deal with this particular dimension, we find an impressive list of contributors, forming a volume "which essentially presumes the death of the foundational approach to political analysis and offers a variety of new perspectives to look forward to the postmodern social world." It is frequent but nonetheless ironic that the foundational approach should be associated with modernity—after all, modernity (above all the Enlightenment) aimed to cut itself loose from the theological foundations that preceded it. Anyway, the real problem with this approach to postmodernity is by now recognizable: is there any connection in linking this momentous view of modernity (crises, disintegration, death, etc.) and the analysis in the report written by Lyotard for the Canadian government? Isn't it an approach more akin to those bombastic diagnoses of scientific revolutions and the like? If we look back at the history of philosophy, we find (as in that of theology or religion) the announcement of "crises" to be a constant feature, by that designation or by several others (on this subject, by the way, Derrida has an interesting work, published by Galilée in 1983 under the title *D'un ton apocalyptique adopté naguère en philosophie*). As a matter of fact, crisis is the greater grand récit in the history of philosophy and is responsible for some of its most impressive works, like Husserl's Krisis. So, *in nuce*, the crisis pretext is neither original nor specifically postmodern.

At any rate, *The Politics of Postmodernity* is a valuable work. Carefully presented by its editors, the book contains a general introduction and short presentations of each of its three parts, and gathers papers from Quentin Skinner, Zygmunt Bauman, and several other scholars. In a well-reasoned effort to be balanced, the volume also includes a chapter by the outstanding non-postmodernist Raymond Plant. Structured in an efficient, conventional fashion, the first part of the book deals with modernity, the second with the critique of its political thought, and the last ventures into "Technology and the Politics of Culture," which presumably corresponds to "the task of our generation to give some coherence and direction to the kind of world the year 2000 will bring, the kind of world the makers of this book and its readers will have helped to create." Symptomatically, the very chronological display of the three parts reveals a purely modern understanding of time as continuing progress now transported to the postmodern condition, another frequent shortcoming of current postmodernism.

Besides that, the book also reveals the implication of the postmodern condition of knowledge with issues hardly related to it, again by association with other French authors, like in the case of Diana Coole's Foucault-inspired postmodern feminism on the ground of the masculinity of modern grand récits. In a way, the emblematic text of the book is, all things considered,

David E. Cooper's "Postmodernity and 'The End of Philosophy,'" a fairly illustrative summa of all these questions. In his contribution, Cooper upholds the usual aspiration of English-speaking postmodernists to a new and unparallelled radicalism, in which the critique of the "depth" of built-in truth or truth-like theories of modernity draws its power from a "spirit which imbues the general culture of postmodernism." As if it were necessary, the symbolic return of one of the most obvious *grands récits* radically cuts against the traditional aspiration to truth (and as if modernity hadn't established itself against tradition's *auctoritas*).

At this point, we might ask what is Hermínio Martins's relation to this English form of the postmodern condition. In the opening of Part III of the book, his text on "Technology, Modernity, and Politics" stands out by its amiability towards traditions. He writes about two traditions, both of them related to a modern-now-postmodern theme of "domination of nature" and attempting to "bring out the sharp differences between two ideal-typical traditions, the Promethean (particularly marked in the wake of the French Revolution) and the Faustian (culminating in the work of the single most influential contemporary philosopher of technology, Heidegger)." This attention to traditions within a postmodern discussion (that of technology, on which Martins has written consistently in recent years) is decisive, as it reflects the critique of the caesurism (a notion put forward by Martins himself in his essay "Time and Theory in Sociology," in *Approaches to Sociology*, edited by John Rex in 1974) present in all the Anglo-American forms of postmodernism. However, the effort to question the apparently obvious revolutionary, caesura-like nature of (post)modern politics, and to rehearse an alternative to it, stands out more clearly in another of his works that also reveals the scope of the work to be done on modernity in the present postmodern condition. I'm referring to a volume of essays on contemporary Portugal entitled *Classe, Status e Poder* (*Class, Status and Power*), just issued by ICS, a new Portuguese academic press.

As Hermínio Martins himself notices in his introduction to this book, there is a connection between the more theoretical analysis of the sort of "Time and Theory in Sociology" or "Technology, Modernity, Politics" and his more empirical essays, such as those collected in *Classe, Status e Poder* (with the exception of the last of these, the one which entitles the volume, as it is extremely theory-laden by comparision with the others). Here we find a Portuguese version of texts already published in English in several collections, all of them on the subject of Portuguese politics and society prior to the current democratic regime established in 1974. This is a valuable contribution to the understanding of what I mentioned above about the work to be done on modernity: written by a Portuguese exiled in England, it offers something extremely rare in Portuguese-related works—an ability to make them part of the Western framework of political studies. Teaching abroad and deprived of access to most of the data usually consulted in this line of research, Martins wrote what is even today an accurate description and evaluation of (1) the democracy overthrown in 1926; (2) the regime of Salazar and Caetano; (3) the opposition to that regime; and (4) the structure of Portuguese metropolitan society until 1974. At the very least, this is a remarkable achievement, but there is something else more relevant to my point.

The interest of a book such as this in the context of postmodern politics is that it brings out the fact that much, and perhaps most, of the work on modernity is still waiting to be done; the postmodern condition, moreover, with its free flow of information, is the appropriate time to do it. The Portuguese case examined by Martins is only one of the many all over the world that display the tensions and contrasts that make modernity in such a binding way that even the postmodern condition did not put an end to them. That is why the analyses in these essays are almost entirely valid today. The simple possibility of access to works like *Classe, Status e Poder* is in itself an indicator of social modernity, as it is proven by their publication in English much earlier than in Portuguese editions. And it is this existence of modernity, simultaneous with what is premodern and postmodern, this idiosyncratic capacity of modernity to endure prolonged, unresolved, and even ignored tensions within itself, that should constitute a serious reason to reassess the meaning and use(s) of the notion that Lyotard made famous.

Of course (or in Derrida's way of saying it, of coarse) it is highly unlikely that such a reassessment will ever take place. As long as polemics such as the Sokal affair set the pace, I tend to sympathize with Rorty's suggestion simply to discard the use of the word "postmodernity" altogether. Nevertheless, and despite all the noise around postmodernism, it is evident that the works such as those of Hermínio Martins, Hans Jonas, Niklas Luhmann, and precisely those above the wrestling of modernists and postmodernists will remain in the future as a legacy of our days.

Rosa Lobato de Faria. *O Romance de Cordélia*. Lisboa: Edições Asa, 1998.

Leonor Simas Almeida

Rosa Lobato de Faria, de há muito figura mediática, só mais recentemente trouxe até nós a *persona* de poeta e romancista. Desde 1983 vem com efeito consolidando a sua personalidade literária, tendo até à data publicado quatro livros de poesia e outros tantos romances. É do último destes, *O Romance de Cordélia*, há apenas alguns meses editado, e já sendo traduzido para inglês (dois dos anteriores, *O Pranto do Lúcifer* e *Os Pássaros de Seda* foram-no em alemão), que aqui se traz notícia.

Trata-se de uma narrativa em primeira pessoa, autobiografia ficcional, como fora aliás também o caso dos romances precedentes, todos de uma forma ou doutra elegendo técnicas destinadas a pessoalizar memórias, num registo narrativo profundamente marcado pela oralidade e pleno de emoção revivida.

A escrita de *O Romance de Cordélia* revela-se de uma transparência enganadora, o trabalho de elaboração da linguagem mal se deixa entrever no efeito obtido de fluidez e leveza que faz corredia a leitura, depressa nos empolga e só nos permite dar conta de certas complexidades ocultas quando já de todo nos envolvemos em múltiplos relatos entrecruzados. Falo de multiplicidade porque a estória da protagonista Cordélia, centro da consciência narrativa deste romance, é atravessada de várias outras em *mise en abîme*, tão relevantes para o resultado final que os principais sujeitos delas merecem alusão logo na dedicatória do livro: "Às reclusas do Estabelecimento Prisional de Tires cuja verdade tornou possível esta ficção"(6).

Mas ocupemo-nos da figura nuclear, presente já no título, investida de funções especiais de narradora de si própria, ou da sua própria história, mas também dela figurativamente leitora por se assumir como sua intérprete e nisso se aproximar de nós, narratários, que seguimos a retrospectiva de uma vida para, como a sua protagonista, lhe atribuírmos um sentido determinado. De resto, os outros contos imbricados no seu, por ela passam necessariamente, através da sua agência ora como ouvinte, ora como leitora (aqui no sentido literal de alguém que lê o relato escrito de ficções criadas por outrem, os "romances de cordel" da Arminda Canivete).

Desde as primeiras páginas se propõe Cordélia rever a sua existência para encontrar o ponto onde "deu o nó cego," o lugar onde deixou de encontrar "a estrada principal, nem o sul nem o norte, nem estrela nenhuma para se guiar" (9). Tendo-se-nos antes apresentado como reclusa prestes a sair em liberdade por ter já cumprido cinco sextos, ou dezasseis anos, da pena a que fora condenada, assim nos dispõe a acompanhá-la no que, quase duas centenas de páginas mais tarde, há-de descrever como "calvário das recordações para ver onde é que a minha vida descarrilou" (162). No decorrer dessa viagem ao passado, Cordélia constantemente regressará ao presente, desdobrando-se no eixo temporal tanto quanto se desdobra em sujeito e objecto do discurso narrativo. Segue uma cronologia linear desde a infância ao fim da vida, repartida em dois grandes momentos; o primeiro, até ao dia de deixar a prisão de Tires, ocupa 170 páginas (cerca de 4/5 da narrativa), o segundo apenas 48. O próprio texto torna explícita esta demarcação, não em termos de alteração da técnica narrativa, mas na ocorrência de um desvio considerável na perspectiva psicológica do eu-narrador: "Aqui neste lugar onde me encontro agora (não perdi o vício de *rever a matéria* e rememorar todo o meu percurso, apenas com uma serenidade muito diferente da angústia com que o fazia na prisão)" (180).

O que nos alerta de novo para a duplicidade do eu, narrado e narrador, e me permite destacar alguns elementos determinantes da leitura que proponho. A análise retrospectiva das duas macro-sequências em questão revela-nos na primeira delas uma maior dissonância entre as duas metades do eu, porquanto o contador se distancia do contado, dissecando e julgando em função de uma sabedoria adquirida posteriormente à experiência; não faltam então os juízos do tipo "saltei pelo meu pé para o altar do sacrifício" (155) ou "O que é que me fez agarrar a uma situação insustentável que não fazia senão piorar? Por que é que (...) não me libertei de tudo aquilo? Talvez porque fiz sempre as escolhas erradas" (128). Por outro lado, a dissonância é menor do que à primeira vista parece, na medida em que o conhecimento e a iluminação se mantêm inalcançáveis: "Afinal subi todo o calvário das recordações (...) e continuo sem resposta" (162); a infelicidade persiste: "Guita coxa. É a minha alcunha de reclusa (...) tanto me faz. Para que serve ter um nome se nem sequer tenho uma vida" (67); e o exorcismo dos fantasmas só redobra o sofrimento "nesta febre de rememorar que me devora as noites e não me ajuda a compreender" (66). Quanto ao segundo grande momento da narrativa, diria que—pese embora a conservação de certa distância analítica (como nesta espécie de sinopse avaliativa: "achei a história daquele homem mais parecida com a minha, isto é, uma sucessão de azares, traições e maldades de que ele fora vítima, com uma inércia que eu muito bem conhecia" (194)—predomina o reforçar-se da coesão entre objecto e sujeito, até ao definitivo abandono do passado verbal seguido de apoteótica fusão na frase que fecha o romance e conclui a viagem: "Arregaço, cantando, a minha saia de estrelas, e lavo os pés na chuva da madrugada"(218).

Se assim me detive nestas duplicidades é porque as vejo entretecidas nas linhas fundamentais de significação da história de Cordélia. Já que se a distância crítica do narrador dissonante relativamente à personagem ecoa a nossa própria impaciência perante a mansidão e passividade que irremediavelmente a sujeitam à condição de vítima, também a consonância, tornada depois tão evidente no final do romance, viabiliza outro tipo de leitura de onde se destaca o papel das forças transcendentes que intervêm no destino da protagonista. Se as duas leituras são conciliáveis ou não, cabe a cada um decidir. Por mim, vejo-as mutuamente se ambiguizando. Lembro só que, sendo verdade que a maior parte do espaço narrativo se ocupa da imanência de Cordélia, com especial relevo para a condenação da inércia que sempre a limitou, não é menos verdadeiro que a presença do sobrenatural se revela desde cedo na figura de Laura, nas quintas-feiras místicas de Alcatruzes, no milagre acontecido à Rita Bandoleira, ou no outro de que é objecto a própria Cordélia e a faz admitir que "os milagres acontecem no limite da culpa, do desespero ou da solidão" (204). Note-se ainda que no momento de epifania coincidente com a chegada ao conhecimento procurado—nomeadamente, a resposta à pergunta de Laura sobre qual a missão de Cordélia na vida—se enumeram as opções que poderiam ter sido, para se concluir enfim: "Eu estaria aqui, neste momento solene da minha morte, fossem quais fossem as escolhas que o meu livre arbítrio me tivesse ditado. Agora que compreendo isso, sinto-me preparada" (217). Por outras palavras, é neste ponto em que definitivamente se abandonou já a ficção realista de primeira pessoa ao colocar-se a personagem narradora relatando a sua própria morte (ou contando o "'sonho incrível' que est[á] a ter"), que a autobiografia ficcionalizada cumpre a função anunciada quando Cordélia reflectia sobre a condição humana: "somos o fio que não conhece o desenho em que está inserido e a que vai dando forma, inexoravelmente, até cumprir o seu destino de fio de teia, de tecido" (132). Porque, cumprido que foi o destino, o fio achou o desenho.

Enquanto elemento de uma organização cósmica, Cordélia aproxima-se da sua homónima shakespeariana, a heroína a quem deve o nome, aquele que o pai "trazia no coração e tinha a ver com o único momento de glória da sua vida, em que representara o papel de rei Lear no teatro de amadores da sua terra" (12). Dela se aproxima pelo fatalismo trágico que sem apelo lhe determina a existência, tanto como pela sua condição de vítima inocente.

Mas a história de *King Lear* tem raízes populares profundas; no caso do folclore português encontramo-las no conto daquele rei cuja filha mais nova, indagada sobre o amor que tinha ao pai, declarou para desgraça sua querer-lhe tanto "como a comida quer ao sol." Lembro como a analogia entre esta princesa e a nossa Cordélia, cujas capacidades de criação culinária são realçadas ao longo do romance, é por ela mesma assinalada: "uma analogia encantadora entre o culto do paladar de que eu dava testemunho e aquela princesa do mesmo nome, para sempre ligada à simbologia do sal" (33). Só que na tradição popular em causa, bem como nos "romances de cordel," género também popular com que este livro joga não apenas ao nível do seu título mas igualmente no do tecido textual (onde ironicamente tais romances se entretecem de forma lúdica, humorística e profundamente criativa, sob a forma de fragmentos dispersos obedecendo a uma fórmula única), sempre "os maus foram castigados e os bons foram felizes para sempre" (113). Isto é, obtém-se a retribuição que o leitor, condicionado sobretudo pela unidimensionalidade das personagens é levado a desejar. No caso de Cordélia tal retribuição, embora podendo integrar o nosso horizonte de expectativas—afinal os oponentes da personagem a quem a narrativa nos alia não são menos unidimensionais do que os protagonistas de qualquer melodrama reduzido à simplicidade máxima—não chega nunca a concretizar-se. Porque se trata de uma personagem de tragédia? Porque encontra a redenção noutra esfera, espiritualizada, melhor definida dentro de uma ética cristã, tendo sobretudo em conta a forma de salvação achada ao cabo do seu *calvário*? Mais uma vez cabe ao leitor achar as soluções que melhor se adequem à sua experiência prévia como actor e espectador tanto das criações artísticas quanto da sua própria existência.

Duma coisa se pode, porém, estar certo: apesar de quaisquer aparências em contrário, as respostas do romance a esta e outras questões não são nem simples nem óbvias. É verdade que o leitor é de várias maneiras seduzido pela narrativa de Cordélia, apresentada como verosímil pelo contraste com as fantasias "de cordel," ou pela sua coexistência com os relatos extraordinários das outras reclusas de Tires, ou ainda pela conclusão de que "afinal é mais fácil do que parece perder tudo na vida, deve haver no mundo milhares de histórias iguais à nossa, que nós, enquanto estávamos no quentinho das nossas casas e na fartura das nossas mesas nem conseguíamos imaginar" (198). Mas nem por isso a verdade ou a verosimilhança da sua versão é menos problematizada: "Quando cheguei aqui e disse às minhas colegas que estava inocente, elas responderam a rir, ai filha, não te canses, estamos todas! A burla que me trouxe aqui? Foi o meu patrão que a cometeu (...) A heroína que apanharam no aeroporto no forro da minha mala? Foi o meu namorado que a lá meteu. (...) O tiro no meu amante? Foi o meu pai que o deu (...)" (162). Como não menos problematizada se acha a plausibilidade de um discurso quase inteiramente determinado pela subjectividade mnemónica: "e vivo com este redemoinho dentro da minha cabeça, a perguntar-me se a minha memória me atraiçoa, se foi tudo assim ou se foi tudo diferente, se estou a atenuar os meus erros e a ampliar as culpas dos outros. Não sei" (162). Nenhum de nós, assim colocado perante uma narrativa consciente da sua própria ambiguidade, poderá sabê-lo ao certo. Mas vale a pena cada um procurar averiguá-lo directamente, que decerto achará proveito e prazer na leitura de *O Romance de Cordélia*.

Com este livro e os que o precederam, todos tão inteligentemente inventivos e emotivamente envolventes, já Rosa Lobato de Faria nos compensou de mão larga por, até há quatro anos atrás, ter guardado de nós a revelação do seu extraordinário dom de romancista, sabedora das verdades da arte e dos artifícios da vida.

Luísa Costa Gomes. *Educação para a Tristeza*. Lisboa: Editorial Presença, 1998.

Maria Eduarda Vassallo Pereira

O leitor tem nas suas mãos e sob os olhos o quarto romance, em dez anos, de Luísa Costa Gomes. De 1981 até 1988, ano da saída de *O Pequeno Mundo*, o primeiro romance, dois livros de contos, uma narrativa, um conto em co-autoria. Depois, mais dois romances, *Vida de Ramón* (1991) e *Olhos Verdes* (1994)—e ainda um terceiro, em co-autoria—*O Defunto Elegante*, com Abel Barros Baptista, em 1996.

A seguir, de novo contos—exactamente intitulados, no volume que os reúne, *Contos Outra Vez*.

A completar a obra, teatro, que, infelizmente, não conheço na totalidade. Mas vi *Nunca nada de ninguém*, numa encenação de Ana Tamen (Acarte, Fundação Calouste Gulbenkian, 1991), e gostei muito de todo o espectáculo, nas diversas proporções encontradas para o fazerem teatro (a encenação, o texto, o trabalho dos actores, a cenografia, a iluminação).

Afirmo que a sucessão dos títulos assinados por Luísa Costa Gomes constitui uma obra; sugiro que, nela, alguma centralidade deve ser reconhecida ao romance.

Os três primeiros ocupam aquilo que, neste momento, é o seu centro geométrico e temporal—os anos de 88, 91 e 94. Sucedem-se, a intervalos regulares, sem a interrupção dos contos, colocados nos extremos. *Educação para a Tristeza* iniciará, talvez, uma nova sequência de romances. E digo sequência, porque os três primeiros não se organizam, de facto, como um ciclo.

Este que agora leio retoma um tema que está presente em *O Pequeno Mundo*, o da casa. Com a Casa vem o Falanstério; a estes dois se liga o da loucura.

Todos presentes em *O Pequeno Mundo*, eram aí integrados na estrutura de uma narrativa epistolar que os tornava úteis—rentáveis para a economia da narrativa, recuperados e tratados no interior de um trabalho de apresentação das personagens, com alguma função, afinal, no avançar e no concluir da trama ficcional proposta—mesmo se essa trama afirma que pouco se avança e nada se conclui; mesmo se e, particularmente, porque aparenta passar-se noutro lugar romanesco que não o que por tais temas é delimitado.

Educação para a Tristeza, que os elege, decepciona-me, como leitora, porque os deixa fugir. Confinando-se-lhes, e confinando-os inicialmente ao conhecimento de uma personagem, deixa escapar o tema da casa e não me leva ao conhecimento dessa personagem.

Maria de Santa Bárbara Travinha entra por engano na Casa Velha e lá fica. A Casa fascina-a e fá-la prisioneira, impede-a de se afastar. Dito de outro modo: Maria constrói, em relação ao espaço, aos seus habitantes e ao passado e história de um e de outros, o fascínio e a prisão.

Quando, enfim, foge, as circunstâncias da viagem que empreende em direcção a Lisboa, ao trabalho e ao apartamento onde mora, impedem-na de chegar. De facto, impedem-na de partir completamente: a viagem mal começa, imediatamente interrompida por um desastre de automóvel que a põe no primeiro hospital.

Aí, Maria de Santa Bárbara tem acesso a pessoas e a documentos. Umas e outros juntam-se aos que trouxe da Casa, àquilo que lá viu e à história daqueles que lá encontrou e a quem se prendeu.

Permanece, porém, o mistério do espaço: o bisavô do Arquitecto, o trisavô do Sancho Simplicíssimo que Maria ama, construiu a Casa sobre um plano e uma ideia que o seu Diário—o documento que Maria trouxe da Casa sem saber o que era—descreve. Sucede que faltam espaços na casa tal como Maria a conhece; correlativamente, faltam partes à história que quer construir.

O romance termina com a segunda chegada da personagem à Casa dos Sabe-Mais e descoberta final da sua totalidade: ao conhecimento que tinha da Casa, Maria acrescenta o que sabia ter de existir nela—o que está para lá da parede que derruba.

Fecha-se o romance, de facto, sobre o embalo do Menino, filho do Sancho Simplicíssimo que Maria já não ama: com o avô arquitecto, o menino vem acordá-la do sono no jardim enfim reencontrado.

Se este resumo é correcto, põe-me questões: porquê o fascínio pela Casa? Que relação há entre a Casa e os seus habitantes, o fascínio pela Casa e o amor afirmado de Maria pelo filho e herdeiro? E ainda: o fascínio de Maria de Santa Bárbara é partilhado por alguma outra personagem? Alguém mais o sente, ou Maria de Santa Bárbara quer dá-lo a conhecer a algum outro?

Para tornar inteligíveis estas perguntas, é necessário dizer que a narração que abre o romance e vem a constituir a sua primeira metade—a dos três meses vividos por Maria na Casa—é feita a partir da memória da personagem, que o desastre desencadeia, e cujo processo e conteúdos expressos se desenrolam ao longo da noite em que Maria tarda a chegar ao hospital.

A descrição do espaço é conduzida pelo olhar da personagem. À personagem que rememora entrega ainda qualquer coisa que é mais do que a narração—que surge, de facto, na terceira pessoa; qualquer coisa que é mais do que o mero encadeamento temporal dos factos narrados.

A personagem Maria de Santa Bárbara está encarregue de estabelecer a causalidade dos episódios narrados, de dizer *post hoc, ergo propter hoc*, dando às relações que assim cria um peso de verosimilhança, não psicológica, mas simbólica.

Com a causalidade, a personagem deve apontar os símbolos. O Menino veio por causa das lágrimas: as lágrimas que o trouxeram foram uma Anunciação.

Maria lava o Menino na banheira em que também entra: simultaneamente o concebe—"e sem pecado," acrescenta o texto (Capítulo VI, 73)—e o baptiza. Diria então que duas vezes o baptiza, uma vez que o ensina a falar, descobrindo o Menino, como primeira palavra, o seu nome próprio, Afonso—que ele diz "A-pon" (Capítulo VII, 88).

Um encadeamento de sucessos, um espaço, os seus múltiplos significados, as personagens que estão no espaço e nele fabricam os acontecimentos, tudo é deixado à criação da personagem de Maria de Santa Bárbara. Dela fica o leitor a saber tudo, no duplo e perigoso sentido de que todo o conhecimento lhe vem dela e de que sobre Maria de Santa Bárbara Travinha nada mais há a saber. Tudo é expresso, nada pode ser inferido.

Os documentos que Maria lê no hospital dizem ao leitor muito mais sobre a Casa do que tudo aquilo que a personagem antes alinhavara. São, sem dúvida, o momento feliz do romance, aquele em que o leitor pode estar com a sua personagem sem hesitações e com todo o proveito.

Constroem eles, além disso, do ponto de vista narrativo, a possibilidade do regresso de Maria à Casa, iluminados ambos, regresso e Casa, pelo conhecimento adquirido pela leitura do diário de Afonso Imaginário.

Pelo regresso se permite a Maria a apropriação da totalidade desejada do espaço; o sono no jardim finalmente encontrado; o tomar o menino nos braços.

Regressar ao Menino significa retomar a linhagem do Avô Imaginário por quem Maria se apaixona de corpo e alma:

> (...) Maria de Santa Bárbara apercebeu-se de que exibia todos os sinais físicos e mentais da paixão. Concluiu que essa paixão se destinava a um homem que morrera há quase cem anos. Teve de sorrir a esta ideia (...). (Capítulo X, 182)

Não ocorre no texto uma palavra para a substituição do amor por Sancho Simplicíssimo pela paixão pelo trisavô Afonso; nem para a construção desta. A paixão é afirmada, mas não é mostrada: o leitor não pode acompanhar o sorriso da personagem, está privado da possibilidade de se entender com ela.

É este o lado decepcionante de *Educação para a Tristeza*, que também por isso não é o romance de Maria de Santa Bárbara Travinha, mas o do espaço sonhado por Afonso Imaginário.

Do encontro da Casa à sua descoberta pela personagem vai um processo de conhecimento que se consubstancia na leitura do diário.

Por este se liga o espaço—a Casa que se sonha construir—ao sonho do Falanstério e ambos, espaço/Casa e Falanstério, à questão da educação.

Tornada tema que, desde o início do romance, Eduardo, o cavalo que fala, formula—"Pode o escopro da educação moldar uma natureza irredutivelmente malévola? Ou, pelo contrário, não deverá ser a educação uma forma de aproveitar o instinto, ainda o mais vil, tornando-o socialmente produtivo?" (Capítulo II, 22)—, para ele se encontra, no texto do diário, com extrema felicidade, uma formulação narrativa e textual.

Saindo para comprar azeite, Afonso Imaginário bate a um casebre para saber "dos da casa" se vai no bom caminho. A mulher miserável que lhe abre a porta queixa-se do tempo e da vida. Ao fundo, três crianças:

> À lareira em que os morrões se apagavam, sentavam-se três pimpolhos moncosos e seminus, descalços, esguedelhados, as caras sujas e negras como tições. Chamei pelos da casa e acorreu de dentro uma mulher ainda nova, arrastando os chinelos na terra batida que lhe valia de sobrado, embrulhada no xaile, a tiritar. (...)
> —Só miséria, só desgraça.
> Queixou-se à vontade enquanto eu assentia, observando pelo rabo do olho as crianças atemorizadas (...) E pelo caminho de volta, ia pensando nesta tremenda educação para a tristeza que é a pequenez, a exiguidade e a miséria destas choças, sujas, fumarentas, sem ar corrente, sem outra luz que a do fogo aceso, onde a tristeza das paredes decreta a ignorância e a miséria dos pensamentos. (Capítulo X, 193).

A seguir, sobre a queixa da mulher:

> (...) O que mais me afligia ainda era o comprazimento na queixa e no murmúrio, na tristeza que desconfia da vida, incapaz de imaginar sequer que é possível sacudir o jugo dos limites. (*Ibidem*)

Educação para a Tristeza, romance que desta passagem tão bem colhe o seu título, poderia abundar da felicidade, da clareza e da contenção com que ela está escrita. Perde-se, pelo contrário, como disse, na personagem de Maria de Santa Bárbara, que não tem reservas que a permitam levar a cabo um romance gótico dos nossos dias; muito menos quando se lhe entrega, e a ela se limita, a construção do espaço e a procura da história que o fez.

Esses, espaço e história, são pertença do sonho de Afonso Imaginário, que quer o Falanstério na Benquerença e dá o filho a educar à avó—"No fundo do meu sangue, sei que o quero educado como um fidalgo" (Capítulo XI, 215).

Só no diário de Afonso, que é o da construção da Casa, espaço e história ficam perfeitamente mostrados nas suas contradições e, o que é uma mais valia, na sua relação com a História.

O nó entre a personagem de Maria de Santa Bárbara e o conhecimento de que pretende apropriar-se não deixa, porém, de ser feito, e com alguma felicidade. O pesadelo da fuga falhada impede a personagem de regressar a Lisboa, à sua casa e ao seu emprego. No que impede a fuga da Casa e faz o pesadelo está o que naqueles se recusa: o espaço da casa de Maria, o apartamento em vizinhança e promiscuidade com outros.

Diz-se, num momento do romance em que a personagem antecipa, pela imaginação, o regresso:

> E vê-se agora a entrar no pequeno apartamento próprio, olhando em panorâmica a sala de humildes dimensões que atravessa em poucos passos para se ir sentar na sua cama, no seu quarto. (...) Pela janela que lhe mostra as traseiras dos encardidos prédios e outras infinitas janelas de outros quartos em que hão-de descansar, noite fora, outras tantas como ela (...). (Capítulo VIII, 135)

Na mesma sequência, na página anterior:

> No outro devaneio está já em Lisboa, rodando a chave de sua casa na fechadura um pouco perra e entrando para encontrar os seus móveis de uso universal, baratos, feitos de pinho humilde, as gravuras anódinas que pendurara nas

> paredes, os cactos, a revista de decoração cuja capa se cobrira entretanto de um pó resistente e inventava a atmosfera toda da sua vida anterior, que nenhuma onda romântica podia estarrecer. (Idem, 134)

É a tacanhez, a exiguidade, o que aqui se recusa. Aponta-se, e recusa-se, o carácter mesquinho construtor da tristeza. Aponta-se a tristeza como único resultado possível da organização do espaço. O espaço como uma educação para a tristeza.

O texto do diário de Afonso Imaginário faz emergir no romance um regime narrativo que leva a que se sintam como ineficazes as personagens do Arquitecto e de Sancho Simplicíssimo. Quase inúteis parecem as do médico e de Cristovão Cabeçudo, semelhantes que são a um *deus ex machina* surgido para levar a Maria um conhecimento completo, a que só se põem dúvidas metódicas. Afinal, a personagem já não precisa dele; ou poderia obtê-lo em fontes mais interessantes, ou por meios mais imaginosos.

O que atrás digo coloca o romance—este e o género de que provém—como criador de um processo de conhecimento que o leitor deverá perfazer, desejando o que se lhe acrescenta, o que partilha com as personagens ou o que delas obtém por subtracção—sejam respostas, interrogações ou hesitações.

A centralidade que apontei ao romance na obra de Luísa Costa Gomes é oriunda da colocação geométrica na sucessão temporal e da geometria daquela obtenção, se entendermos geometria como espaço, reflexão e sabedoria.

Pensando em tudo isto, diria que li *Educação para a Tristeza*; que gostaria de ter lido mais, no sentido em que desejaria ter encontrado mais para ler e muito mais ainda para ficar a saber; e, enfim, que desejaria ter lido com uma paixão diferente da que, a maior parte do tempo, pus no romance; paixão que apenas a personagem de Afonso Imaginário, e o texto das passagens que lhe são atribuídas, completamente desperta e merece.

Helder Macedo. *Pedro e Paula*. Lisboa: Editorial Presença, 1998.

Isabel A. Ferreira

Pedro e Paula, o romance mais recente de Helder Macedo, coloca em cena o espaço português de aquém e além fronteiras numa sucessão de quadros vivos da última metade deste século. Inserido numa linha novelística que encara com especial atenção um espaço romanesco múltiplo e descentrado, a narrativa examina a pátria como lugar de passagem e renovação, país em trânsito entre passado e futuro, registando os labirínticos caminhos portugueses principalmente pela Europa e pela África.

Romance de espaço(s), mas igualmente romance de personagem(ns), a obra aposta no duplo enquanto imagem unificadora, linha de interpretação que privilegiamos entre as fecundas possibilidades de leitura oferecidas pela narrativa. Exemplo do duplo são os gémeos não idênticos que dão pelo nome de Pedro e Paula, cuja diferença se define desde a primeira infância pelos olhos verdes e carácter frugal dela e pelos olhos castanhos e personalidade imperiosa, egocêntrica dele. Os gémeos, no centro da intriga romanesca, representam o conflito, a irreconciliação e, sobretudo, os caminhos antagónicos do Portugal dos últimos cinquenta anos. Paula personifica a pureza das intenções e o idealismo revolucionário dos anos 60 e 70, bem como a arte e a liberdade. Pedro, pelo contrário, corporiza o egoísmo, o conservadorismo político e a corrupção. Metáforas dum eu dividido e dum universo fragmentado, este duplo pós-moderno não forma uma unidade nem tão-pouco possui um perfil dualista.

Representando, enquanto gémeos, a forma mais antiga do duplo na arte e na literatura, Pedro e Paula sugerem outros paralelismos e remetem não apenas para a leitura intertextual de *Esaú e Jacó*, de Machado de Assis, menção explícita no texto e em epígrafe, mas também aludem à figura de Janus (149), deus romano protector das entradas e saídas, cujos dois rostos apontam para a imagem do duplo, fio condutor em *Pedro e Paula*. Assim, sob o signo de Janus, deus do início, bem como das pontes e passagens, abre o primeiro capítulo do romance precisamente intitulado "Entradas e Saídas," que consiste na revisitação do Portugal de meados dos anos 40. O país surge aqui como espaço de trânsito e confluência, ponto de entrada e saída de levas de refugiados em final de guerra, cruzamento de viagens simultaneamente eufóricas e desencantadas com destino aos exílios e às terras de emigração. No título, sem dúvida sugestivo deste capítulo, afluem conotações de passageiros em trânsito e de saída da guerra, celebrada justamente no dia em que os gémeos dão entrada no mundo. Explicitamente o texto refere "as entradas e saídas do corpo humano" (19), e implicitamente deixa entrever a inauguração de uma nova era na enfática escolha daquela significativa data para o dia do seu nascimento.

Mas se a imagem do duplo preside à construção do enredo de *Pedro e Paula*, quer na forma de gémeos não idênticos quer nos percursos diferenciados das várias personagens, a essa imagem cabe também estruturar o processo de narrar que toma como alicerce a ironia, a paródia e a multiplicidade de "verdades" ou a miscigenação das "verdades" e das "mentiras." Estamos de facto perante uma narrativa tecida de "verdades mentidas com mentiras verdadeiras" (55), em que a mentira "é a verdade de um eu alternativo" (54). Neste romance repartido em 12 partes, com fronteiras nem sempre nítidas, misturam-se o género epistolar e a crónica de família formando por recomposição o "corpo orgânico" a que Cesário Verde alude em epígrafe. Resulta este todo da reinvenção dos fragmentos da memória individual e colectiva que nos chegam através do olhar e da voz do narrador/autor que é simultaneamente "leitor" e "espectador" da estória de Paula e da (H)história do seu tempo; a este cabe a função de "confiante cronista de incertezas" (122) e "cauteloso inventor de probabilidades" (122), dando assim início à sua história: "O que certamente não aconteceu foi talvez o seguinte (...)" (11). Neste sentido, também o escritor possui as características de Janus uma vez que é observador, *voyeur* de um tempo passado e de um futuro que adivinha e/ou inventa.

Como inicialmente se apontou, o romance Pedro e Paula evoca igualmente os espaços de dispersão portuguesa pelas partes da Europa e de África. Os destinos do exílio, emigração, evasão e retorno fragmentam-se pela cidade de Londres, Paris, Lourenço Marques e, especialmente, por Lisboa, configurada como *topos* de onde irradiam as referências culturais e ideológicas do período que abarca os anos 40 e a década de 90, incluíndo obrigatoriamente o antes e o depois da revolução de Abril. Pontos de referência geográfica fundamentais no imaginário português, estes espaços enformam os caminhos percorridos pelas famílias Montês e Vasconcellos que se entrecruzam no enredo da obra, representando o percurso múltiplo e diferenciado dos portugueses de aquém e além-mar.

Exemplos dum espaço romanesco plural e descentrado são Londres e Paris, configurando os trajectos paralelos de exílio e expatriamento das personagens

Gabriel Vasconcellos e Paula Montês. Paris, lugar de evasão e deambulação de Paula, sem as peias da colónia africana e do domínio familiar, simboliza a experiência da liberdade (43) vivida junto de expatriados portugueses, de artistas e de objectores das guerras de África durante as manifestações do Maio de 68.

Aludindo à residência do narrador/autor, também ele voyeur (47-48), Londres surge, por sua vez, como a terra de "hibernação" (52) de Gabriel, personagem que se define como o espectador (36)—estrangeirado que observa o país-berço à distância—e como o intelectual estrangeiro embora português (73), de regresso a Lisboa com vista a resolver os males da pátria (81) num tempo de verdades adiadas. Londres constitui ainda o espaço de aprendizagem e de "regeneração" (127) de Paula que se realiza na descoberta do amor materializado no encontro com Gabriel. Novamente se problematiza aqui a temática do duplo nos possíveis laços filiais entre Gabriel (padrinho-pai; amante-pai) e Paula com sugestões de uma relação incestuosa entre ambos. De facto, paira sempre no ar a ideia de "incestuosa submissão filial ao desejo" (127) que, mesmo que não seja real, possui imenso poder psicológico sobre as personagens, funcionando ora como entrave ora como factor motivador do desejo no romance.

Passando por África, referência obrigatória no imaginário português, e que *Partes de África* (1991) já revisitara, *Pedro e Paula* regressa a Lourenço Marques e a um nostálgico domingo de janelas abertas de onde exalam os cheiros a caril e ressoa a mesma e prenunciadora canção, "Adeus, cidade..." (50), emitida pela Rádio Clube de Moçambique. Espaço, sem dúvida, claustrofóbico, a capital da colónia seria para Paula o lugar onde se imaginava "o que poderia haver do outro lado da rede protectora" (50), esfera opressiva das relações familiares num "tempo colonial em suspensão" (95).

Estamos assim perante uma imagem de África, cujos significados apontam para lugar de opressão, segundo Paula; e de alienação e perversão, segundo Ana, mãe dos gémeos. Para Pedro, cujo perfil de colonialista exibe os traços do pai, África representa o afastamento da irmã ou a "expulsão" da identidade do gémeo, o Outro que constitui parte do seu eu (96). Remetendo o leitor para o título do primeiro capítulo, mas agora com conotações diferentes porque inserido num discurso proferido por Pedro, as "Entradas e Saídas" assumem a forma de princípio simbólico de "ingestão e expulsão" (98-101). Segundo a personagem, esse é o princípio que rege a sobrevivência humana; segundo o leitor, pode aplicar-se à relação de Pedro e Paula e, em última instância, à relação entre portugueses e africanos. Por último, África metaforiza, no caso do pai dos gémeos, o espaço de evasão e oportunidade, tornado lugar de perdição e suicídio.

"Espíritos e Corpos (1969-1974)," sem dúvida, um dos capítulos centrais na obra, toma por tema a política ultramarina de construção de uma sociedade multirracial em África. Relatando a experiência africana da família Montês e, particularmente, as actividades de José Montês, no cargo de governador de distrito, e enquanto membro integrante do aparelho de controlo e repressão das populações autóctones, o romance denuncia as medidas portuguesas de "pacificação" e "recuperação" (85) dos africanos. Os núcleos implementados com o apoio das técnicas persuasivas e vigilantes da PIDE, corporizada na personagem de Ricardo Vale, remetem-nos mais uma vez para o tratamento do espaço no romance. Trata-se porém, desta vez, do espaço de contenção e tortura de africanos submetidos à "conversão" ideológica designada por "metamorfose," que a tatuagem de uma borboleta no braço esquerdo assinala.

"Depois da Festa (1997) (1974-1975)" evoca a entrada de Portugal numa nova era após a saída da ditadura, da guerra de África e do passado colonial. Este capítulo não deixa, no entanto, de transmitir uma visão desencantada da trajectória portuguesa na fase após a Revolução, especialmente pela referência dos eventos que culminaram na descolonização e no deflagrar das guerras civis em África. *Topos* onde se entrecruzam os caminhos do passado e do presente, Lisboa é, no romance, o lugar da "Revolução dos brandos costumes" (105), cuja emergência a obra enfatiza num "capítulo" sem estatuto de capítulo, repleto de reticências e precisamente intitulado "Festa É Festa (1974)."

Em *Pedro e Paula*, a Lisboa do pós-25 de Abril configura o lugar de regresso de exilados e de "consolidadas amizades" (126) e o porto de abrigo de retornados de África, que proliferam pelas partes da cidade. Entre estes conta-se Pedro, cujo futuro anuncia a nova mentalidade capitalista em Portugal que vingará através do "crescente império imobiliário" (152), criado por Fernanda, sua mulher. A cidade de Lisboa é igualmente pano de fundo das artes plásticas de Paula, bem como cenário de meditação sobre as transformações sociais entretanto ocorridas no país, que nos chegam através das digressões desta por Campo de Ourique, Lapa, Jardim das Amoreiras, Jardim da Estrela e Cemitério dos Prazeres e que a levam a concluir: "Uma chatice não poder andar à solta na cidade, ver aquelas cores a mudarem sempre, a transformarem as coisas mais familiares em novas combinações. Uma cidade pintura" (169). Por fim, é ainda em Lisboa que se verifica o conflito entre os gémeos, desencadeando a consumação do incesto, descrito em versão dupla—uma "sucinta," outra "grotesca"—pelo narrador (184).

"Pois é...(1997)," o último capítulo do livro, revisita precisamente a cidade de Londres. Espaço de encontro com o narrador/autor, Londres surge agora como possível pátria adoptiva de Paula e de sua filha Filipa. Eterno círculo de "entradas e saídas," a estória contada por Paula transforma-se na ficção que o narrador/autor converte em memória de um tempo e em homenagem aos dois amigos (203), Paula e Gabriel. Incesto psicológico, incesto figurado das personagens em harmonia, contraposto ao incesto real de Pedro, a união de Paula e Gabriel completa o círculo das "entradas e saídas": a morte de Gabriel no interior do corpo de Paula (205), para de dentro dela tirar toda a morte que o irmão lá pôs (206). O final do romance retoma assim a imagem do duplo que atrás associámos ao mito de Janus, jogando de novo com o princípio de "ingestão e expulsão" do corpo. Note-se que tendo-se anunciado no primeiro capítulo o nascimento dos gémeos (expulsos do corpo da mãe) se conclui a estória de Paula, atribuindo-se especial relevo à morte de Gabriel enquanto regresso ao corpo dela.

George Monteiro. *The Presence of Pessoa. English, American, and Southern African Literary Responses.* Lexington: The University Press of Kentucky, 1998.

Silva Carvalho

The Presence of Pessoa, um dos últimos livros publicados por George Monteiro, é constituído por um breve prefácio, nove capítulos, e um apêndice onde se reproduz pela primeira vez o que Roy Campbell deixou do seu *Fernando Pessoa*.

No prefácio o autor explica o que pretende fazer com este livro (essencialmente mostrar, como sugere o seu título, as marcas de Pessoa em autores de língua inglesa, sobretudo americanos, ingleses e sul-africanos).

Dos nove capítulos, o primeiro é genérico e panorâmico, englobando uma brevíssima biografia de Pessoa e depois um historial da fortuna crítica do poeta português nos países de língua inglesa, com os seus sucessos e os seus falhanços, assim como as motivações que levaram os poetas a lê-lo ou a traduzi-lo muito antes dos críticos e dos *scholars*, sumariando desta hábil maneira os assuntos que vão ser tratados nos capítulos seguintes.

Imediatamente o leitor se dará conta de um traço fundamental desta obra, bem visível no final do capítulo, quando George Monteiro arrisca como hipótese de origem da última frase escrita de Pessoa ("I know not what tomorrow will bring") as escrituras sagradas: a sua vasta informação, fruto de uma investigação inteligente, paciente e cuidada. Mas uma informação que é servida por uma finura de observação onde inesperadas conexões são estabelecidas, dando do problema tratado, em pequenos apontamentos, uma leitura por vezes ligeiramente diferente daquela a que se está habituado. E como se nada fosse, isto é, muito casualmente. Aliás, será este aspecto o que me parece mais discutível nestes capítulos a todos os títulos notáveis, e ver-se-á mais tarde porquê, pois se se adquire uma certa ilusão de objectividade quando simplesmente "se mostra" o que teve lugar ou aconteceu, às vezes vale a pena também "dizer-se" alguma coisa, pela afirmativa ou pela negativa, do que justamente se está a considerar. Ou quererá George Monteiro deixar esse trabalho aos seus leitores, como se o seu propósito fosse apenas de dar conta de factos literários mais ou menos históricos, sem neles introduzir opiniões ou pareceres? A verdade, porém, é que pelas suas observações Monteiro toma, as mais das vezes, implicitamente ou explicitamente, partido (veja-se o caso de João Gaspar Simões em relação à biografia de Pessoa, ou todo o capítulo dedicado a Allen Ginsberg). O problema consiste em saber se o comum dos leitores (para não dizer dos mortais) saberá ou poderá ler o que se sugere sem ser devidamente sublinhado.

Mas é melhor dar-se um exemplo, para que se perceba o que está em questão neste reparo. Quando se fala da segunda oportunidade de promover Pessoa em Inglaterra, tentativa frustrada de Sena junto de Edith Sitwell, o que mais ressalta ao olhar, ao ponto de se ficar estarrecido, não é a generosa tentativa de Sena tentando dar a conhecer ao estrangeiro o poeta que ele pensa ser o mais importante de Portugal no século vinte antes do seu advento (de Sena, é claro), mas o tratamento que Sena oferece ou dedica a Edith Sitwell. Aquele *her genius* para uma poetisa inglesa de segunda ou terceira categoria (e tenhamos a coragem histórica de um Harold Bloom, mesmo a de sermos parciais—e injustos—neste preciso momento, mas isso é que é a crítica, como disse há já tanto tempo Baudelaire) e o facto de a citar como autoridade para ajuizar do valor dos sonetos ingleses de Pessoa, deixa muito a desejar, introduzindo uma nota dissonante na capacidade valorativa e estética que Sena mostrou nessa altura. Ou, pelo menos, levanta um outro problema. Um leitor de uma língua estrangeira, mesmo se reputado escritor na sua, será capaz de possuir uma percepção estética idêntica à que mostra na sua língua e cultura? Ora nada disto merece um comentário, expondo-se apenas o *matter-of-factness* da situação.

Considere-se, já agora, um outro exemplo. Trata-se da segunda edição do *Oxford Book of Portuguese Verse*, de 1952, a cargo de B. Vidigal. George Monteiro tem a perspicácia de escolher duas citações, do que será uma introdução ou prefácio de Vidigal à antologia, que me parecem fundamentais. A primeira por mostrar que Pessoa foi, além de um grande poeta, um grande crítico, estabelecendo melhor do que ninguém o cânone poético do século dezanove numa data em que a inclusão de certos autores não era de todo evidente como nos parece agora, e falo sobretudo de Cesário Verde. Mas a segunda citação, ao dizer "Pessoa paved the way for the generation of poets now writing, and it is through him that their creed is finding a warmer response among the public," é problemática. Porque se é verdade que Pessoa, nas suas três ou quatro variantes, fixou o idioma poético português deste século, quer se queira quer não reconhecer o facto, a verdade é que toda a poesia portuguesa deste século, com raras excepções, foi escrita de costas viradas para a experiência pessoana. E a possível resposta calorosa do público, quando se pensa em poetas como José Régio ou Miguel Torga, possivelmente vivendo então o auge da popularidade, não advém da presença de Pessoa nesses poetas, mas sim da sua ansiosa ou inconsciente omissão, para não dizer dos ecos ainda vigentes de uma poesia finissecular. Aliás, poder-se-ia mesmo discutir se houve na altura, como se há hoje em dia, em Portugal, um público para a obra de Pessoa. Como diz, e muito bem, George Monteiro, Pessoa é "a poet's poet." Restará saber—e o livro de Monteiro neste aspecto, pelos problemas que levanta, é importantíssimo para futuros estudos—se, em língua inglesa, não é ou foi apenas "a mediocre poet's poet."

Mas passemos aos outros capítulos. O segundo, Old School Loyalties, refere-se à importância que Pessoa teve para Roy Campbell. Este, considerado no começo da sua carreira como um dos melhores poetas da sua geração (pressupõe-se que ingleses e não sul-africanos), morre em 1957 em pleno declínio da sua reputação literária. George Monteiro dá-nos o retrato possível deste homem, e o resultado não é muito agradável, apesar de George Monteiro fazer tudo para ser justo e ver as coisas sempre pelo seu lado estético.

Reaccionário, fascista, sente-se em casa num Portugal salazarista. Escreve mesmo um livro chamado *Portugal.* Diz ter estudado na mesma escola que Pessoa, em Durban, só que alguns anos mais tarde. E deixa-nos este apontamento saborosíssimo: ter visto o nome de Fernando Pessoa entalhado numa carteira. Para quem vai pôr em questão a identidade como era concebida no ocidente, não se pode dizer que Pessoa não soubesse que era Pessoa. Se a anedota for verdadeira, é claro.

Os seus grandes poetas portugueses são Camões e Pessoa, mas os motivos para os distinguir parecem-me altamente duvidosos: razões nacionalistas: um por causa do Canto V de *Os Lusíadas* e da sua importância para a cultura sul-africana, como começo simbólico de uma identidade, e o outro porque foi durante algum tempo sul-africano, além de ser também um poeta do mar, como lhe parecia evidente na leitura que fez da *Mensagem.* De qualquer maneira George Monteiro frisa mais de uma vez que, embora a visão que Campbell teve de Pessoa devesse em muito aos trabalhos pioneiros de Gaspar Simões e de Casais Monteiro, isso não impedia que o autor sul-africano não tivesse uma visão muito sua e, por isso, original, de certos aspectos da obra de Pessoa.

O terceiro capítulo, introduzindo mais dois poetas que se sentiram atraídos pela fascinação Pessoa, Edouard Roditi e Thomas Merton, ambos americanos, é dos mais interessantes para o leitor de hoje, quando avança com o conceito de antipoesia, que se deve a Merton. Não porque esse conceito fique bem explicitado, pois só um *strong reading*, para não se falar de um deliberado *misreading*, de Alberto Caeiro, nos poderá fazer dele um *budista zen*, mas porque o conceito de antipoeta ou de antipoesia tinha já aparecido na cultura portuguesa pela pena de Gaspar Simões a propósito justamente de Casais Monteiro, embora por motivos completamente diferentes, isto é, neste caso, por uma recusa do idioma poético então vigente. Se George Monteiro nos esclarece, com a ajuda de Sena e de Hamburger, sobre a impossibilidade de se poder ler alguns traços da poesia de Caeiro como reveladores de uma verdadeira atitude mística, ligando-o intempestivamente a San Juan de la Cruz, como o faz Merton, fica sempre por esclarecer um facto que é do domínio público: Pessoa serve-se de Alberto Caeiro não para criticar a poesia, ou toda a poesia que foi escrita desde os seus primórdios até à sua época, mas sim os poetas idealistas românticos, como o era o seu contemporâneo (e todo um problema se vislumbra, a saber, o que poderá significar em literatura a contemporaneidade) Teixeira de Pascoaes, poeta retardado de cem anos em relação aos poetas românticos ingleses ou alemães, autêntico anacronismo que só culturas débeis ou frágeis como a portuguesa permitem, para não dizer que acariciam ou propiciam.

Interessante notar como a análise que George Monteiro faz da poesia de Merton o leva, e sem dúvida acertadamente, a dizer que, se Caeiro começa por ser o Pessoa que mais interessou Merton aquando do conhecimento que fez do poeta português, Álvaro de Campos assumirá um papel relevante para o fim da sua vida. Mostrando assim, talvez como já o fizera Jacinto do Prado Coelho, que motivos, problemas e temas passavam de heterónimo para heterónimo denunciando compreensivelmente uma raiz ou um fundo comum: o homem em disposição artística e literária chamado Fernando Pessoa.

Não convém esquecer, contudo e também, o papel de Edouard Roditi na apresentação que este faz de Pessoa aos leitores americanos, historicamente falando a primeira. O ensaio crítico chamava-se "The Several Names of Fernando Pessoa," e apareceu na revista modernista *Poetry* em Outubro de 1955. Ele próprio um poeta, verá neste livro de George Monteiro a análise de um dos seus poemas, "Autopsychoanalysis," em princípio um parente próximo do "Autopsicografia" de Pessoa. Mas mais uma vez a acuidade analítica do comentar se revela ao estabelecer as diferenças entre os dois poemas, aduzindo outros poemas do poeta português que ecoam no de Roditi, e, sobretudo, ligando o poema analisado com o de Jorge de Sena, "Em Creta, com o Minotauro." O que não deixa de ser interessante, pois é como se a língua inglesa estivesse ela própria a constituir o cânone poético para este século vinte português, ao escolher estes dois nomes de uma profusão inalcançável de nomes: Pessoa e Sena, um modernista e o outro pós-modernista. Este fenómeno é digno de ser pensado dentro e fora de Portugal, mas até mais dentro do que fora, pelas razões que me parecem óbvias, sobretudo quando se julga (já que utilizar o verbo "pensar," nesta ocasião, seria um desdouro para o pensamento), como alguns julgam, que Portugal é um país de poetas, esquecendo-se sempre de dizer que "de poetas medíocres," insusceptíveis de atraírem as atenções das culturas estrangeiras.

O capítulo quarto é dedicado ao poeta e tradutor Edwin Honig. Mas, sobretudo, de maneira enviesada, já que se trata de "dominoes" e de máscaras, ao problema da identidade. É, talvez, de todos os capítulos, o que mais suscita a reflexão de um estudioso de Pessoa e das suas afluências, pátrias ou estrangeiras. George Monteiro testemunha da importância do trabalho de Honig como tradutor de Pessoa, e realmente tem sido ou foi uma tarefa assinalável e mesmo assinalada por outros poetas americanos, como, por exemplo, Karl Shapiro, que escreve um poema intitulado "On First Looking into Honig's Pessoa." O poema contém este verso assombroso: "Writing in Portuguese and broken English sonnets." Como não se ficar espantado? Então o inglês (a língua, é claro) do Pessoa inglês (ou, pelo menos, sul-africano), dito por tanta gente até agora como excessivamente literário, livresco, mais shakespeariano do que Shakespeare nos seus sonetos, soa a Shapiro, se alguma vez o leu, como "broken English"? Que dizer deste facto? Apenas de que a recepção do mesmo poeta, em várias línguas ou culturas várias recebe tratamentos e juízos diversos, muitas vezes antagónicos. Mas não deixa de ser curioso que um inglês macaqueando o de Shakespeare, com todas as virtualidades de raciocínio de Pessoa, possa parecer deficiente a um poeta americano contemporâneo.

Contudo, a confessada influência do poeta português em Honig, sobretudo no seu livro *Four Springs*, depois deste ter escrito "I saw the possibilities of using a variety of voices to carry to completion a long work of my own," cria uma certa perplexidade no autor de *The Presence of Pessoa*, ao ponto de o fazer dizer: "But specific evidence of how *Four Springs* was influenced by Pessoa's poetry is a rather elusive matter, Honig's own assertion being the strongest evidence there is." Talvez, e desconhecendo-se de todo o livro de Honig, porque George Monteiro estaria à espera de "frases, imagens e conceitos" pessoanos que lá não aparecem, mas que surgirão justamente em alguns dos subsequentes poemas, ulteriores e mais recentes, do mesmo poeta e tradutor americano, analisados mais adiante. O problema que se coloca aqui, não só de Honig, mas também de todos os admiradores de língua inglesa de Pessoa contemporâneos, é muito simples e poderá ser formulado com algumas perguntas: Até que ponto a experiência heteronímica de Pessoa não estará mais que esgotada na segunda metade do século vinte? Como não ver as máscaras pessoanas, contemporâneas das máscaras de um Yeats, antes como culminação de um problema da identidade do e no século dezanove europeu, como tão bem viu Jorge de Sena (escalonando os seus autores e cultores ao longo desse século) e outros investigadores? Logo, essencialmente e terminalmente modernista, mas sem possível significado nem significação na segunda metade deste século. Porque o "eu," se se puder ainda falar nestes termos, voltou novamente, numa espécie de eterno retorno do mesmo, a ser teorizado, isto é, contemplado, como no tempo de Descartes? Claro que não. Mas veja-se neste mesmo capítulo a solução da leitura que Paz faz de Pessoa, e que George Monteiro aceita como válida ao distinguir dicotomicamente um putativo "true self" dos seus heterónimos, como se toda a experiência pessoana fosse um jogo ou uma brincadeira literária (uma mascarada) e não a assunção crítica e sofrida da modernidade do sujeito. Parece-me pois necessário, hoje, distinguir dois tipos de heteronímia. Uma heteronímia horizontal, como já lhe chamei num pequeno ensaio dedicado à situação de Sena na poesia portuguesa deste século, mas em que se discutia, sobretudo, a sua posição em relação ao *problema* Pessoa, e que era, sem dúvida, a de Pessoa e foi a do modernismo, e uma heteronímia vertical, que Sena apenas intui sem a explorar.

Será pois por acaso que Edwin Honig, no panorama das letras americanas, e no da poesia, em particular, apenas merece o lugar de uma menoridade, assinalável mais como tradutor de Pessoa do que como poeta? A poesia americana, na segunda metade deste século, e como diz uma das suas melhores críticas, já que se trata da mulher e professora Marjorie Perloff, "is elsewhere," não nos livros de Honig. É que a aprendizagem ou influência de um grande poeta (sem dúvida como é o caso de Pessoa) não pode consistir na assimilação dos seus temas ou ideias ou formas, que são irremediavelmente passados, mas antes na maneira como ele muda o paradigma estabelecido ou estabelece uma nova e mais recente mutação. Caberia agora fazer-se a pergunta, um pouco indiscreta: E isso aprende-se? (mas será um problema a discutir numa outra oportunidade).

O capítulo cinco, ao tratar do parentesco entre *O Banqueiro Anarquista* e a novela de Lawrence Ferlinghetti, *Love in the Days of Rage*, é não só benvindo como oportuno, pois raramente se vê referências críticas ao texto de Pessoa, lido como uma pirotecnia de raciocínio e não como evidência de um pensamento político. Como se fosse para esquecer, e falo da crítica portuguesa em geral. O facto de vir mencionado e citado o ensaio introdutório de uma mais recente edição de *O Banqueiro Anarquista*, publicada em Lisboa por um K., e intitulado "Fernando Pessoa, O Mito e a Realidade," diz da investigação levada a cabo pelo autor de *A Presença de Pessoa*. Pena é que neste caso as citações sejam escassas. E a discussão desse ensaio preliminar diminuta. Por ser subversivo? Por ser negativo, como se poderá depreender das citações? Por não conter nada que pudesse interessar o leitor americano no que toca a uma perspectiva de Pessoa?

De qualquer modo, a maior parte deste capítulo-ensaio pretende dar a conhecer até que ponto Ferlinghetti foi sensível à problemática que Pessoa introduz nesse seu texto tão desmerecidamente desconhecido. Isso vê-se pelo estudo minucioso que George Monteiro empreende da novela do escritor americano, mostrando em que pontos os dois autores se aproximam ou diferem. Chega-se à conclusão de que as ideias expostas no *Banqueiro* são convergentes com muitas das ideias que Ferlinghetti se faz de um possível anarquismo convivendo com a sociedade capitalista que agora vigora. A forma de exposição dessas ideias é que diverge. Pessoa escolhe um monólogo argumentativo e o poeta americano um enredo ocorrido em Maio de 68, em Paris, França.

O sexto capítulo, onde se exploram as queixas de Allen Ginsberg no que respeita a quem está mais próximo de Whitman, se ele ou se Pessoa, minúsculo como é, pelo que evidencia de como a poesia é ou foi vivida nos Estados Unidos neste século, é uma pequena lição pedagógica sobre a famosa "anxiety of influence" detectada e inventada por Harold Bloom. Se é patética a atitude quase decadente e injusta de Ginsberg em relação ao morto Pessoa, e George Monteiro no-lo mostra à saciedade, não é menos verdade que Ginsberg sabe muito bem do que está a falar e, por conseguinte, do que está em causa no mundo em que vive. A precedência, no estabelecimento de um cânone, é, desde os românticos, isto é, desde há dois séculos, fundamental, e o poeta americano, ao contrário dos poetas portugueses deste século, sabe-o como mais ninguém. Ter havido, numa outra língua que fosse, mesmo se e quando esta língua é desconhecida dos grandes centros de poder intelectual e literário, logo, sem importância, alguém que "descobriu" primeiro que Ginsberg o seu Whitman, é coisa que não se perdoa. É como se toda a vida poética de Ginsberg tivesse sido posta em risco. Daí a reacção intempestiva e mesquinha, mas quando se trata da sobrevivência, mesmo se só literária, as leis da civilidade são esquecidas para emergir apenas o lancinante grito de desespero ou de revolta. Aquela de se apresentar, logo no começo do século, uma encarnação de Whitman na figura de Álvaro de Campos, é muito forte e tem o seu peso. Ginsberg, ao descobrir que não tinha sido o primeiro a reconhecer uma origem ou uma anterioridade, reagiu mal. Não deixa por isso de ser o grande poeta americano da sua geração ou do seu grupo como muitos dos mais conceituados críticos do seu país o consideram ainda hoje. E veja-se como acaba este capítulo (em que George Monteiro, indisfarçadamente, toma o partido do poeta português, não lhe bastando agora "mostrar" para "dizer" abertamente o que pensa de Ginsberg pela comparação que faz entre os seus poemas dedicados ao mestre do século dezanove e a "Saudação a Walt Whitman" de Campos): "Ginsberg continued to admire Whitman, we know, and he continued to assign Pessoa to his students." Se assim foi, Ginsberg não poderia ter deixado, de uma maneira ou de outra, de admirar também Pessoa (embora o verbo "admirar" não seja aqui o mais consentâneo com o que certamente lhe iria na alma).

Curioso e enigmático é o capítulo seguinte, dedicado a Joyce Carol Oates. Nele George Monteiro, num afã quase detectivesco, tenta deslindar o mistério de uma possível mistificação, a da consagrada autora americana, ou do fenómeno mediúnico, se é assim que se diz ou se pode dizer, de um Pessoa do outro mundo enviando emanações fantasmagóricas a uma sensibilidade ímpar. Está em questão o livro de histórias *The Poisoned Kiss and Other Stories from the Portuguese*. Lido o capítulo, infere-se que Joyce Carol Oates conhece ou conheceu o trabalho de Campbell, e que por conseguinte deveria também ter tomado conhecimento das traduções que este fez de Pessoa.

O capítulo oitavo é essencialmente uma leitura das afinidades, não só poéticas mas também idiossincráticas, entre o poeta sul-africano Charles Eglington e Pessoa. É um prazer seguir o comentador na amostragem que faz, com um detalhe quase de verdadeiro *close reading*, como Eglington trabalha os poemas da *Mensagem* de Pessoa para realizar e obter "Homage to Fernando Pessoa," um poema constituído por uma série de vários poemas, da primeira secção do seu livro *Under the Horizon*, intitulada "Compass." Como não poderia deixar de ser, todas as vicissitudes historizantes dessa "Homage" são relatadas proficuamente, como é apanágio do autor no seu normal tratamento das questões literárias que aborda. A salientar o que nos parece ser a *perdição poética* de Eglington, para lá da real que foi o seu suicídio: a sua concepção da poesia, na segunda metade do século XX, ainda como um jogo de um certo "número de frases, imagens e conceitos." Ainda por cima, não da sua lavra, mas derivados de um poeta que se admira. Mas este problema já foi referido.

Finalmente, no último capítulo, surgem os mais recentes nomes de gente escrevendo em inglês e que foi sensível ao *charme* pessoano. São eles Michael Hamburger, John Wain, Andrew Harvey e Dennis Silk.

Convém, antes de mais, assinalar aqui uma das duas imprecisões que surgem neste livro. Álvaro de Campos nunca foi um "Edinburgh-trained naval engineer," pois foi em Glasgow que fez os seus estudos, e, já agora, no primeiro capítulo fala-se de Bocage como poeta português do século XIX, quando só viveu cinco anos nesse século, a sua vida decorrendo muito pré-romanticamente no século XVIII.

Quanto aos quatro autores tratados, a informação que se obtém sobre o poeta inglês John Wain é reconfortante, não porque se diga bem ou mal do seu poema "Thinking About Mr. Person" enquanto poema, mas porque se é informado de que este autor se rebela, num outro escrito, contra o muito admirado em França do século XIX, via Baudelaire, Edgar Allan Poe, introdutor infeliz do conceito de *short poem* que veio a fazer a felicidade do simbolismo francês e outros, não impedindo, no entanto, que o modernismo se consagrasse seriamente ao *long poem* em regiões menos dominadas culturalmente pelo preconceito francês, como o americano, mesmo se em termos diferentes dos pressupostos por Poe. Mas mais não se diz sobre este assunto. Restaria saber se o *long poem*, como foi descrito o poema em questão, que interessa visivelmente a Wain, pois é forma que o seduz e que ele reproduz noutros seus poemas como *Wildtrack*, *Letters to Five Artists* e *Feng*, é espacial ou temporal. Isto é, se é apenas "a suite of interrelated poems" dando conta de diferentes visões estético-ideológicas do mundo, ou antes uma "suite of times or moments" escritas e vividas pela mesma pessoa, sem que o "ego" apareça como uma configuração de multiplicidade de "eus" e de corpos coabitáveis num guinhol imaginário (o Circo Pessoa, como muitas vezes lhe chamo, derrotado por ver que só o fenómeno do espectáculo atrai as multidões, e não o que significa uma vida, os seus actos e os seus gestos), mas antes como uma sucessão de estados ontológicos ou existenciais diferenciados e pertencendo ao mesmo corpo (para não se dizer, à mesma pessoa) em instantes diferentes.

Ainda uma breve referência a Andrew Harvey e à longa citação que dele se faz nas páginas 103 e 104. São tais os "dislates" na apresentação que elabora de Caeiro e Campos, denunciando uma tradição que se está a formar, em língua inglesa, da recepção pessoana, com os seus mitos e as suas degenerescências, nem melhores nem piores, é verdade, que os portugueses ou em língua portuguesa, que é deveras urgente fazer-se novamente uma leitura de Pessoa capaz de o actualizar, mas em termos novos e tendo em conta o que foi feito no ocidente na segunda metade deste século. Não só do ponto de vista meramente estético, mas sobretudo no que diz respeito à teoria e crítica literárias. Caso contrário, Pessoa morrerá, ou será completamente desfigurado, nas mãos daqueles mesmos que dele se aproximam para se salvarem como "criadores" ou "poetas" contemporâneos, imitando-o aqui ou ali, sem uma consciência plena do que se espera da linguagem poética: perpétua renovação.

De tudo o que ficou dito, poder-se-á compreender a importância do livro de George Monteiro. Como se nada fosse, em capítulos-ensaios quase despidos de pretensiosismo, como se apenas se ousasse mostrar este ou aquele pequeno facto concernindo a recepção de Pessoa em língua inglesa, obtém-se um livro recheado de problemas resolvidos ou a resolver. E o diálogo que Pessoa está a estabelecer com outras culturas é estimulante para qualquer leitor, poeta ou simplesmente amante da poesia. *The Presence of Pessoa* é pois um livro que merece ser lido. Espera-se que esta crítica o tenha demonstrado.

Fernando Pessoa & Co. Selected Poems by Fernando Pessoa. Edited and Translated from the Portuguese by Richard Zenith. New York: Grove Press, 1998.

Elide V. Oliver

Fernando Pessoa's poems, as with all good poetry, defy translation. It is a fact, however, that translations of poetry usually work within the limited horizon of what is possible. They are by definition icons of the original, representing it only to a degree as ambassadors and delegates. A faithful translation, then, must reach a consensus of representability capable of indicating the essential characteristics of the original in order to bear the simplest claim of a translation. Cervantes, in a felicitous image, remarked that all translations are the inside out of a tapestry; all the stitches are there, but pale, blurry, with faded colors.

In the case of this present volume, selected, introduced, and translated by Richard Zenith, notwithstanding the praiseworthy effort to put together a book of one of the most important and intriguing poets of this ending century, Cervantes's tapestry, regrettably, fades, blurs, and pulls apart.

Pessoa wrote under a series of what he called "heteronyms," and the fact that these heteronyms consist of powerful "poets" writing under different voices, styles, and diction about equally various themes is complex enough. In Pessoa's own words, we read that, "For some temperamental reason that I don't propose to analyze nor is it important for me to analyze, I've built inside myself many characters, distinct between each other and distinct from me as well, characters to whom I've attributed many poems that are not how I, in my feelings and ideas, would write them" (*Ficções do Interlúdio*, Aguilar, Rio de Janeiro [my translation]). He also adds, "Let's suppose that a supreme depersonalized being, like Shakespeare, instead of creating the character of Hamlet as part of a drama, created him as a simple character, without drama...It wouldn't be legitimate to look into this character for a definition of the feelings and thoughts of Shakespeare unless the character were flawed because the bad playwright is the one who reveals himself" (*ibidem*). This very phenomenon isolates Pessoa among the most original poets of the century and requires a fundamental examination of the crucial relationship between his life and poetic achievement.

It is not without embarrassment, however, that one reads Zenith's "explanations" of Pessoa's subtle dialectics of hiding by revelation and vice versa. He tells us that "Pessoa was sincere in his insincerity; heteronymy was not a game he acquired or invoked along the way, [but] it was woven into his DNA." One infers that the image is not trying to convey that Pessoa was genetically predisposed to heteronymy. Yet, it would be more useful to the reader who does not know Pessoa to be told instead that the poet would be better understood as a creature who, differently from most of us who are content with one personality, cultivated a multiplicity of them. One may even advance the hypothesis that this multiplication was only possible because Pessoa was structurally a "depersonalized" creature without a persona.

The discovery that Pessoa had many more heteronyms (over seventy) than was previously assumed (Alberto Caeiro, Álvaro de Campos, Ricardo Reis, Bernando Soares, Alexander Search, António Mora, Raphael Baldaya, Charles Robert Anon, Jean Seul, Coelho Pacheco, Thomas Crosse) should not come as a surprise. Pessoa not only needed this expansion, but he also needed to make each heteronym "real." In order to do so, more often than not, each was assigned details, like physical and psychological characteristics, philosophical and aesthetic preferences, natal horoscopes; he had them know and correspond to each other and engage in intellectual debates and other sorts of activities. This radically imaginative step should be taken as both a necessity and a play. Like prisms, Pessoa's heteronyms reflected aspects of a manifold world.

In such a context, it strikes one as strange to "justify" Pessoa's depersonalization by affirming that he was "sincere" in his insincerity. The exculpation sounds like a lame defense against a jury of Puritans who caught the poet lying. However, the case is not about sincerity or insincerity at all. In order to grasp Pessoa, one has to do two things: to meditate in the many senses of the concept of paradox and, as in the occult disciplines that Pessoa knew so well, not to try to understand, but to accept. Pessoa asks us to accept his paradoxes not because he felt he was particular, but because these paradoxes are those of the universe as he saw it.

O poeta é um fingidor.
Finge tão completamente
Que chega a fingir que é dor
A dor que deveras sente.

[Literally: The poet is a pretender. / He pretends so completely / That he reaches the point of pretending it is pain / The pain he really feels.] In Zenith's versions:

The poet is a faker
Who's so good at his act
He even fakes the pain
Of pain he feels in fact.

The existential condition of the poet for Pessoa resides in this paradox. The poet pretends so completely (in such a complete imitation of nature), that even when he pretends he is suffering, his suffering becomes real. This situation can only occur under some given conditions; for instance, the full condition of mimesis in which the poet lives, a condition of imitation that is so *faithful* to reality, *becomes* reality. Seen in this light, the paradox seems less paradoxical, it is true, but there is still the tension between the fact that the poet is so complete a pretender that his pretension of pain covers his real pain. The anti-platonic refusal contained in the paradox is remarkable. Plato condemns the poet because he considers him to be not one step removed from the world of ideas, but two. For Plato, the poet was despicable because he was an imitator of the imitation. He was not looking directly into the world of ideas as the philosopher, but imitating the already defective world in which we live.

In this sense, Pessoa's poet, in imitating so completely, in being so completely a pretender, ends up opposing the *truth* of Plato's assumptions. And the reason why is that the act of pretending is so *complete* that it accomplishes in itself a true mimesis. Pessoa's poet advances one step in the direction of the world of ideas, facing Plato's theory against its own *contradictions*.

This is a philosophical step that has important connections with many modern theories of poetry. Pound and Eliot, among others, favored a conception of poetry that puts in relief a clear perception of reality conveyed in equally clear wording. Actually, the project is not far from a classic conception of poetry, as opposed to the romantic view in which the relationship between words and nature is mediated by the emotion of the voice orchestrating the poem. Pessoa's conception is *both* at the same time. It requires a fine mimetic quality in the poet, or rather a mimesis, so complete that it becomes real, and its reality equals the feeling of the poet.

There is a considerable distance between this paradox and the simplistic generalization of the "sincere in his insincerity" and the "DNA" theory advanced by Zenith. Going deep into his point, he states that "the only way Pessoa could conceive of being a poet was by not being, by pretending, by achieving complete insincerity." This is an altogether twisted understanding of Pessoa's enterprise. It was precisely because of Pessoa's radical capacity for *imagination* that he could and would write under any voice that he judged appropriate to convey his *necessary imagination*. This has nothing to do with "sincerity" or "insincerity," qualities that alone do not offer a warranty against good or bad poetry. As a matter of fact, according to the well-known saying by Keith Waldrop that "a bad poem is always sincere," it may be that "sincerity" is not a proof of good poetical behavior. Actually, what Waldrop emphasizes with his line is not that sincerity is bad, but that it is *irrelevant* for the quality of a poem.

Zenith is not alone in responding to the challenge: many other translations have failed just the same. Edwin Honig and Susan Brown are not happier. Their version runs:

> The poet is a faker. He
> Fakes it so completely,
> He even fakes he's suffering
> The pain he's really feeling.

This version is more attentive to punctuation, whereas Zenith is more careless. But it, too, has lots of imbalances despite its undeniable cadence. The merit of the stop after the first verse, as in the original, should not be underestimated. Pessoa's assumption in the poem is very affirmative: the poet is a pretender. STOP. The rest is complementary to the statement, working as a predication. This is very clear in the Honig-Brown version and not at all clear in the translation by Zenith, which engages the verse in a longer predication that does not exist in the original. The second verse in Portuguese begins with a hidden subject: *he, / (the poet) pretends so completely… that…* etc. This is the skeleton structure in which Pessoa wrote his paradox-verse, to which the Honig-Brown version is more faithful. Both versions, however, lack the sparking of clarity, which in Portuguese is so unambiguous and is responsible for the element of surprise and strength conveyed by the originality of the statement: *The poet is a pretender. (He) pretends so completely that he even pretends it is pain, the pain he really feels.*

Another problem is the difference in conception between "pretender" and "faker." The word in Portuguese, *fingidor*, means "pretender"; in the context of the poem, it is someone who pretends any feeling, including the feeling he already has. The word for "faker" is *falsificador*. "Faker" carries in it an intentionality of action that the adjective "pretender" does not. A pretender is more introspective. It might seem a trifle, especially when one considers the "freedom" with which poetry must be translated, or as some prefer, "transcreated." But as there is nothing free in free verse, there is also nothing "free" in translation. Actually, the skill of a translator is always evident when given the least "freedom" with which to work.

Zenith's translations often fail to convey with clarity Pessoa's images. English-speaking readers can get puzzled by some of Zenith's resolutions, such as:

> I'm nothing.
> I'll always be nothing.
> I can't want to be something.
> But I have in me all the dreams of the world.

> [NÃO SOU nada.
> Nunca serei nada.
> Não posso querer ser nada.
> À parte isso, tenho em mim todos os sonhos do mundo.]

Comparing Zenith's translation with Jonathan Griffin's, we have:

> I am nothing.
> Never shall be anything.
> Cannot will to be anything.
> This apart, I have in me all the dreams of the world.

Zenith's translation is inaccurate and untrustworthy. It is not difficult to see that Pessoa's rhythm disappears in Zenith's translation. The poem in question, signed by the heteronym Álvaro de Campos, is not colloquial. It is lyrical, and it requires sensitivity to syntax that Zenith simply does not exhibit. Of course, it is impossible to repeat the word "nada" three times, as Pessoa does, and this is already a formal difficulty to be surmounted. But to complicate things, the double negative, usually accepted as a simple negative in Portuguese, implies logical and philosophical assumptions that are out of hand in Zenith's version. In any case, after the utterly radical statement about

Being and Nothingness of the three first verses, Pessoa takes a radical turn that Zenith misses.

The fourth line of the stanza, "À parte isso, tenho em mim todos os sonhos do mundo," Zenith translates: "But I have in me all the dreams of the world." It is a key verse because it introduces a suspension of the poet's judgment about himself as being nothing. It introduces an ironic distance to the previous statements. After a three-time confirmation of nothingness as an opening for his *Tabacaria* (The Tobacconist's or the Tobacco Shop), the poet surprises the reader with an ironic turn that is introduced by the phrase "*This apart*" (I have in me all the dreams of the world).

In other words, *Apart the fact that I am nothing and will never be anything I have in myself all the dreams of the world.* The strength, originality, and beauty of the construction, and I mean here the existential and poetical construction together, are completely missing in Zenith's version.

There is nothing in English against the literal use of "this apart" (À parte isso). Why, then, instead of following Pessoa's words did he change them and erase Pessoa's fundamental irony?

Imprecisions are a constitutive part of Zenith's translations and impair on many levels a faithful rendering of Pessoa into English. His translations lack clarity.

Faithful translations usually strive to raise this luminous apprehension. They also try to preserve the wholeness and harmony of the original for which they stand.

A translator must create mechanisms of compensation; otherwise, the result of his work is unfaithful, poor, anemic, and doomed to pass around an utterly false image that does not correspond to the original. Much has been said about the commonplace of the *traduttore traditore*, and how sometimes a "good" betrayal works in favor of the original and not to its detriment. When Zenith betrays, however, as we have seen with the "This apart" question, he betrays for the wrong reasons.

The general impression caused by this volume of translations is that it is incomplete, hasty, and clumsy. The poems sound muffled, the images turn to be odd or trivial, and the translation of syntax lacks consistency. Moreover, there is no conscientious work with alliterations and assonances, nor is there concern for rhythm. The reader who knows the originals will also be able to detect problems with punctuation and errors in the accents in Portuguese. The notes are sparse and could be a lot more informative.

In many situations, Zenith's translation does not follow the punctuation of the original poems, and one is left with many conjectures. Is this part of his "free" translation, or has he had access to freshly uncovered manuscripts that would justify some of his daring punctuations?

Example:

A lavadeira no tanque
Bate roupa em pedra bem.
Canta porque canta e é triste
Porque canta porque existe;
Por isso é alegre também.

Zenith:

The washwoman beats the laundry
Against the stone in the tank.
She sings because she sings and is sad
For she sings because she exists:
Thus she is also happy.

The colon introduced by Zenith in the fourth line introduces a forcefulness that makes the fifth line look like an overemphatic consequence of the previous two verses. Yet, the verse here is light, and a less limiting punctuation like the semicolon of the printed editions would serve the poem better. However, what is even more important here is that the poem is written in a playful and musical rhythm, and Zenith is very uncomfortable with both. If the reader wants to have an idea of how playful and rhythmical the poem is, he will have to read Griffin's version:

The laundress at the pool
Pounds clothes upon stone truly.
Sings because sings, is grieving
Because sings because living;
Therefore is cheerful too.

The mistakes in Portuguese are related to diacritics. Pessoa's name was written *Pessôa* and not *Pêssoa*. This may seem a trifle for those who do not speak the language, but the mistake alters considerably the pronunciation of Pessoa's name. This mistake comes at the very first line of Zenith's introduction and should be mended, for it suggests an embarrassing carelessness. Dr. Pancrácio and Dr. Gaudêncio, too, among others, each deserves his accent.

The only book Pessoa published in his lifetime is *Message*, written under his own name or orthonym. It was published in 1934, one year before his death. *Message* is probably the only true epic achievement of the twentieth century. In it, Pessoa conceives a nation somehow anthropomorphically represented whose identity is transformed from action into essence, from history into timeless myth. The poem is divided into three parts and bears analogies with heraldic symbols. The first part, "Blazon," has five sections: "The Fields," "The Castles," "The Inescutcheons," "The Crown," and "The Crest." The second part, "Portuguese Sea," is composed of a sequence of poems. The third part, called "The Hidden One," also has three sections, "The Symbols," "The Warnings," and "The Times," that repeat the structure of the whole poem.

Probably in order to fit the size of the volume, only some poems from *Message* were translated. Nonetheless, there is neither a warning note nor a comment explaining to the reader why the original numbering of each poem has disappeared in these versions, nor is there any explanation to help the reader contextualize the poems. The original numbering of the poems, with their reference to the section in which they appear, if only preserved, would have been enough to call the reader's attention to the close-knit structure of *Message*. It would have been an informative service to the reader as well to have offered a note explaining the internal divisions and titles of the sections of Mensagem if not, at least, to give some idea of the nature of Pessoa's accomplishment in writing it.

A remarkable characteristic of *Message* is that it is written with "archaic style" orthography. The impact of such use in Portuguese should not be ignored because it provides a certain specific tone that completes masterfully the epic atmosphere. If the translator makes no attempt to create an equivalent of this feature (which is understandable), there is no reason why, again, at least a note couldn't have been written explaining Pessoa's motivation in the choice of such particular orthography.

One of the most famous poems Pessoa wrote from *Mensagem* is translated in this present selection. It is called "Portuguese Sea" ("Mar Portuguez") and stands as a compelling example of all the best verse Pessoa could write: rhythm and rhyming seem to spring from the same source of the theme, a powerful conjunction that adds to the complete naturalness of the epic pathos invoked by the title.

The whole of *Message* was translated by Jonathan Griffin in a book published in 1991. His rendering of "Portuguese Sea" preserves rhythm, inversions, timing, and the difficult rhyme schemes, especially in a crucial moment of the poem in which Pessoa rhymes the verb "to give" in the past (deu) with the noun, "sky/heaven" [céu]. Griffin translates the rich rhyme as follows:

> Peril and abyss has God to the sea given
> And yet made it the mirror of heaven.

This represents quite an achievement. Here the reader has not only Pessoa's inversions, but also the rendering of the original rhyme scheme: a verb (given) and a noun (heaven), not to mention the success of the faithful rendition.

Zenith's attempt, however, is pedestrian and altogether deprived of poetry; all the inversions of the original, as well as the rhymes, are lost, without a sober reason. The result is anemic and uninspired:

> God placed danger and the abyss in the sea,
> But he also made it heaven's mirror.

There is no effort to work with linguistic compensations, creating equivalences where the encounter between the two languages, Portuguese and English, fails. The recourse to the syntax in direct order in both lines, where Pessoa placed an inversion, is merely a procedure to curb the translator's own inability to render the verses faithfully.

Compare the original:

> Deus ao mar o perigo e o abysmo deu,
> Mas nelle é que espelhou o céu.

As for the presentation of the book, there are major issues that should be considered, especially if we take into account that this volume is meant for a public that has no access to the original Pessoa. Thinking of this, the idea of appending Pessoa's orthonym and heteronyms with epithets (such as Álvaro de Campos, The Jaded Sensationist, or Fernando Pessoa-himself, the Mask behind the man, etc.) is misleading. One cannot understand the purpose of such arbitrary and gratuitous intrusion, since Pessoa's orthonym and heteronyms speak for themselves and do not need pseudo-didactical management to make them more revealing. Zenith's procedure works against itself, weakening what it attempts to reinforce, doing a disservice to the poet, and misleading the reader.

It also strikes a dangerous precedent. Imagine if the fashion is adopted by inexperienced scholars of our new Dark Ages. It may tag Yeats or Wordsworth, for instance, with any arbitrary "facilitating" epithet, such as "The Inventor of Ireland," and so on and so forth.

In translating Pessoa and his heteronyms, Zenith is usually pedestrian and confused. It can be clearly noticed that there is no coherence in his choices. Poems are translated according to the whim of the moment, with no regard to rhyme or internal rhyming, alliterations, assonances, rhythm, repetitions, and punctuation. We are, then, faced with an Alberto Caeiro who speaks a dull, pseudo-philosophic rant. A Caeiro who is miles away from the poet's direct and sensible common-sense in Portuguese; an Álvaro de Campos sounding hysterically banal; a Ricardo Reis whose elegantly classic inversions and rare words framing his Horatian odes seem to struggle against vapidity and commonplace.

This is most unfortunate. The reader who does not speak Portuguese is deprived of yet another occasion to get acquainted with one of the most original and imaginative poets of the twentieth century. Cervantes's tapestry is pulled apart, and Pessoa goes on waiting for a good weaver.

***Portugal heute. Politik. Wirtschaft. Kultur.* Edited by Dietrich Briesemeister and Axel Schönberger. Bibliotheca Ibero-Americana Vol. 64. Frankfurt a.M.: Vervuert Verlag, 1997.**

Paulo de Medeiros

The nearly one thousand-page volume edited by Dietrich Briesemeister and Axel Schönberger is both a *tour de force* and one of the most important manuals for students and researchers in Portuguese Studies today. As the editors rightly claim in their introduction, this is the first work to attempt such a broad overview of twentieth-century Portugal. Before actually referring to its contents, I think that a bit of contextualization might help to place this volume and assess its significant contribution. The tradition of German scholarship on Portuguese Studies is long and distinguished. Names like those of Friedrich Bouterwerk, Carolina Michaëllis, or Wolfgang Kayser have long been recognized as fundamental for any understanding of the field. More recently, a series of publications has attested to a renewed vitality of Portuguese Studies in Germany which, in spite of institutional shortcomings, has been expanding exponentially. This development is all the more remarkable considering that the interest of most German Lusitanists in the literature and culture of Portugal and other lusophone areas is less than officially recognized—suffice it to say that the only Chair in Portuguese Studies, at Trier, was just inaugurated a few years ago with the nomination of Henry Thorau. A new interest in matters Portuguese can be attributed to a variety of factors ranging from the end of the colonial wars and the resulting international isolation of Portugal to the integration of Portugal in the European Union. But all too often the image of Portugal still tends to oscillate between that of a cheap vacation paradise to that of an exotic place within Europe's borders—indeed, the designation of Portugal as border, frontier, or margin, appears over and over again in varied publications geared to the public at large or even the educated middle classes. Thus, a special issue of the Swiss cultural magazine *Du* on Lisbon as a literary city still was entitled "The Center at the Margin" ("Zentrum am Rand," Vol. 9, 1996).

In this last decade, however, German scholarly works have contributed greatly to disperse such romanticized idealizations of Portugal and Portuguese culture. Among these, the following deserve special mention: two volumes of essays edited by Rainer Hess on the contemporary Portuguese novel

(*Portugiesische Romane der Gegenwart: Interpretationen*, 1992, and *Portugiesische Romane der Gegenwart: Neue Interpretationen*, 1993) as well as one book edited by Elfriede Engelmayer and Renate Heß on contemporary women writers (*Die Schwestern der Mariana Alcoforado. Portugiesische Schriftstellerinnen der Gegenwart*, 1993); and also Gesa Hasebrink's Ph.D. dissertation on post-1974 novels, *Wege der Erneuerung. Portugiesische Romane nach der "Nelkenrevolution"* (Berlin: Tranvía, 1993). Scant distribution even within Germany, however, certainly limited the reception of these works by a non-academic public. But this should no longer be a problem. Coinciding with the 1997 Frankfurt Book Fair, which featured Portugal as a special theme, the prestigious publisher Suhrkamp issued as a pocket book a collection of essays edited by Henry Thorau on *Portugiesische Literatur*. This volume, which gathers a collection of important essays by distinguished Portuguese and German scholars, is undoubtedly the best concise and rigorous introduction to twentieth-century Portuguese literature currently available in any language. Indeed, even the excellent volume on *After the Revolution: Twenty Years of Portuguese Literature, 1974-1994*, edited by Helena Kaufman and Anna Klobucka also in 1997, appears far more uneven in comparison.

Even a few years ago, the literary scholar with little or no Portuguese who might have wanted to check Portuguese literature would still be confronted by an almost complete lack of materials; however, this is clearly no longer the case. The works just mentioned all make important contributions for Portuguese Studies and also for comparatists and students in general. What had been lacking still was a rigorous and broad approach to contextual aspects such as social and economic devolpments. With the publication in 1998 of *Modern Portugal*, edited by António Costa Pinto (see the review by Michael Baum in the previous issue of *Portuguese Literary & Cultural Studies*), a significant step was taken to redress that shortcoming. And with the publication of *Portugal heute* the international scholarly community and students (at least those with reading knowledge of German) have also gained an indispensable tool for study and research.

The editors explicitly refer to *Portugal Today* as a reference work that does not pretend to be encyclopedic. Its subject matter, implied in the title, is contemporary Portugal, even though in some articles, by necessity, the authors must also refer to historic material. This is especially evident in one article by Axel Schönberg, who attempts to trace with large brushstrokes the most important points in Portugal's history up to 1974 (119-58). Thus, essays of varying length over a large number of topics have been assembled, and while some treat their subject matter in general terms, others assume a much more specialized perspective on a limited topic. Obviously, as with any such enterprise, there are differences from article to article, although the quality of them all is quite even. Another exemplary trait is the clarity and sobriety of all the articles. The dissemination of information and not polemics rightly guides the authors. The book is divided into four thematic parts: economy, land, and population; history, state, politics, society, and religion; language, culture, education, and science; and cultural relations between Portugal and Germany. Among the forty-seven articles, nine are signed by Briesemeister and two by Schönberg themselves. A constant in all articles is the inclusion of selected bibliographic lists which, with few exceptions, already would make the volume quite valuable inasmuch as they provide easy access to sources in a variety of disciplines and thus facilitate further interdisciplinary inquiries. Of the four parts, the most extensive is the one on language, culture, education and science, which by itself accounts for over half of all the articles. Indeed, it is here that one finds essays on linguistic and specific cultural topics as well as overviews of literary genres. As such, this is also the most uneven of all sections, for it mixes not only highly divergent topics such as the "Acordo Ortográfico" (429-60), Fernando Pessoa (561-76), and "Fado" (673-98), but it also includes long articles such as the one on peculiarities of Brazilian Portuguese (365-90) and very short ones like the one on Portuguese architecture (699-704). And, of course, there are inevitable repetitions that the editors account for as facilitating the comprehension of individual essays. These are common constraints of edited volumes, and this one, in comparison with others, seems to have successfully achieved a good balance. Indeed, it is doubtful that any readers will actually read this volume from cover to cover. More likely they will use it selectively to look for information on a given topic, something at which the volume excels. If there is any complaint to be voiced, it is simply the desire to have a CD-ROM version of this book that would provide convenient access to the information.

One could quibble with organizational decisions, but that is not my intention. For instance, the nine articles on linguistic aspects could well have formed a separate, formal division. After all, that is also the number of articles in the last part on the cultural relations between Portugal and Germany, which appears more coherent than the much larger part on language, culture, education, and science. What interests me, however, is the way this book begs for a consideration of the field of Portuguese Studies. The editors defend the gaps in the volume by saying that they necessarily reflect the way the discipline is practiced in Germany, and this argument is both credible and critical. Take, for instance, the large section of the book on cultural relations. It is obviously of more restricted interest than the others because it more specifically reflects the country of origin (or at least the linguistic space) of the book and its intended primary audience. Especially the article on German Studies in Portugal might even appear to exceed the purposes of strict information about contemporary Portugal, yet it is a readily understandable and very pertinent chapter. On the whole, even though these chapters by themselves are also of general interest for an understanding of Portugal, one can well imagine that if the book were produced, say, in the United States, it would be replaced by others either geared to a Luso-American audience or reflecting the relations between the United States and Portugal.

Another point of contention pertains to the way in which literature has been treated in this volume. Understandably, given the wide scope of the volume (and even perhaps reflecting the fact that the volume edited by Henry Thorau had just been published), the chapters on literature are focused either too specifically or too broadly on genre. Still, one wonders why there is one article on the post-1974 novel in Portugal, two on theater—one on theater in general, the other on post-1974 drama—one on lyrical poetry post-1974, and one on Pessoa. One can think of all kinds of reasons for such a choice, like the desire to concentrate on developments after the Revolution, to present more facts about theater since this genre has had less critical attention in general, and even to trace the indelible influence of Pessoa in this century. But why is there no mention of other genres like the short story, the essay, epistolography, or diaries? Why a chapter on Pessoa but none on Saramago, whose importance even before the Nobel prize was clearly recognized and who enjoys wide reception in Germany? Obviously, these questions are not so much directed only at the book in question but to the way the field of Portuguese Studies is conceived—or better, to the way that no consideration is given to what Portuguese Studies in theory, or even in practice, is or should be.

The gaps, in other words, might not just be a reflection of Portuguese Studies in Germany. Rather, they may be symptomatic of wider methodological gaps in the field at large. At least, for this reader, it is very interesting and pertinent that the volume opens with one large introductory essay on economics and another on population issues, and it is gratifying to see these subject matters considered together with historical, political and literary issues. Likewise, having chapters on philosophy (759-80), cinema (637-52), the internet (653-62), and archives and libraries (741-48) in Portugal points to a wider consideration of Portuguese Studies besides providing very pertinent information. And yet, one can only wonder why there is no consideration of feminist studies in Portugal, the position of women in Portuguese society, or the roles of television (besides the brief considerations in the short article on modern media, (627-35), and advertising. Clearly, in a volume of this nature, cultural items are included because of the need to transmit to students certain key elements of Portuguese society beyond the strictly historical and literary. And my questions are not meant to indicate any shortcoming of the book in itself. Rather, besides offering us an extremely useful and important reference work, Briesemeister and Schönberg also make explicit how much Portuguese Studies needs a serious consideration of its goals, methods, and practices. That the editors do not attempt to do so in an introduction or preface is quite understandable, as they would inevitably exceed the already quite broad parameters of the present publication. And although the questions will remain with all of us committed to the development of Portuguese Studies in the meantime, we have one more indispensable tool. The present volume should not only be in all institutional libraries, but with its affordable price, it should also find a place on our shelves as well.

Abstracts / Resumos

(Re)Telling History: Lídia Jorge's *O Dia dos Prodígios*

Lígia Silva

Lídia Jorge's first work *O Dia dos Prodígios* (1980), crystallizing crises of identity and History, raises questions about the concept of a coherent and unified subject, totalitarian systems, the discursive construction of the subject, and the concept of discourse. Taking into account Bakhtin's sociolinguistic approach to the novel, this study attempts to show that the narrative structure, constructed as a patchwork of different discourses, offers an appropriate place for a better understanding of the diverse relations between the different social subjects in a particular society. Bakhtin's concept of "dialogism" is examined to show the emphasis given to the role of the reader, and close textual readings explore the techniques through which the marginalized experience, of a rural community and of women, is articulated in the novel. To read some of the female characters, psychoanalysis is used as a tool to reveal how the text deconstructs female identity, in an attempt to unveil a discourse that engages with a protean concept of individual identity. I demonstrate how Lídia Jorge's novel, confronting a universalistic reason, acts as a mode of rewriting History, contradicting absolute claims to truth, which grants the novel a place within a framework of post-modernist aesthetics.

Sex and Success in *Notícia da Cidade Silvestre*: A Tale of Two Cities

Cláudia Pazos Alonso

This article deals with the portrayal of women in *Notícia da Cidade Silvestre*. It discusses how in this compelling modern-day *bildungsroman* Lídia Jorge questions whether equality feminism, represented in the novel by Anabela Cravo, is necessarily the best or most successful way forward for women. It argues that, through the use of a first-person narrative interspersed with diary entries and through various other significant narrative devices, the author is able to revalue and construct a powerful subject position for Júlia Grei, whose actions and thoughts ultimately reflect the potential subjacent in difference feminism.

A Costa dos Murmúrios: Uma Ambiguidade Inesperada

Paula Jordão

Desde a sua publicação que *A Costa dos Murmúrios*, de Lídia Jorge, tem provocado grande interesse, tanto por parte do público laico, como do literário. Para tal contribui não só a escolha da guerra colonial em Moçambique nos anos 60 como tema central do romance, mas principalmente a problematização que Lídia Jorge faz desse mesmo tema. Uma problematização que, através do discurso da narradora Eva Lopo, passa pela desmistificação de questões como a Verdade, a História ou a Escrita, atingindo assim aspectos essenciais da ordem dominante. Considerando, no entanto, as relações entre as várias personagens, podemos perguntar-nos se elas não reflectem uma certa ambivalência a essa ordem dominante. Ambivalência essa que, no caso particular de Evita, nos pode fornecer uma imagem bastante diferente da habitual, como se pretende mostrar neste estudo.

Memória Infinita

Paulo de Medeiros

A Costa dos Murmúrios de Lídia Jorge é, sem dúvida, um dos seus romances mais importantes e que mais atenção crítica tem recebido, especialmente no que diz respeito ao questionamento da História por parte das estratégias narrativas do romance. O foco deste ensaio é sobre o conceito de memória e como no romance ele é diversamente explorado. Distinguindo-se de outros romances sobre a guerra colonial, neste observa-se uma desconstrução rigorosa e uma reconceptualização do que significa escrever sobre a guerra. A memória é assumida como ingrediente essencial para evitar quer a submissão ingénua ao processo de desvalorização, contaminação e evasão do passado, quer a colaboração plena ou parcial nos mecanismos de repressão. A memória é tão necessária para evitar essa colaboração quanto excessiva, sendo também necessário, para a sobrevivência da identidade individual, um certo processo de esquecimento. A esse desejo de esquecimento, quer individual, quer nacional, opõe-se sempre um excesso de memória.

Back to Nietzsche: The Making of an Intellectual/Woman—Lídia Jorge's *A Costa dos Murmúrios*

Hilary Owen

This study of *A Costa dos Murmúrios* aims to reassess the perspectives the novel affords on feminism, postmodernism and post-colonial critical debate. Jorge's subversion of the teleological master narratives of History, departs from the representation of women as emblematic of marginal "anecdotal" histories. This effectively means that the "feminine" (explored through the identity dialectics of the sexually ambiguous Evita/Helena relationship) operates as deconstructive figure, undermining western humanist epistemology. Taking a cue from post-Nietzschean antihumanism, Eva's de-authorizing of post-Enlightenment historiography works through a poetics of radical displacement, in the manner of Deleuzian deterritorialisation and theories of nomadology. The study concludes by discussing the dilemma which the novel poses between marking the end of Portuguese colonialism as specific historical experience, and unmaking the European philosophical foundations of historical narrativization, in the context of self-reflexivity occasioned by Portugal's (re)turn to Europe.

Donning the "Gift" of Representation: Lídia Jorge's *A Instrumentalina*

Ana Paula Ferreira

Published separately in 1992, Lídia Jorge's short story *A Instrumentalina* draws upon the form of the parable to explore the impasse of representation within a postmodern and, specifically, post-revolutionary epistemological context. Read in conjunction with the author's other fictional works, this apparently unpretentious fictional autobiographical memoir assumes a critical-theoretical depth that makes it a privileged, indeed "instrumentalist" (John Dewey), illustration of a practice of textuality centered on the simultaneously liberating and treacherous "gift" of representational language. Attendant on the way the story—as Jorge's both previous and posterior works—both evokes and deflects historical, sociocultural and personal referentials, the present analytical "un-wrapping" of *A Instrumentalina* highlights the aesthetic and political implications of a "gift," namely language freed from censorship, that in fact can only be not.

Da *Performance* Como Retórica (e Vice-Versa)

Maria Lúcia Lepecki

Pretendo argumentar que em *O Jardim sem Limites* de Lídia Jorge se encontram nítidos traços do discurso filosófico. Tento circunscrever o que me parece caracterizar esse tipo de discurso e mostrar como Lídia Jorge converge na escrita filosófica. Para isso analiso alguns tópicos retóricos e procuro mostrar de que modo uma dada escrita serve à veiculação de determinada realidade tanto ficcional como histórica, num quadro de sistemática construção especulativa.

Contingency and Loss in *Marido e Outros Contos*

Ellen W. Sapega

This article analyzes Lídia Jorge's *Marido e Outros Contos* (1997) in light of current theories of the short story. After commenting on this genre's implicit relationship to the novel, I demonstrate that the volume in question can be read as a loosely organized short story sequence. The common thematic thread that links the various stories emerges from the author's consistent investigations into the role of random circumstance and violence in the construction of the female characters' subjectivity. While this is particularly evident in "Marido," "Espuma da Tarde," and "O Conto do Nadador," I conclude that the collection in general focuses on multiple manifestations of female desire, drawing explicit attention to this desire as both controlled and conditioned by the prevailing male hegemony.

Picturing Time: Some Photographs of Lídia Jorge by Luís Ramos

Memory Holloway

This article deals with four photographs of Lídia Jorge taken by Luís Ramos in 1990 and critiques the conventions of photographs of writers, including the commemorative photograph, the writer's work place, ways of seeing the relationship between the child and adult, and the role of the family archive in constructing an image of the self in a network of social relations. The author argues that the photographs are literally and figuratively framed in ways that bring into question issues of *voyeurism* and spectatorship.

O Romance e o Tempo Que Passa ou A Convenção do Mundo Imaginado

Lídia Jorge

Quando o império da comunicação e do pragmatismo pareciam anunciar o declínio do romance, de súbito, o género de novo renasce e se impõe como espaço de encontro dos imaginários comuns a partir das realidades diversas. No caso português, o romance actual, fortemente ancorado na realidade social e histórica do país, contribui, através das várias vozes dos seus intérpretes, para a criação desse novo imaginário sem fronteiras, onde se encontram os anseios mais íntimos e os sonhos mais secretos relacionados com o conhecimento e o afecto dos homens. Sítio de refúgio e lugar dinâmico de mitos e imagens fundadoras da inquietação moderna, o romance português de hoje oferece um contributo importante para a convenção do imaginário deste fim de século, mesmo a nível de autores ainda pouco divulgados.

Contributors / Colaboradores

Cláudia Pazos Alonso is a Lecturer in Portuguese and Brazilian Studies at the University of Oxford, England. She is the author of *Imagens do Eu na Poesia de Florbela Espanca* (Lisbon: INCM, 1997) and editor of *Women, Literature and Culture in the Portuguese-Speaking World* (Lampeter: Edwin Mellen Press, 1996). She has also published articles on contemporary women writers, including Lídia Jorge, and on Brazilian writers José de Alencar and Rachel de Queiroz.
E-mail: claudia.pazos-alonso@modern-languages.oxford.ac.uk

Silva Carvalho, Leitor de Português da Universidade de Massachusetts Dartmouth, é autor de vários livros de poemas (dos quais se destacam os que formam a *Pentalogia Americana* e a *Trilogia Porética*), de um livro de ensaios (*A Linguagem Porética*) e de um romance (*Palingenesia*). Actualmente prepara a edição de um volume intitulado *Tetralogia Fática*, constituído por quatro livros. O seu trabalho consiste essencialmente no estudo das condições culturais e literárias que testemunhem e propiciem a passagem de uma linguagem poética para uma linguagem porética.
E-mail: acarvalho@umassd.edu

Stephanie d'Orey graduated in Social Anthropology from the London School of Economics. She lived in Portugal for several years, where she taught at the Instituto de Arte e Design in Lisbon. She works as a translator and interpreter in Portuguese and French. She is currently working on *O Vale da Paixão*, the most recent novel by Lídia Jorge.
E-mail: Stephdorey@aol.com

Elfriede Engelmayer nasceu em Viena da Áustria. Doutorou-se na Universidade de Viena com uma dissertação sobre as canções de José Afonso. Colabora regularmente na revista berlinense *Tranvía*. Tem trabalhado e publicado em torno de literatura de mulheres e literatura contemporânea portuguesa. Numerosas traduções. É leitora na Faculdade de Letras da Universidade de Coimbra.
E-mail: iea@cignus.ci.uc.pt

Ana Paula Ferreira is an Associate Professor of Portuguese, Critical Theory and Women's Studies in the Department of Spanish and Portuguese at the University of California, Irvine. She has published widely in the areas of Neo-Realism and Portuguese women writers and is currently finishing a manuscript titled *Homebound: Femininity, Women Writers and the Nationalist Order*.
E-mail: apferrei@uci.edu

Isabel A. Ferreira é doutoranda no Departamento de Estudos Portugueses e Brasileiros na Brown University, onde lecciona na qualidade de Teaching Fellow. Prepara a sua tese de doutoramento relacionada com o tema da imagem de África no romance português do século XX. As literaturas portuguesa e africana contemporâneas e a autobiografia brasileira constituem as suas áreas privilegiadas de interesse, tendo artigos publicados sobre o romance de João de Melo e os diários de Fernando Aires.
E-mail: Isabel_Ferreira@brown.edu

Memory Holloway teaches 20th-century Art History at the University of Massachusetts Dartmouth. She has written *Picasso in the Collection of the National Gallery of Victoria* and *Max Klinger: Love, Death and the Beyond*, also for the National Gallery of Victoria. She is currently preparing an exhibition on the work of Paula Rego and is working on a book on 20th-century Portuguese art.
E-mail: mholloway@umassd.edu

Paula Jordão ensina na Faculdade de Letras da Universidade de Utrecht, na Holanda. Entre as áreas de ensino e investigação a que se dedica contam-se as de literatura portuguesa contemporânea e literatura brasileira. Presentemente encontra-se a preparar a sua tese de doutoramento sobre a escritora Lídia Jorge. E-mail: paula.jordao@let.ruu.nl

Maria Lúcia Lepecki é brasileira de origem. Vive em Portugal desde 1970, sendo professora catedrática da Faculdade de Letras da Universidade de Lisboa desde 1981. Trabalha em literatura portuguesa (sécs. XIX e XX) e em teoria da literatura. Foi professora catedrática convidada na Universidade de Paris--Sorbonne (Paris IV) durante um ano. Tem numerosos ensaios publicados em revistas especializadas em diversos países e seis livros de crítica de literatura portuguesa, brasileira e africana. Foi Prémio Nacional da Crítica no Brasil em 1977, com o seu livro *Autran Dourado: Uma Leitura Mítica* (São Paulo, Editora Quíron).
E-mail: spqr@esoterica.pt

Carlos Leone has a BA degree in Philosophy from Lisbon's Universidade Nova. Since 1995 he has been working as literary critic and translator. He is now finishing a Master's dissertation in Sciences of Communication. A book of critical essays on Portuguese contemporary authors, *Dez Críticas*, is coming out in May 1999 by Edições Colibri, Lisbon. At the moment, Carlos Leone writes regularly for NON!, www.interacesso.pt/non, and *Ciberkiosk*, http://alf.ci.uc.pt/ciberkiosk.
E-mail: mleo@mail.teleweb.pt

Paulo de Medeiros, Professor Catedrático e Director do Departamento de Português da Universidade de Utrecht, tem escrito sobre vários temas de literatura comparada e teoria literária. Presentemente desenvolve um projecto sobre diarística e continua a investigação no campo da identidade nacional, sendo da sua coordenação o número 13 (Outubro de 1996) da revista *Discursos*, sobre "Literatura, Nacionalismos, Identidade."
E-mail: Paulo.deMedeiros@let.uu.nl.

Elide V. Oliver is assistant-professor at the University of Minnesota. She has taught at the University of São Paulo and the Pontifícia Universidade Catolica also in São Paulo. Most recently she has been a visiting scholar at Yale University. A poet and translator, she has published translations of Nerval, Dujardin, Swift, Hawthorne, among others, as well as critical articles in numerous journals. Her complete commentary and translation of the "Third Book" of Rabelais into Portuguese awaits publication. She is currently writing a book on time, immortality and literature.
E-mail: lelaval@pantheon.yale.edu

Hilary Owen is a Senior Lecturer in Portuguese (since October 1999) in the Department of Spanish and Portuguese Studies at the University of Manchester, England. She is the editor of *Gender, Ethnicity and Class in Modern Portuguese-speaking Culture* (Lewiston: Edwin Mellen, 1996) and has published articles on Portuguese and Brazilian women writers including The Three Marias, Agustina Bessa-Luís, Hélia Correia, and Clarice Lispector. She is currently doing research for a book on women's writing in Mozambique.
E-mail: hilary.owen@mcmail.com

Maria Eduarda Vassallo Pereira é doutorada em Literatura Portuguesa pela Universidade de Lisboa, em cuja Faculdade de Letras foi assistente e recentemente iniciou um projecto de pós-doutoramento. *Visiting scholar* na Brown University, prepara a edição de *A Constituição da Ficcionalidade em Eça de Queirós* e estrutura novos planos de investigação sobre prosa oitocentista e a Geração de 70.
E-mail: M_Vassallo-Pereira@brown.edu

Ellen W. Sapega is an Associate Professor of Portuguese at the University of Wisconsin-Madison, where she is also co-editor of the *Luso-Brazilian Review*. Author of *Ficções Modernistas: Um Estudo da Obra em Prosa de José de Almada Negreiros* (Lisboa: ICALP: 1992), she organized and wrote the preface to Volume III (*Artigos no Diário de Lisboa*) of the *Obras Completas* of José de Almada Negreiros (Imprensa Nacional-Casa da Moeda) and has published articles on Portuguese literature and culture in such journals as *Colóquio/Letras*, *Discursos*, and the *Luso-Brazilian Review*.
E-mail: ewsapega@facstaff.wisc.edu

Lígia Silva graduated in English and German Languages and Literatures from the Faculdade de Letras, Universidade do Porto. She completed a Masters in Education and later on a Masters in European Languages and Culture at the University of Manchester. She was a Camões *leitora* and now is a temporary Lecturer at the University of Manchester, where she is preparing her Ph.D. thesis on Lídia Jorge.
E-mail: Lígia.Silva@man.ac.uk

Leonor Simas-Almeida é Senior Lecturer no Departamento de Estudos Portugueses e Brasileiros da Brown University e tem publicado trabalhos na área da sua especialidade, a literatura comparada, o mais recente dos quais, "Des emotions qui (et qu') inspirent *Madame Bovary*, Luiza et Edna Pontellier," sairá no próximo número dos *Arquivos do Centro Cultural Português*, de Paris. Tem publicado também outros ensaios sobre literatura dos séculos XIX e XX, como por exemplo "Ser e Não Ser: Eis a Ambiguidade como Substância e Princípio em Machado de Assis" (*Espelho. Revista Machadiana*, 1998) e "A Redenção pela Palavra em *Terra Sonâmbula*, de Mia Couto" (*Revista da Faculdade de Letras*, Lisboa, 1996).
E-mail: Onesimo_Almeida@Brown.edu

University of Massachusetts Dartmouth
Center for Portuguese Studies and Culture

Founded in 1996, the University of Massachusetts Dartmouth Center for Portuguese Studies and Culture is designed as a forum for the interdisciplinary study of the language, literatures, and cultures of the Portuguese-speaking world. The publication of a scholarly journal at this juncture, in the third year of the Center's existence, underscores our research goals in the field of Portuguese Studies. The Center aims to serve as a liaison between the University of Massachusetts Dartmouth and other institutions involved in Portuguese Studies in the United States and abroad. It proposes to develop pedagogical materials to aid in the teaching and learning of the Portuguese language at all levels of instruction, while fostering the development and dissemination of knowledge about the Portuguese-speaking communities of the United States.

The agreement recently signed between the University of Masschusetts Dartmouth and Rádio Televisão Portuguesa (RTP) will allow for the establishment of RTPi North America in the television studios of the campus. Locally produced programming will be transmitted internationally to more than 20 million homes, including 1.1 million in the United States. As part of the agreement, the University will receive a complete collection of the RTP Video Library. These materials will be available at the University Library.

The Center is currently preparing a textbook (Encontros) for the teaching of both Brazilian and European Portuguese, to be published by The McGraw-Hill Companies Finally, the Center's planned development of a Graduate Program in Portuguese stresses its commitment to the intellectual preparation of students at the highest level. The Summer Program in Portuguese, founded in 1994, will hold its sixth annual program this year (June 28-July 30), offering eight different courses, from beginning language to seminars on literature and culture. The Center also sponsors international colloquia on topics and authors related to the Portuguese-speaking world. The conferences on Almeida Garrett (22-23 October 1999) and on Eça de Queirós (14-15 October 2000) exemplify our commitment in this area. In addition, the Center organizes an annual lecture, concert, and dance series, and art exhibitions, accentuating its responsibility to the university community and to the region. This fall, the University Art Gallery will host an exhibition on the art of Paula Rego. The Center also supports a Visiting Distinguished Scholar program and promotes the exchange of students and faculty with universities in the seven countries whose official language is Portuguese, as exemplified by the University's agreement with the University of the Azores.

The Center's objectives and endeavors are made possible by the generous support of the following individuals and institutions: Chancellor Peter H. Cressy, University of Massachusetts Dartmouth; Rui Chancerelle de Machete, President of the Luso-American Development Foundation; Foreign Minister Jaime Gama and Secretary of State for the Communities José Lello, of the Government of Portugal; Ambassador Fernando Andresen Guimarães and Cultural Counselor José Sasportes, of the Embassy of Portugal in the United States; Jorge Couto, President of the Camões Institute, José Blanco, Administrator of the Calouste Gulbenkian Foundation and of the National Commission for the Commemoration of the Portuguese Discoveries. In addition, the Center gratefully acknowledges the financial support of individuals and institutions in Massachusetts and Rhode Island, such as Lawrence Fish, President of Citizens Financial Group; Anthony Andrade, President of Universal Press; Manuel Fernando Neto, President of Neto Insurance Group; and Frank B. Sousa, President of Colonial Wholesale Beverage Corp. In particular, the Center wishes to thank Representative Robert Correia, of the State House of the Commonwealth of Massachusetts, for his tireless efforts in the development and funding of the Center for Portuguese Studies and Culture.

Portuguese Literary & Cultural Studies 3

Alberto Caeiro

Outono 1999

Depois de *Borders/Fronteiras* (Outono de 98), *Lídia Jorge in Other Words / por Outras Palavras* (Primavera de 99) e antes de *Brazil 2000* (Primavera de 2000), a revista *Portuguese Literary & Cultural Studies* dedica o seu terceiro número à obra do heterónimo de Fernando Pessoa, Alberto Caeiro, o Mestre dos outros heterónimos e um dos poetas mais influentes na poesia portuguesa do século XX. A função de Caeiro na economia da obra pessoana, os seus precursores, a sua recepção em Portugal e no estrangeiro, a filosofia, a antropologia e a teologia de Caeiro, a concepção da interpretação, Caeiro e a cultura, os sentidos na poesia de Caeiro, o poema longo e o *serial poem*, Caeiro e a poesia actual, o estado dos Estudos Literários e dos Culturais na análise deste *corpus* breve, são apenas sugestões de tópicos para a submissão de artigos que visam refrescar a leitura crítica desta poesia *sui generis* no contexto das poéticas e correntes de pensamento do século XX e mostrar o estado das disciplinas das humanidades na análise de uma curta série de textos. Inglês e português são as línguas principais desta publicação.

Contacto:
Victor J. Mendes, Editor
Portuguese Literary & Cultural Studies
Center for Portuguese Studies and Culture
University of Massachusetts Dartmouth
North Dartmouth, MA 02747 USA
Tel. 508-999 8338 Fax 508-999 9272
E-mail: vmendes@umassd.edu

Portuguese Literary & Cultural Studies Subscription

Center for Portuguese Studies and Culture
University of Massachusetts Dartmouth
Dartmouth, MA 02747 USA
Tel. (508) 999 9270 Fax (508) 999 9272 E-Mail greis@umassd.edu

Name

Address

City **State** **Zip**

Country

☐ **Annual Individual Subscription $ 20 (2 issues)**
☐ **Annual Institutional Subscription $40 (2 issues)**
☐ **Single Issue $15 (Issue Number __)**
Outside of the USA add $12.00 for shipping and handling

Payment enclosed
☐ **Check** ☐ **Visa** ☐ **Mastercard**

Credit Card Number **Expiration Date**

Signature **Date**